DIY
3D paper
Alphabet

Alphabet papier 3D
à faire soi-même
by **Sofs**

1

CUT

couper

3 types of lines

3 types de lignes

easy facile

plier vers le haut

fold upwards

2

score your fold lines before folding!

cut, fold and assemble

couper, plier et assembler

marquer vos lignes avant de plier!

You will need:
Scissors, or craft knife and cutting mat.
White glue or a glue stick or double side tape.
A ruler and something not too shrap to score your lines.

3

plier vers le bas

fold downwards

Vous aurez besoin:
- couteau xacto et tapis de coupe ou ciseaux
- colle blanche, bâton de colle ou ruban double face
- règle et objet pointu pour marquer vos lignes de pliage

Look over the template first to check for important information such as where to start or finish.

Veuilliez regarder les notes sur le patron pour des infos importantes comme par ou commencer et finir.

4

glue tabs to matching numbers on inside

collez languettes vers les numéros correspondant et à l'intérieur

HOW TO   LE COMMENT

3D paper model

modèle papier 3D

SEE next pages for detailed instructions
VOIR pages suivantes pour instructions détaillées

page 3-6
page 7-10

We are here to help you!

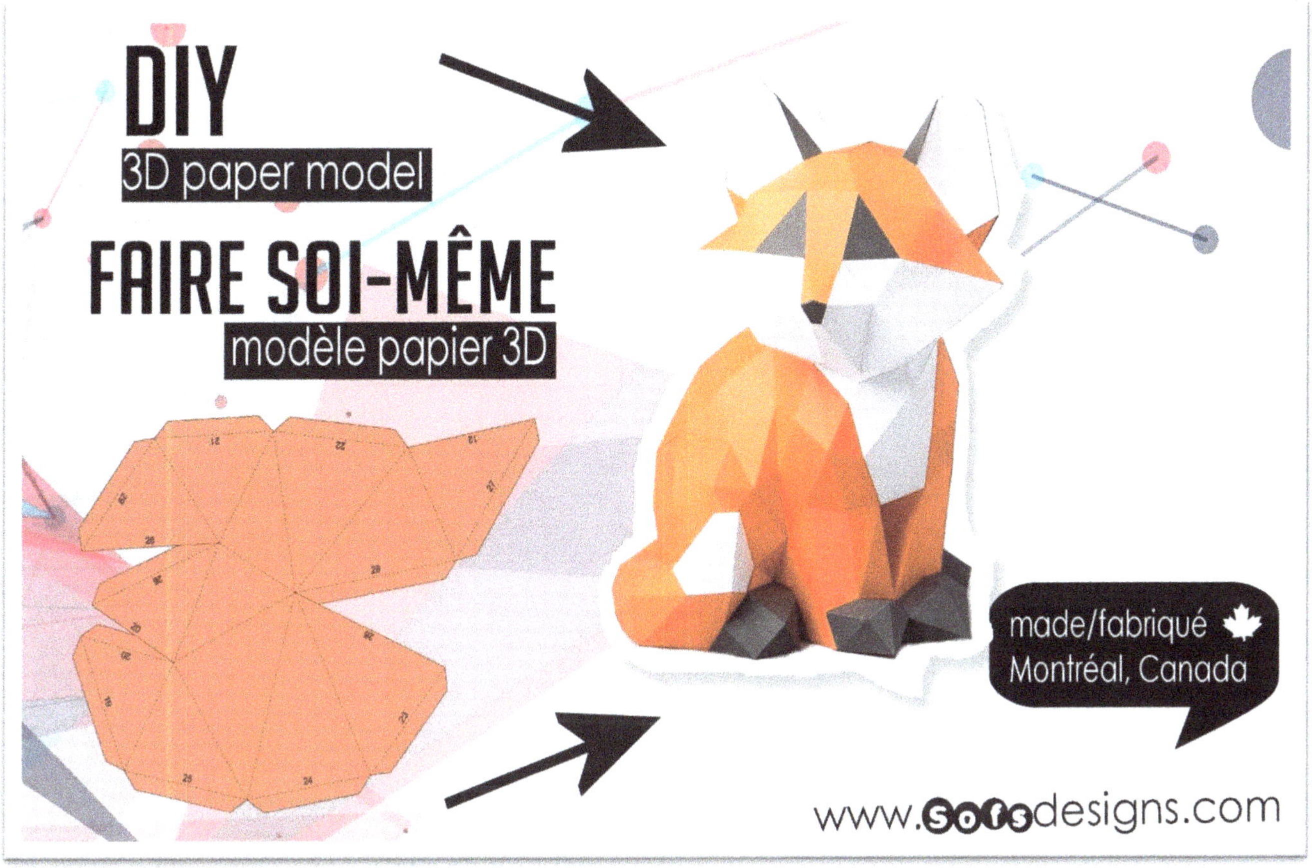

the instructions apply to every models!

READY?

Before you begin, please know that its always the first one that is the longest but once you get the hang of it, it gets easier and easier and SO satisfying. Also, you can always go on www.sofsdesigns.com where you'll have the link to our many HOW to pages!

Let's get started!

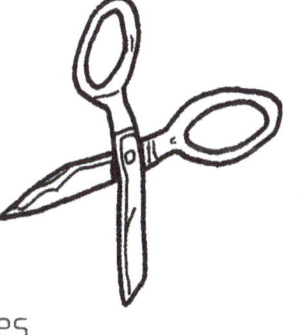

What you need to get started:
- Craft knife and cutting mat or scissors
- Ruler and something sharp-ish to score your fold lines
- Glue stick, white glue or double side tape (hot glue doesn't work well!)

how to make your papercraft

1   You will need to prepare your pieces first by cutting them (#1, #2) and scoring them (image #3 notice the knife is upside down using the back of the knife to apply a score line not cutting the paper) Scoring allows for a clean fold line.

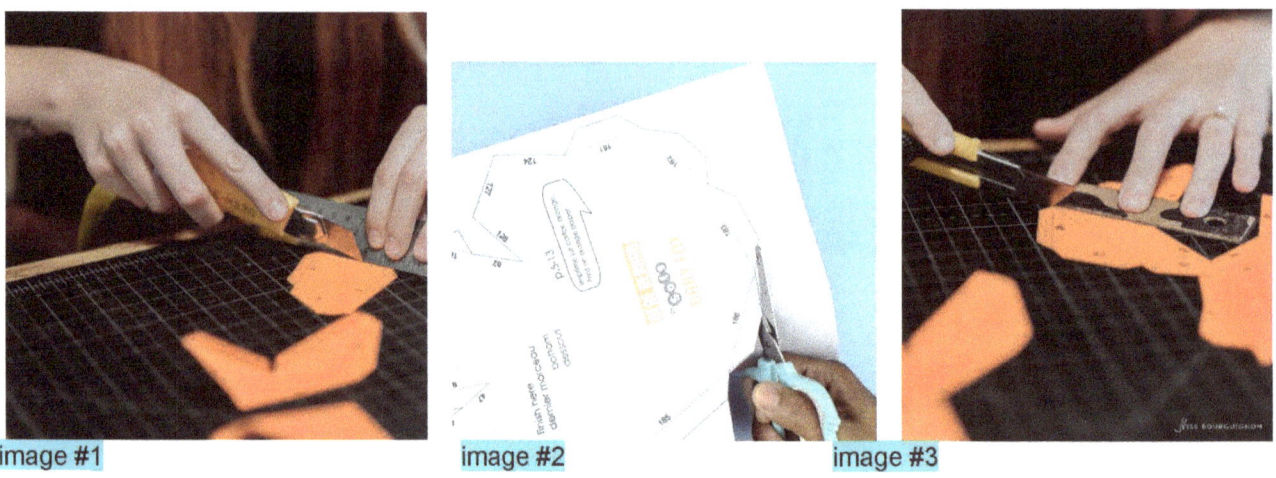

image #1   image #2   image #3

Notice that the Assembly lines (see images #4- #7 below) make mountains (fold up) and valleys (fold down) on 'clean' side.

2

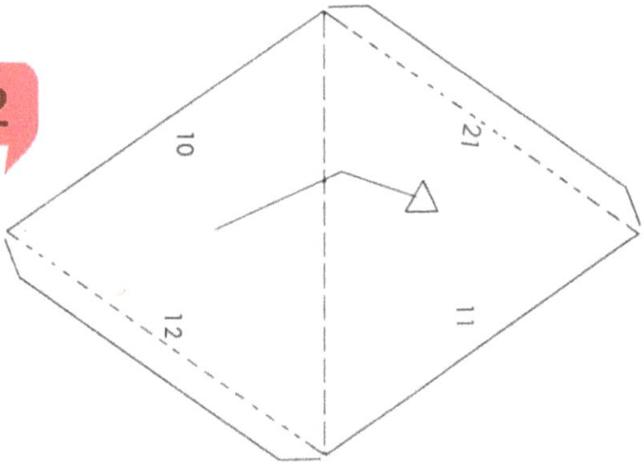

make mountain on 'clean side'

image #4

3

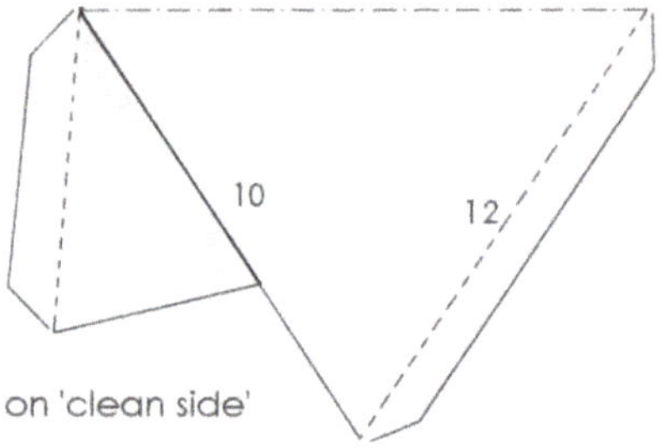

make valley on 'clean side'

image #5

image #6   image #

4 Once that's done you need to find the matching numbers on your tabs (image #8-9) as this is where you will glue the two same number tabs together. You glue (or use double side tape) the tabs on the printed side so that your model has no trace of the template on the clean side once complete (image #10).

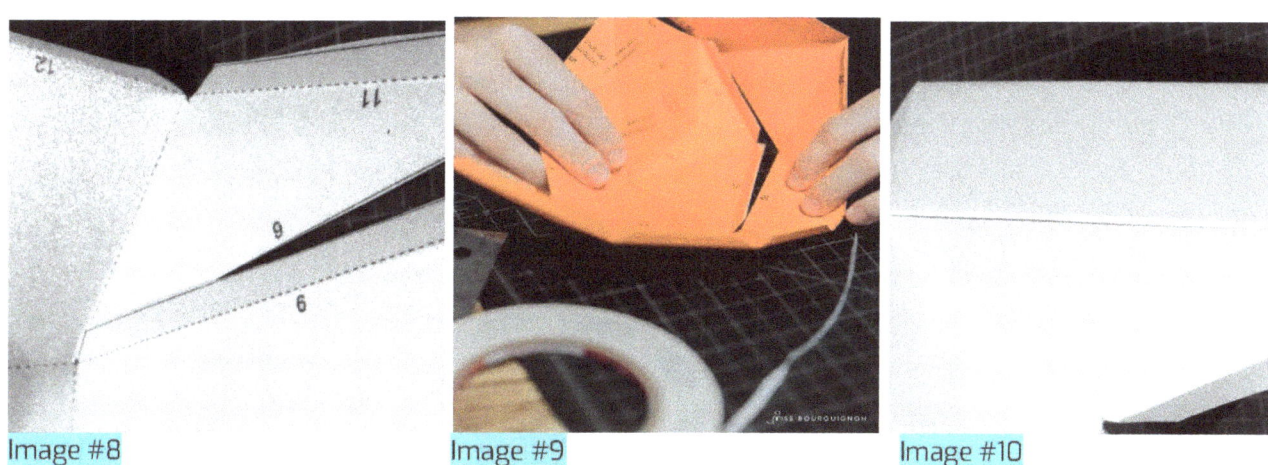

Image #8   Image #9   Image #10

You may get into corners where your glue stick can't reach so you can use a toothpick to apply the glue (image #12) or use a different kind of glue which will have better reach (image #13). Using 'strong' double side tape is also a good technique (images # 14-15).

Image #11   Image #12   Image #13

Image# 14   Image #15

When you start it's good to plan ahead a little bit, for example sometimes the template will have specific instructions on the pages themselves so take a look first.

WE RECOMMEND that you start with the top of the model and work your way down adding one piece at a time. For example, starting with a piece from the head and add one piece until the head is done then continue on your way around body until you reach the last piece at bottom (or against the wall). Often time that last piece will offer the option to cut a whole so you can reach inside so its easier to glue. The parts are written on the pieces or pages so you can tell which is which. Organize them a little bit so you know where you are going ahead of time.

Keep in mind that this is a bit like making a puzzle. The activity does take some time and should not be `rushed`. Take your time and enjoy the flow.

If you want to make your papercraft stronger, you can use mod podge,or resin. You can also stuff it with scrumble newspapers or plushie stuffing.

Voila! Now you know all about making 3d papercrafts.

The rest will come with experience!

Don't forget to recycle when done!

Nous sommes ici pour vous aider!

DIY
3D paper model

FAIRE SOI-MÊME
modèle papier 3D

made/fabriqué 🍁
Montréal, Canada

www.sofsdesigns.com

Vous êtes prêts?

Les instructions sont pour tous les modèles.

Avant de commencer, vous devez savoir que c'est toujours le premier qui est le plus long à fabriquer, mais une fois que vous savez comment faire, ça devient de plus en plus facile et si satisfaisant. Aussi, vous pouvez toujours aller sur www.sofsdesigns.com où vous aurez des liens vers nos nombreuses pages 'Comment Faire'.

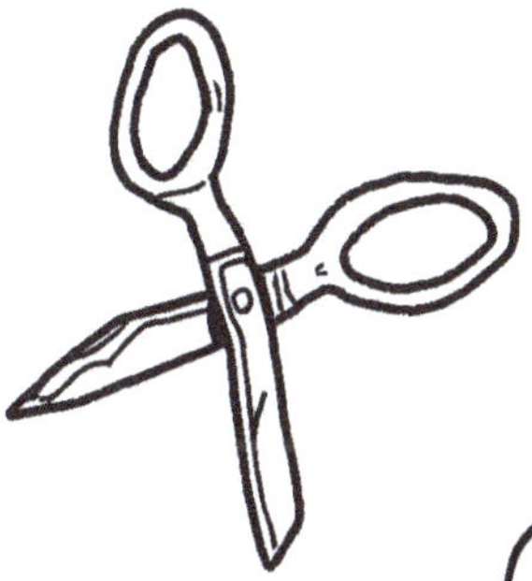

Allons-y!

Voici les choses dont vous aurez besoin:
- couteau exacto et tapis de coupe ou ciseaux
- règle et objet pointu pour marquer (scorer) vos lignes de pliage
- colle, un bâton de colle ou certains préfèrent du ruban double face.

Comment Faire vos modèles papercraft 3D

1 Vous devrez d'abord préparer vos pièces en les coupant (#1, #2) suivant la ligne pleine et en marquant les lignes pointillées (image #3) Remarquez que le couteau est à l'envers en utilisant le dos du couteau pour marquer le papier (sans couper le papier) Le marquage (scoring) permet une ligne de pliage propre.

image #1   image #2   image #3

Notez que les lignes de votre patron (voir les images #4- #7 ci-dessous) font des montagne (pliez vers le haut) et des vallées (pliez vers le bas) du côté « propre ».

2

10   21   11   12

make mountain on 'clean side'

image #4

3

10   12

make valley on 'clean side'

image #5

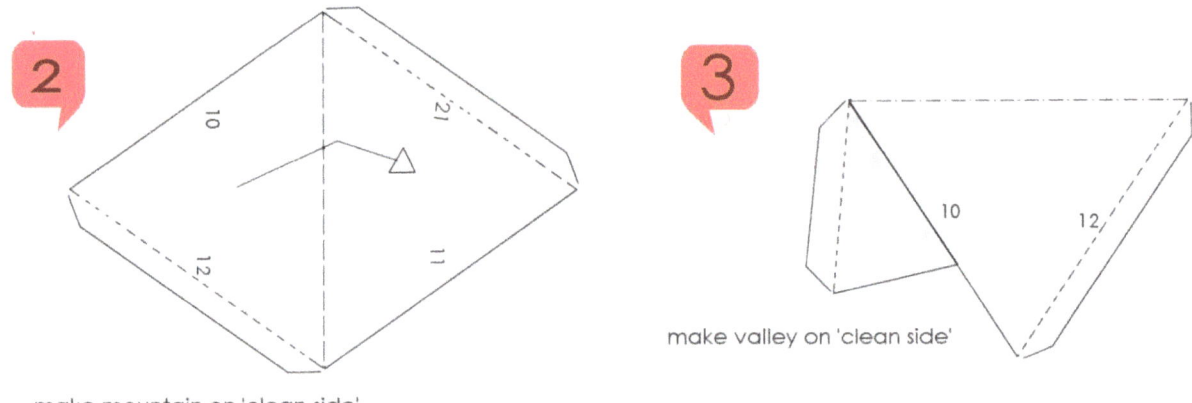

image #6   image #7

4

Une fois cela fait, vous devez trouver les numéros correspondants sur vos onglets (image #8-9) car c'est là que vous collez les deux mêmes onglets de chiffres ensemble. Puisque vous avez un « côté patron » et un « côté propre », vous collez ou utilisez du ruban adhésif double face sur tous les onglets du côté patron afin que votre modèle n'ait aucune trace du modèle une fois terminé (image #10).

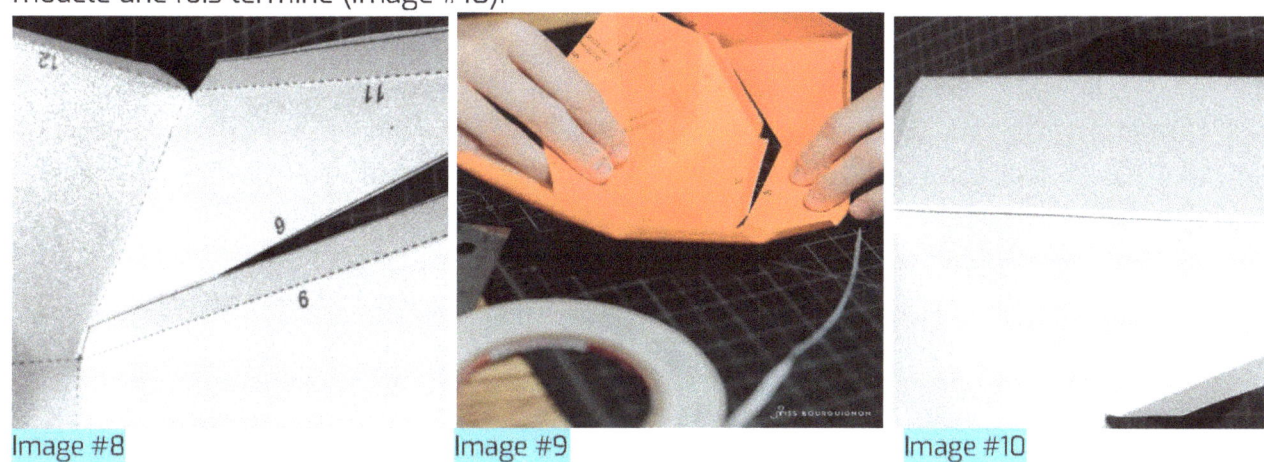

Image #8 Image #9 Image #10

Vous pouvez avoir des coins où votre bâton de colle ne peut pas atteindre, donc vous pouvez utiliser un cure-dent pour appliquer la colle (image #12) ou utiliser un autre type de colle qui aura une meilleure portée (image #13). L'utilisation de ruban adhésif double face « fort » est également une bonne technique (images # 14-15).

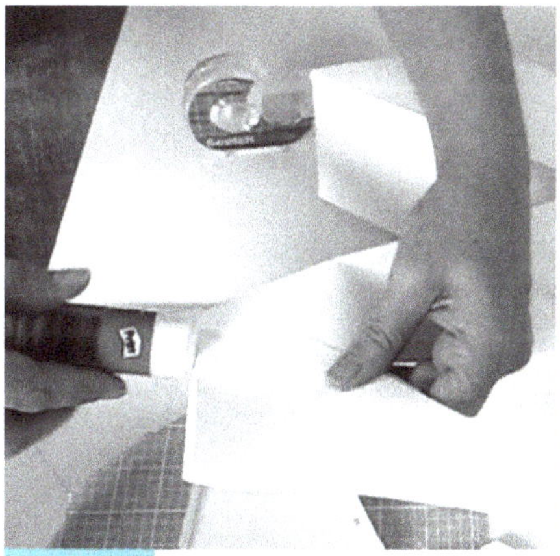

Image #11  Image #12  Image #13

Image# 14 Image #15

Trucs et Astuces :

Lorsque vous commencez, il est bon de planifier un peu à l'avance, par exemple parfois le modèle aura des instructions spécifiques sur le patron lui-même.

Aussi, NOUS VOUS RECOMMANDONS de commencer par le haut du modèle et de vous digérer vers le bas en ajoutant une pièce à la fois. Par exemple, commencez par une pièce de la tête et ajoutez une pièce jusqu'à ce que la tête soit terminée, puis continuez votre chemin avec les morceaux du corps jusqu'à ce que vous atteigniez la dernière pièce en bas (ou contre le mur). Souvent, cette dernière pièce vous offrira la possibilité de couper un trou afin que vous puissiez atteindre l'intérieur pour qu'il soit plus facile à coller. Les parties du patron sont écrites sur les pièces afin que vous puissiez dire laquelle est laquelle. Organisez-les un peu pour savoir où vous allez à l'avance.

Gardez à l'esprit que c'est un peu comme faire un casse-tête. L'activité prend un certain temps et ne doit pas être « précipitée ». Prenez votre temps et profitez du moment!

Si vous voulez rendre votre papercraft plus solide, vous pouvez utiliser du mod podge ou de la resine. Aussi vous pouvez insérer du papier de journeaux froissés.

Voilà! Maintenant, vous savez tout sur la fabrication de papercraft 3D. Le reste viendra avec l'expérience!

Recyclez lorsque vous avez terminé!

IDEA

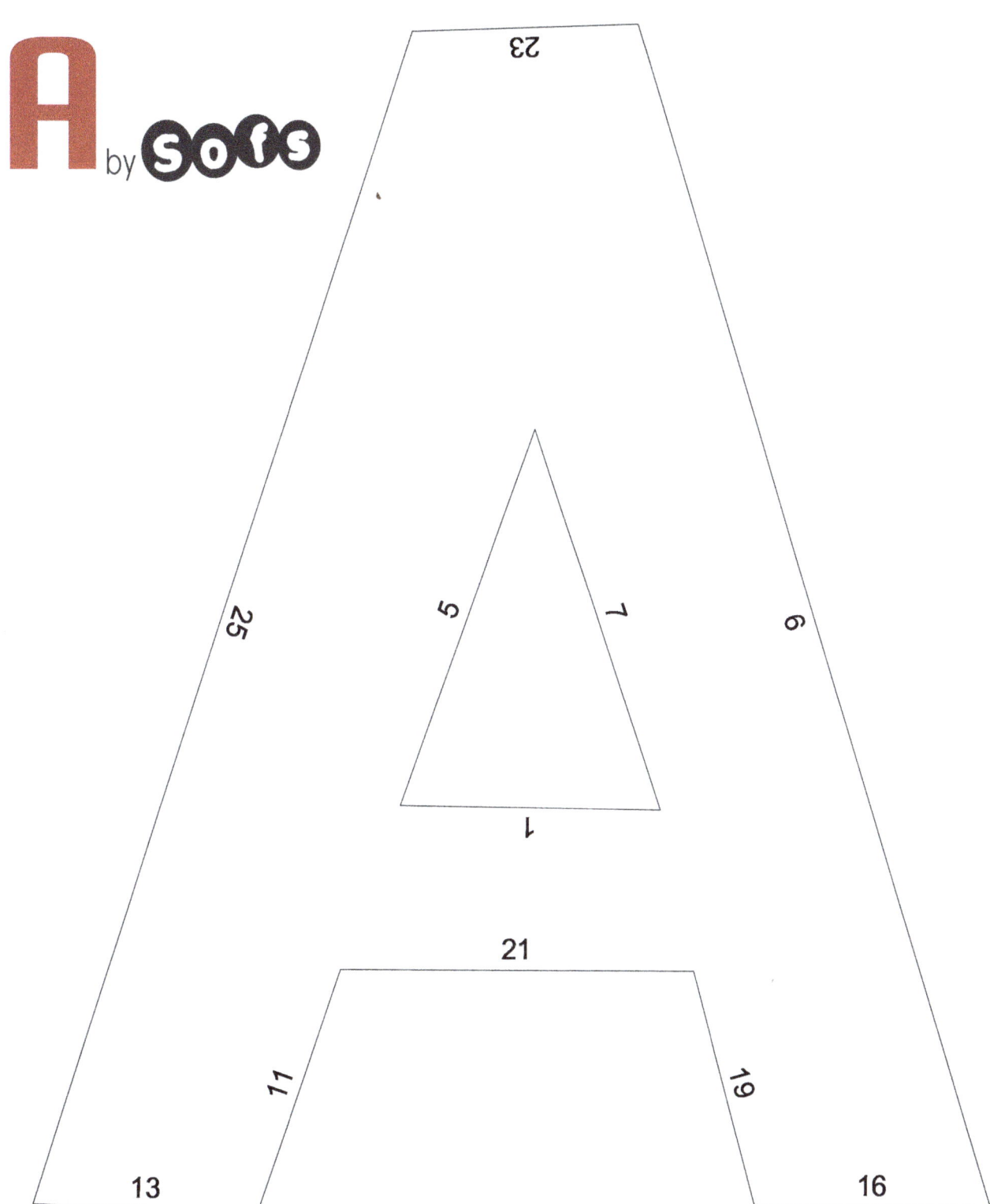

A by Sofs

p.1/4

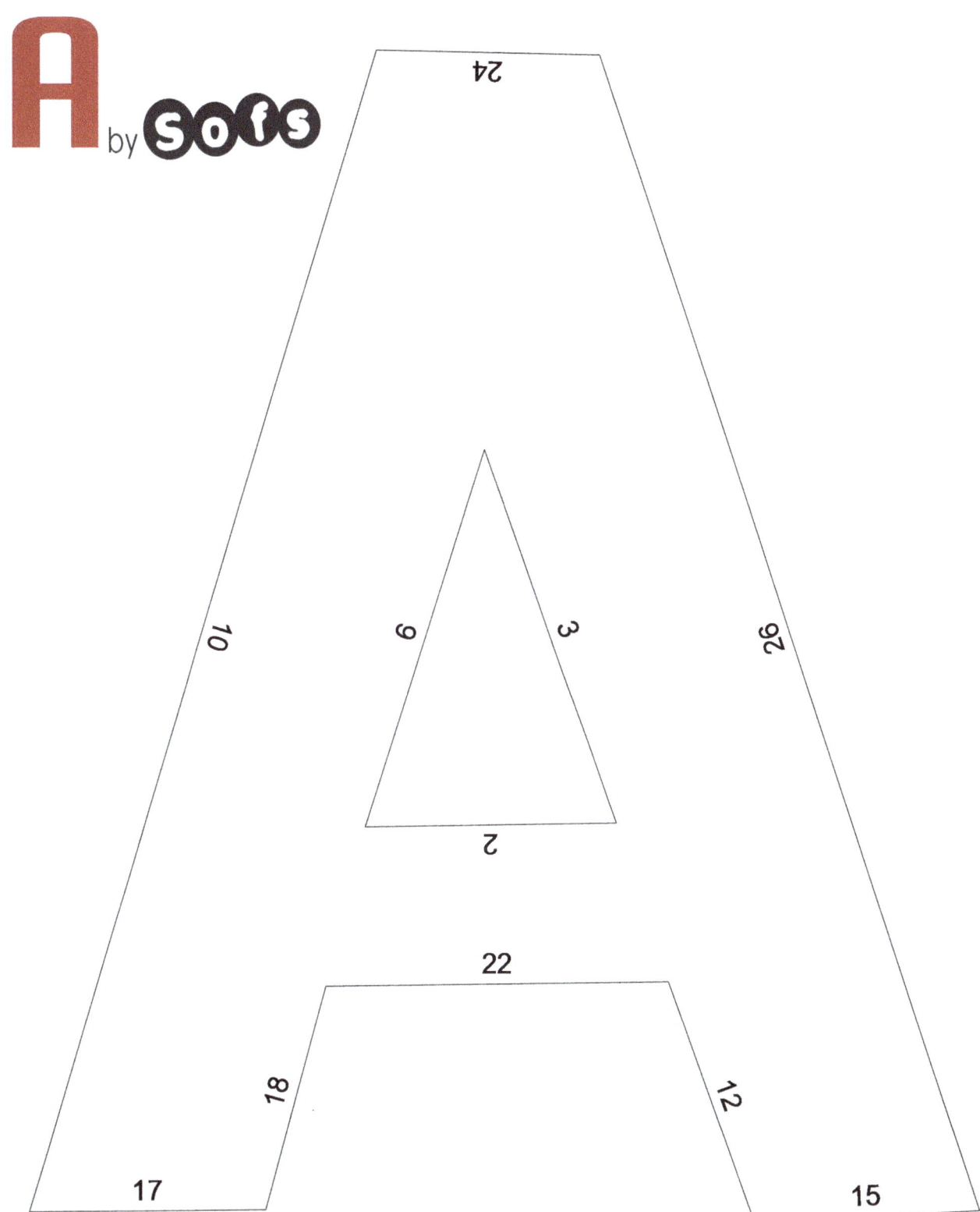

A by Sofs

p.2/4

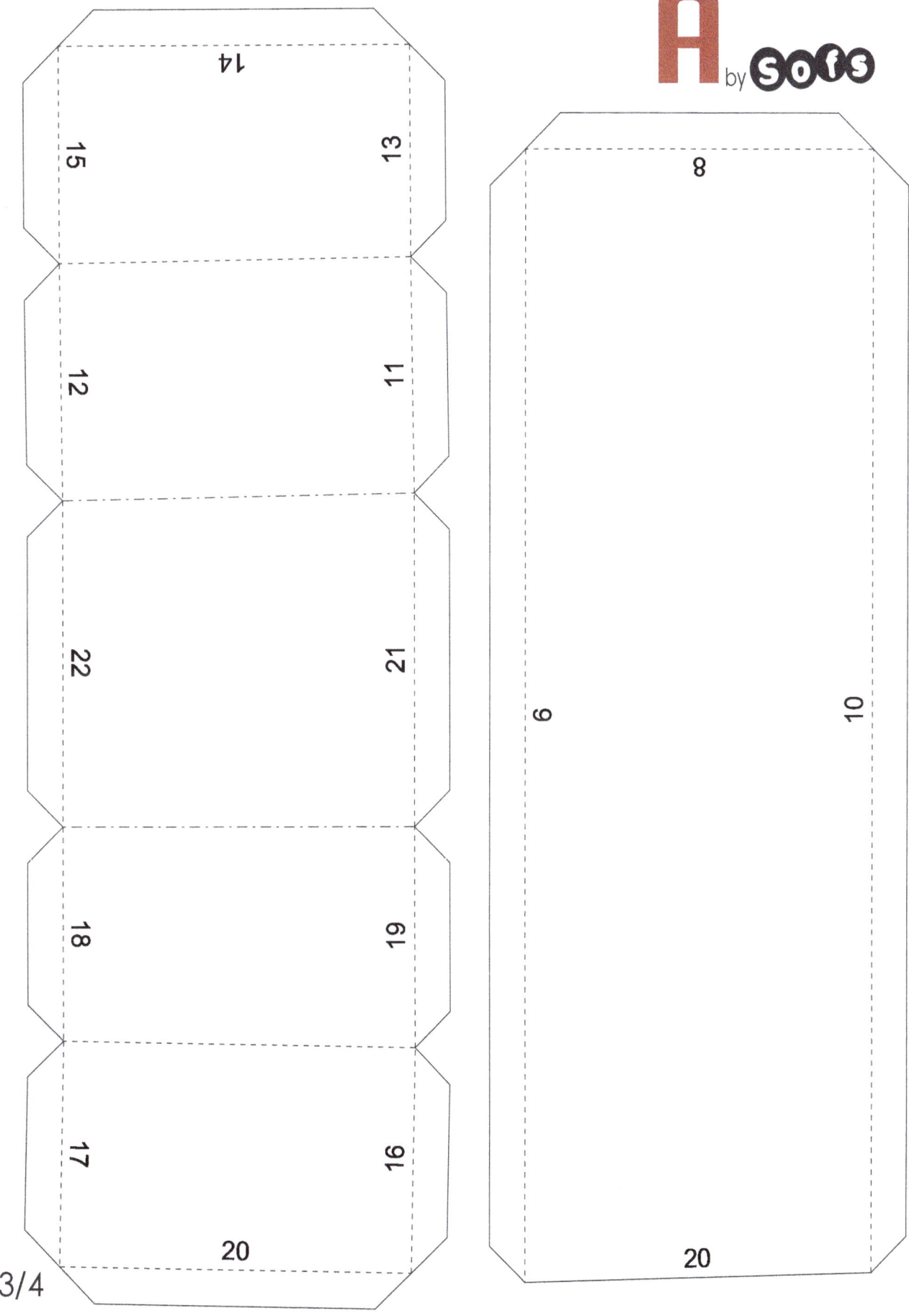

p.3/4

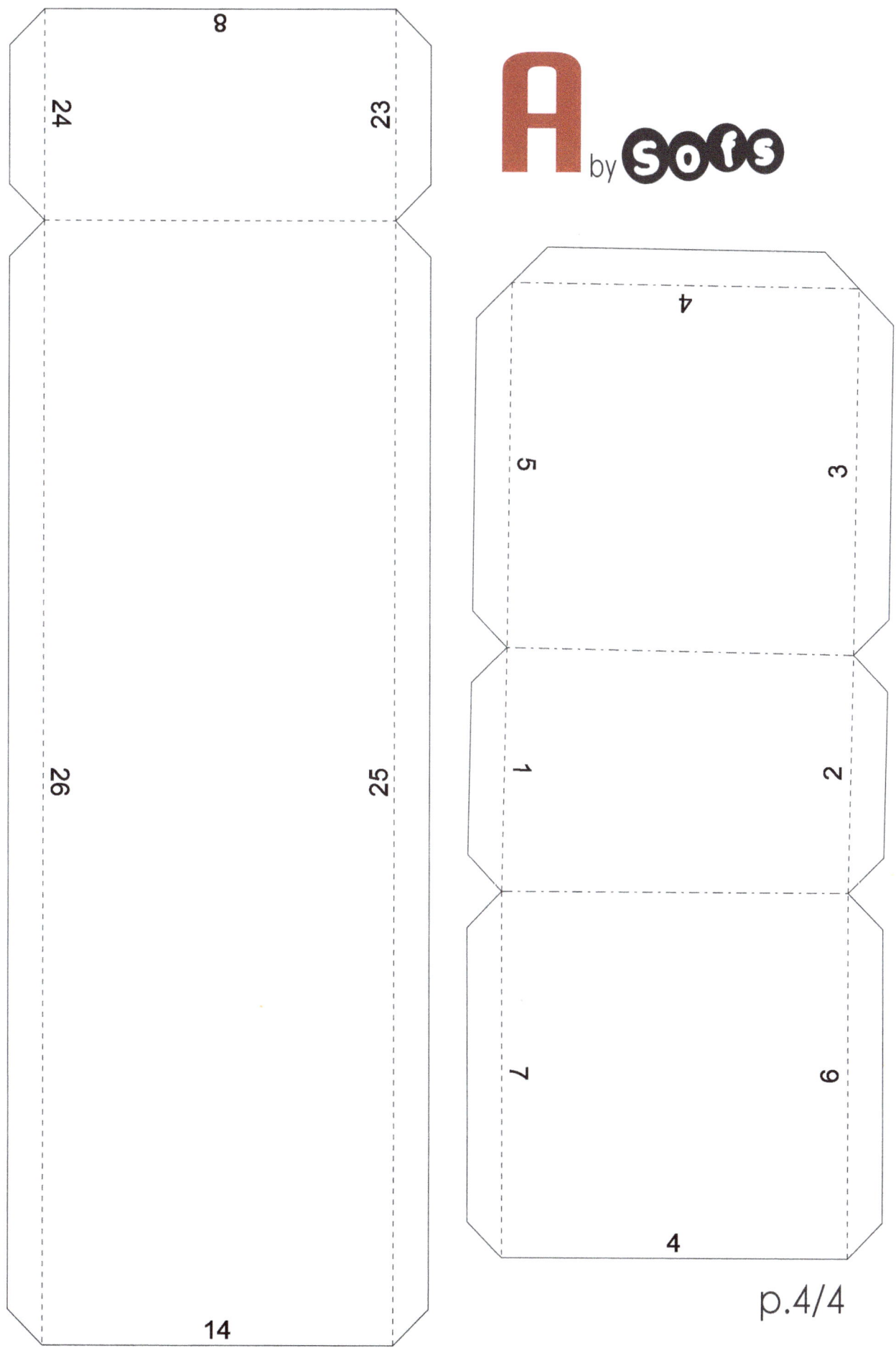

A by Sofs

p.4/4

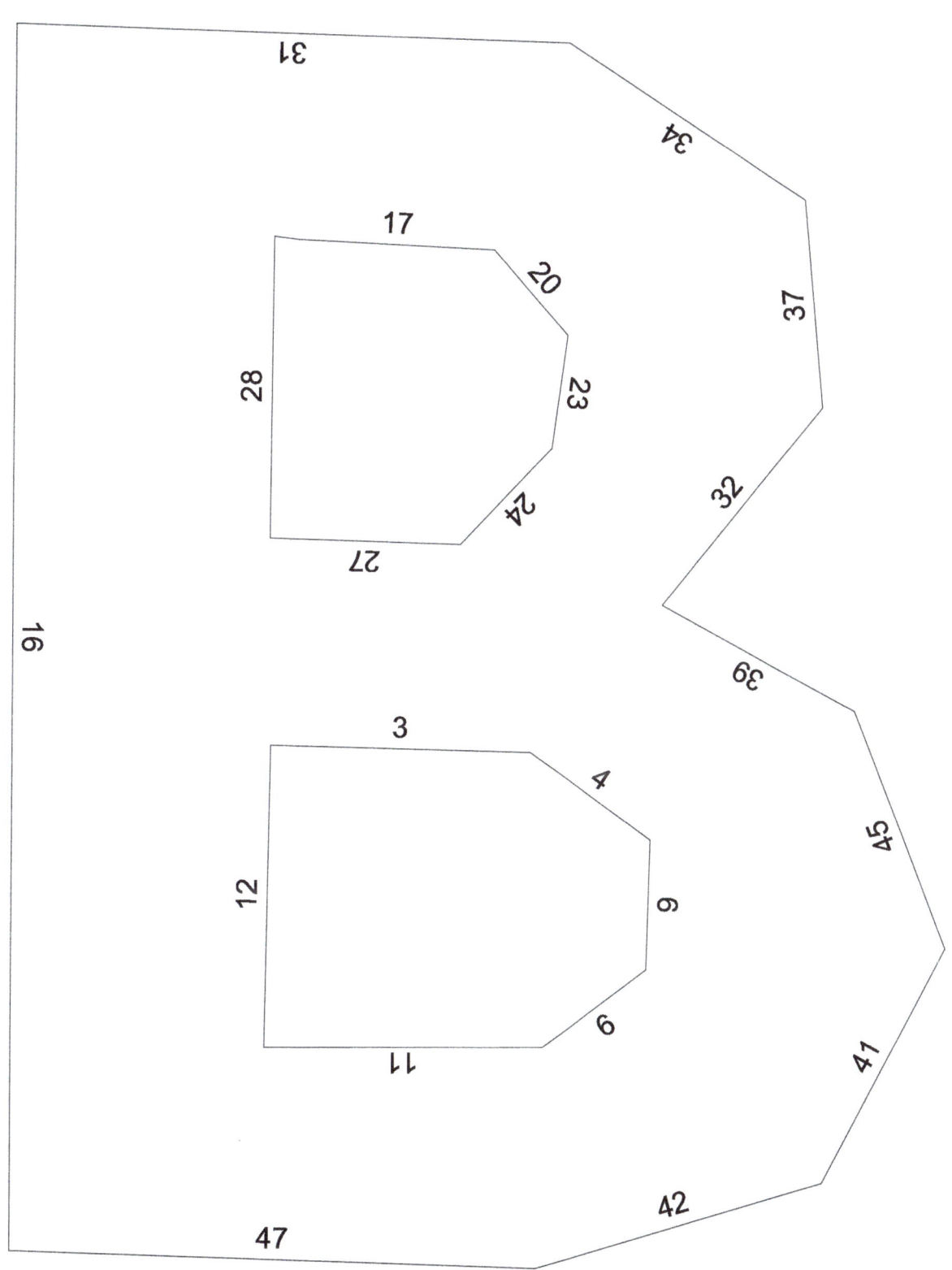

B by Sofs

p.1/5

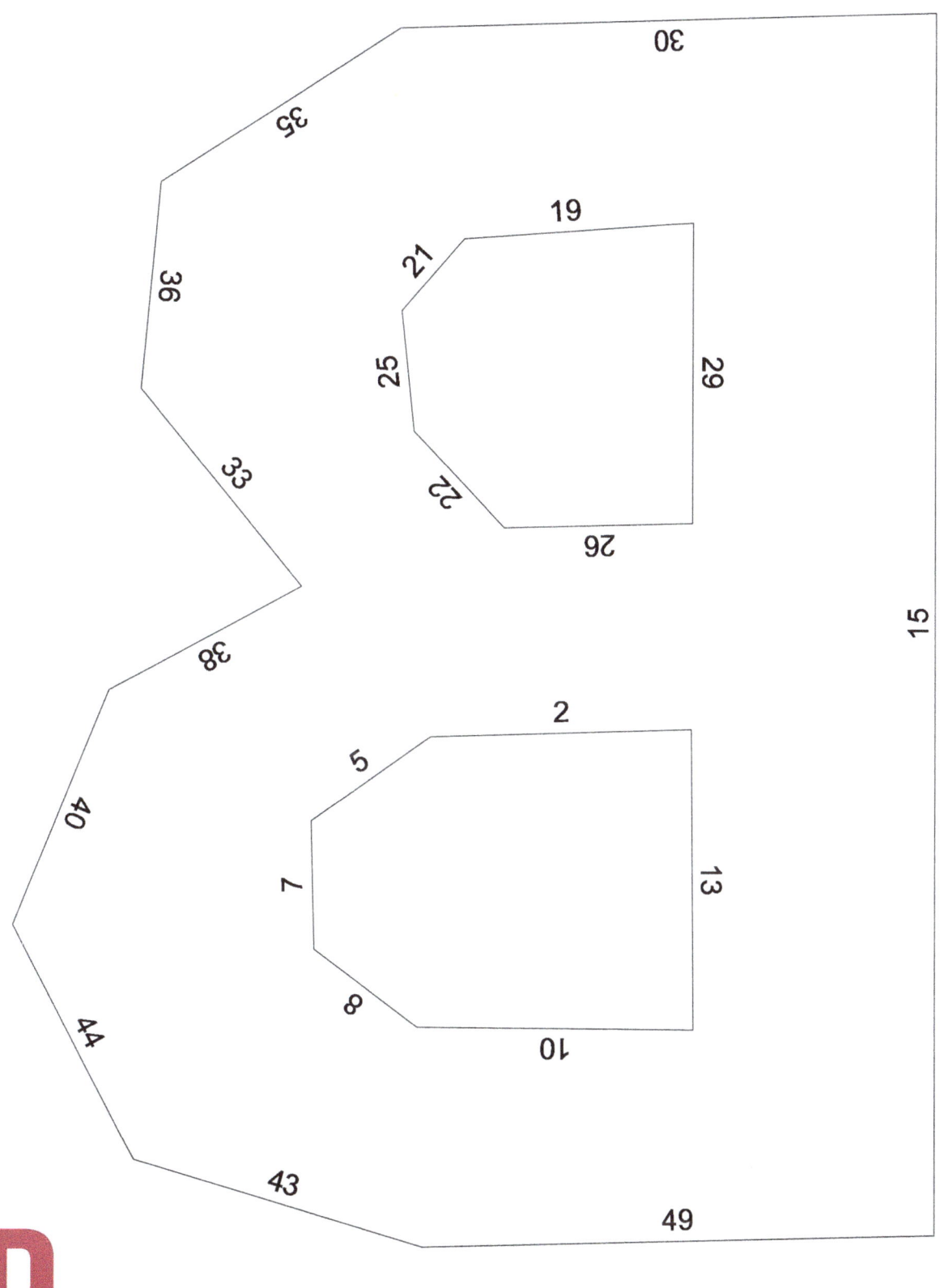

B

by Sofs

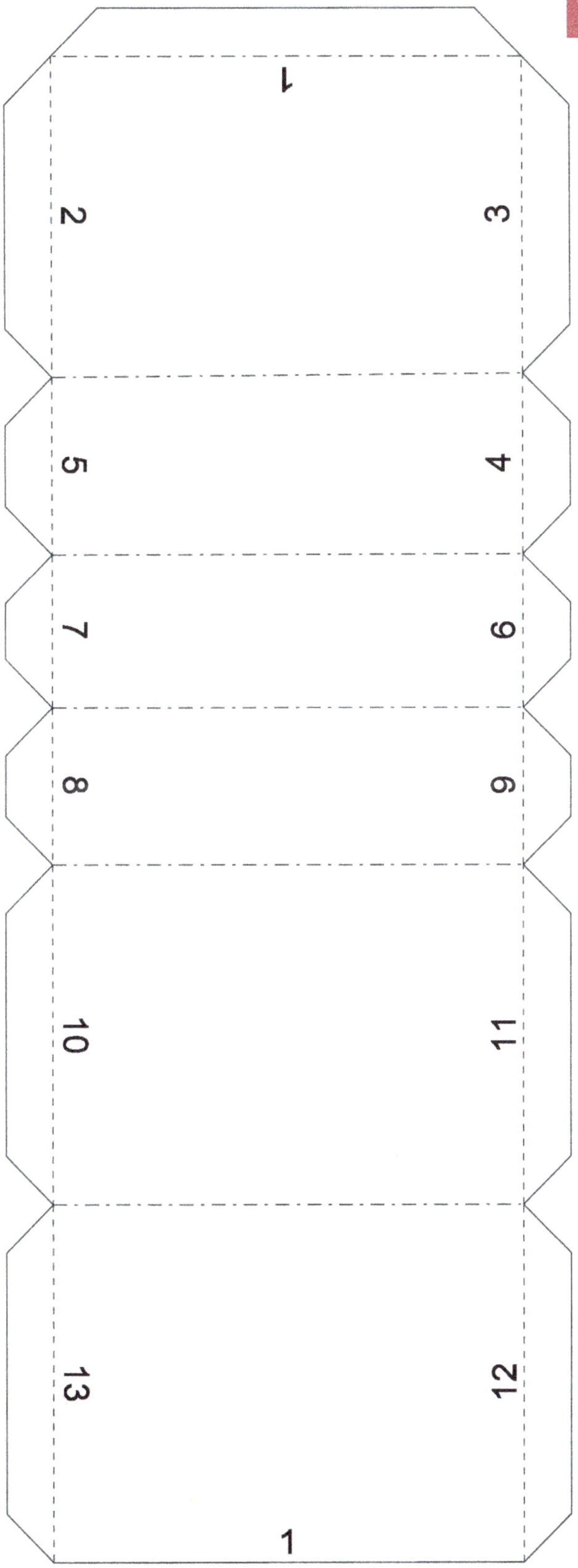

1

2

3

5

4

7

6

8

9

10

11

13

12

1

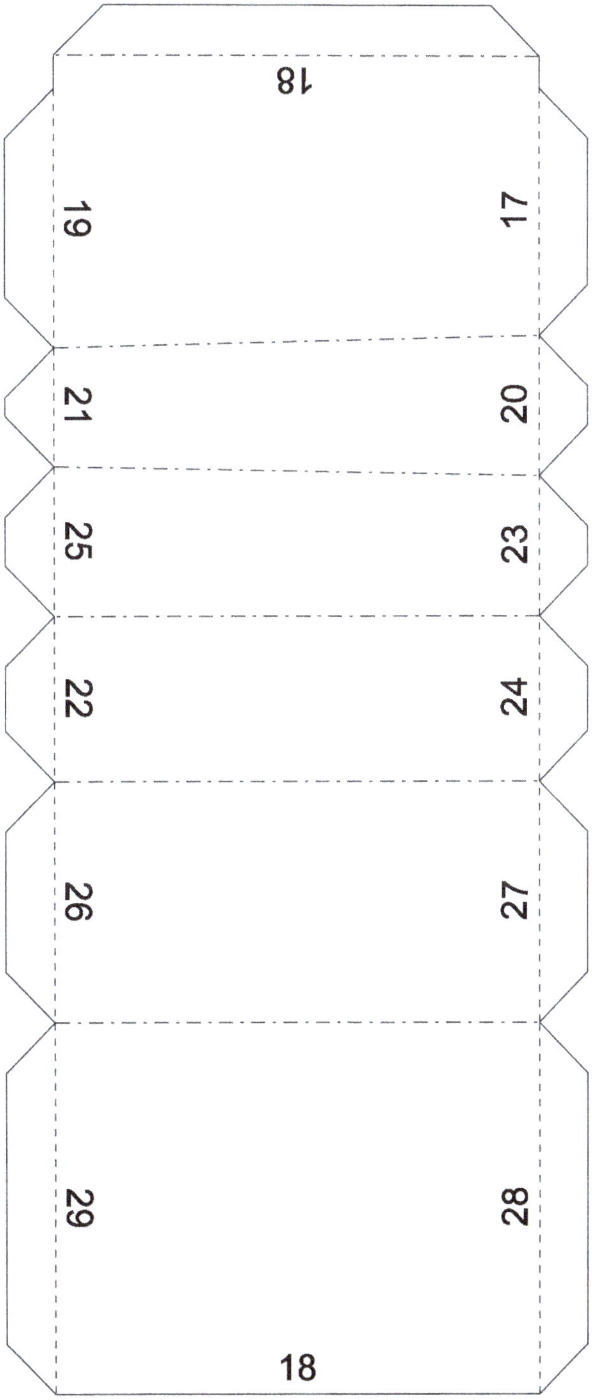

18

19

17

21

20

25

23

22

24

26

27

29

28

18

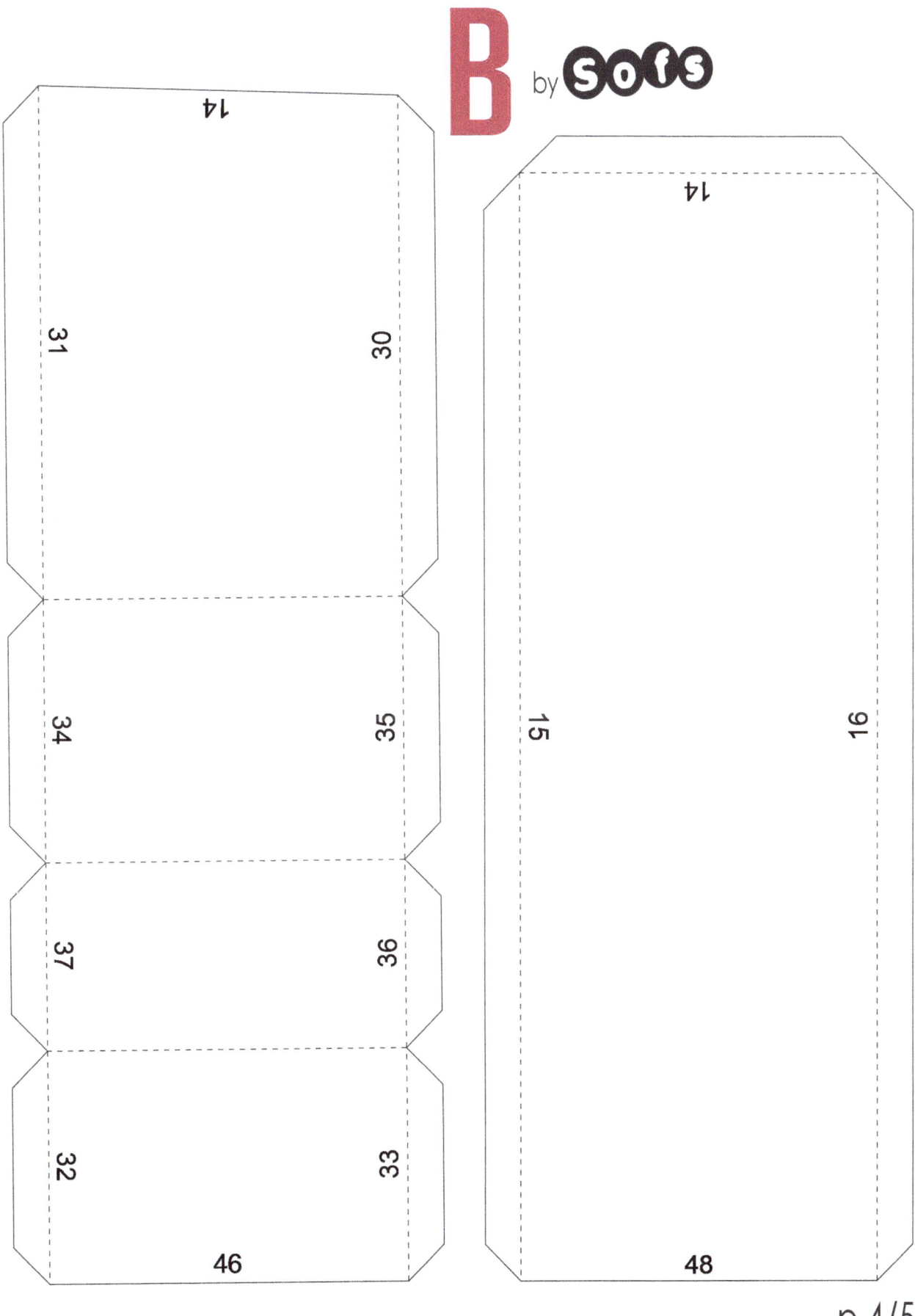

B by Sofs

p.4/5

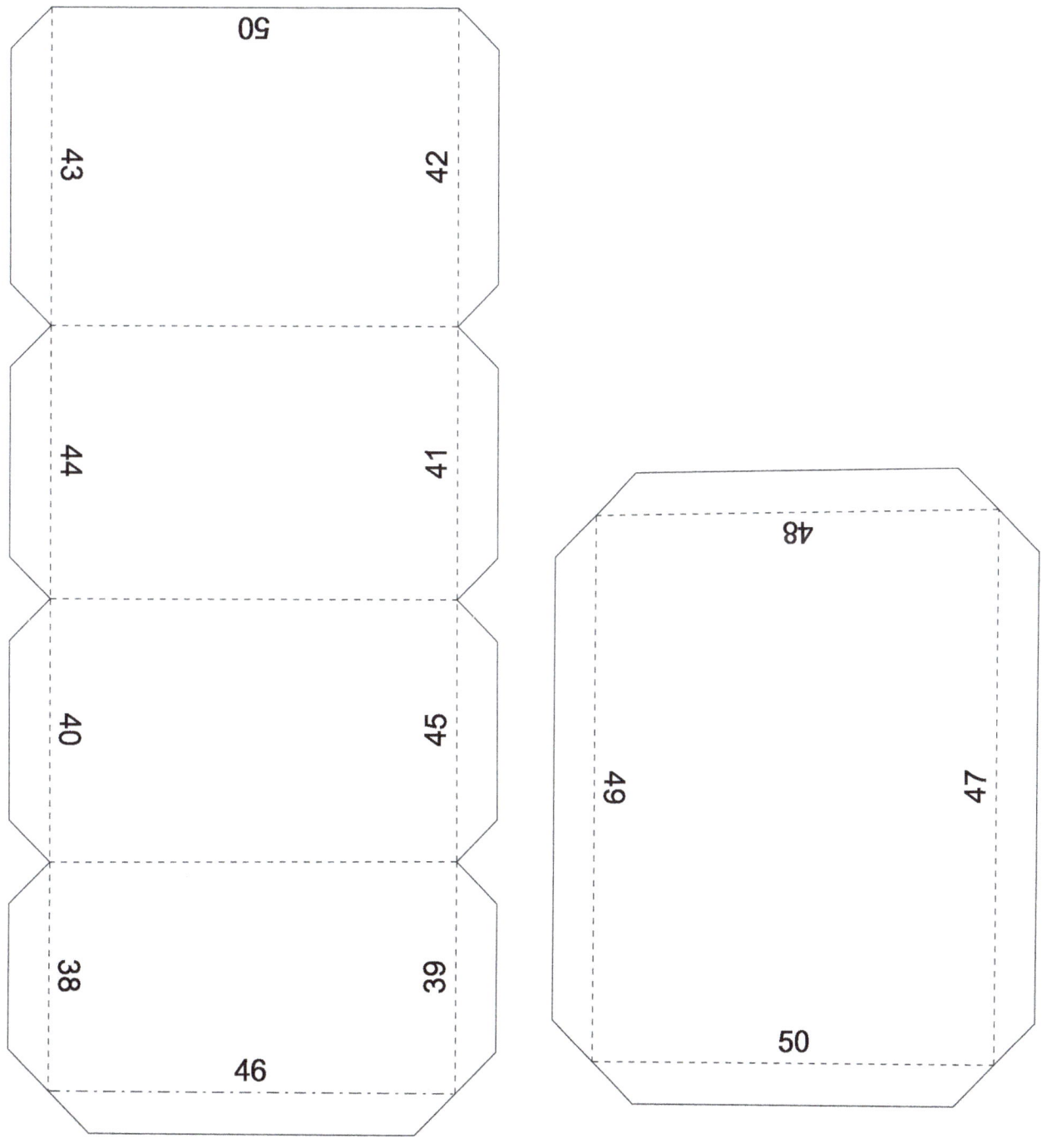

50

43

42

44

41

40

45

38

39

46

48

49

47

50

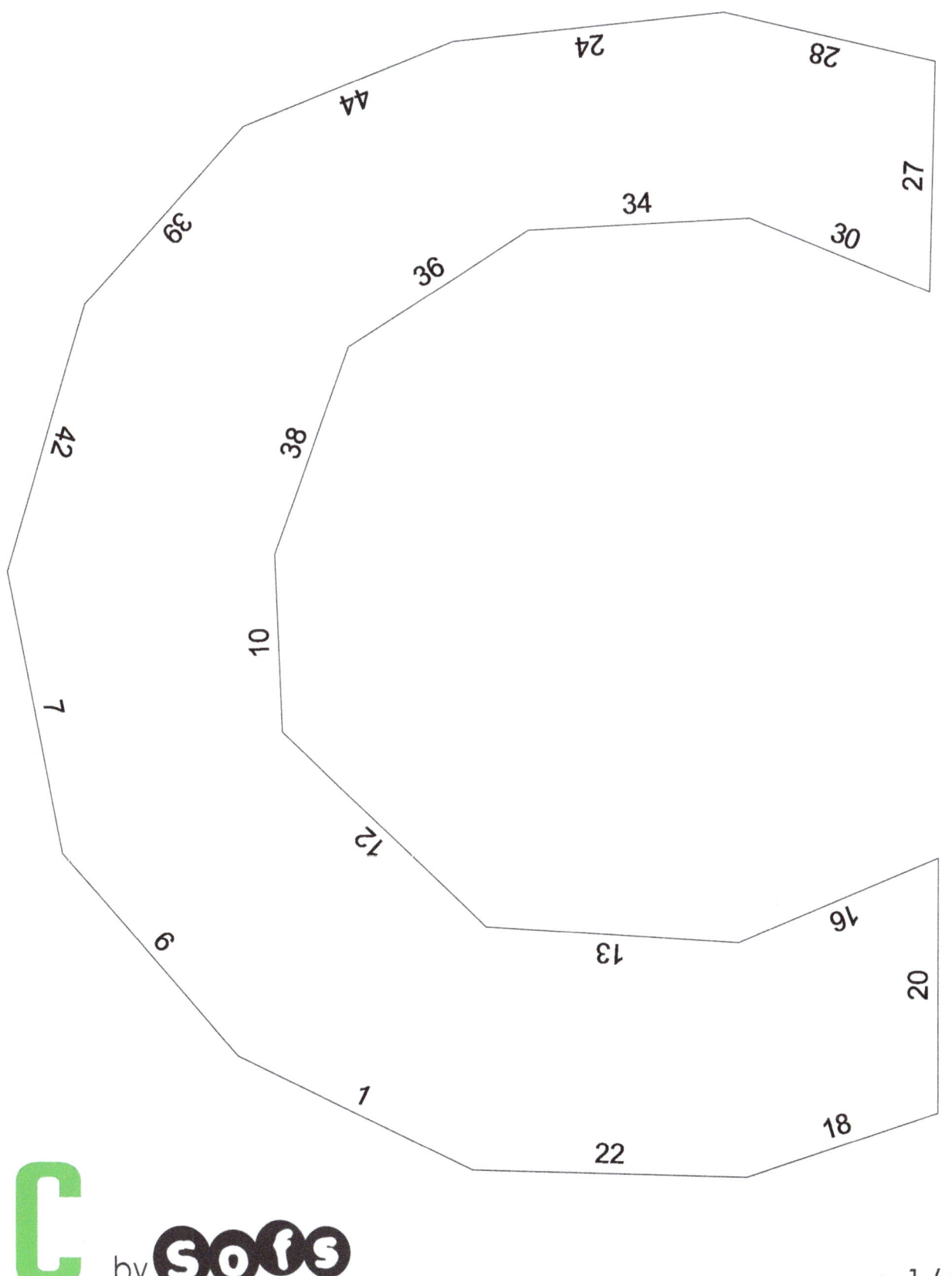

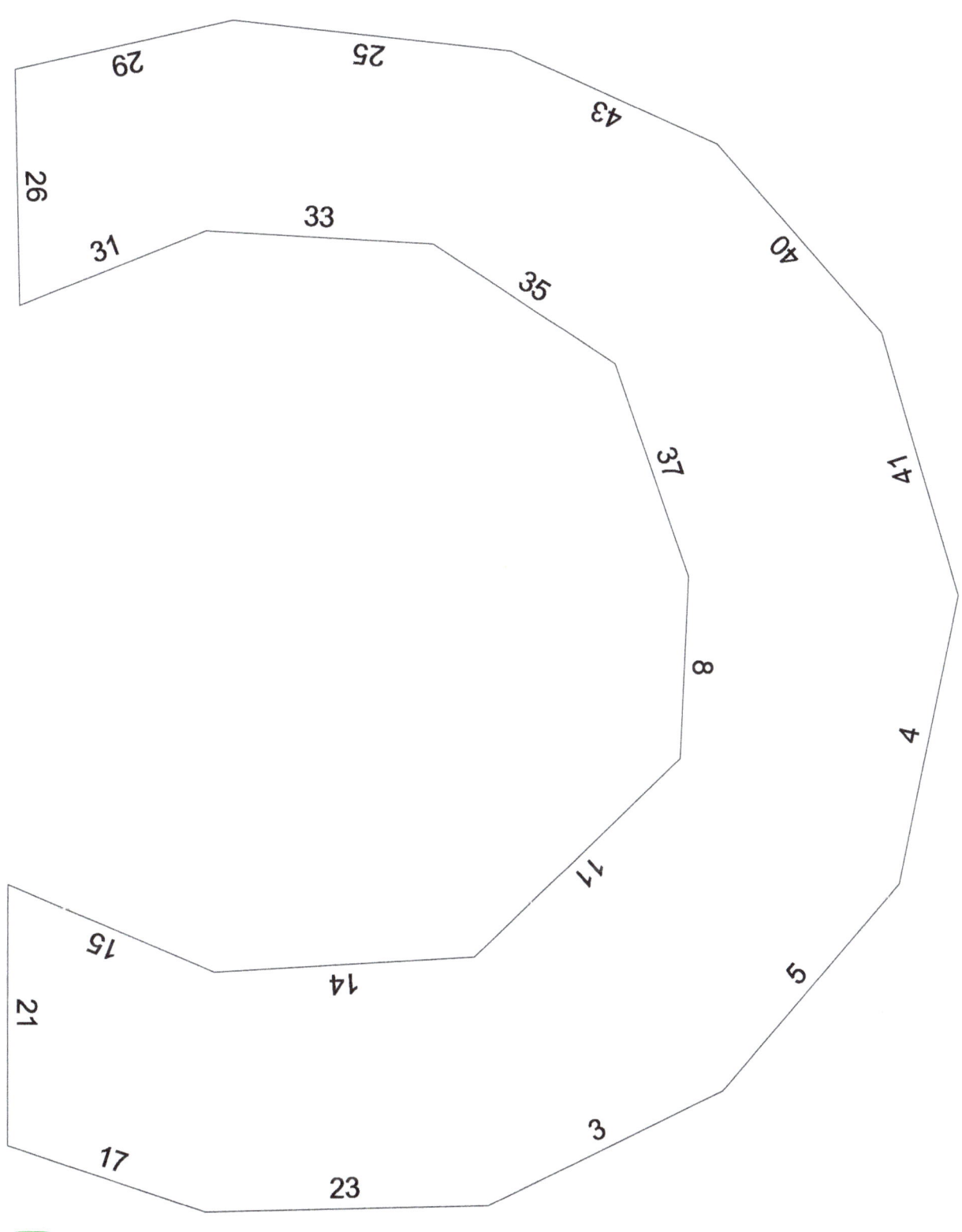

C by Sofs

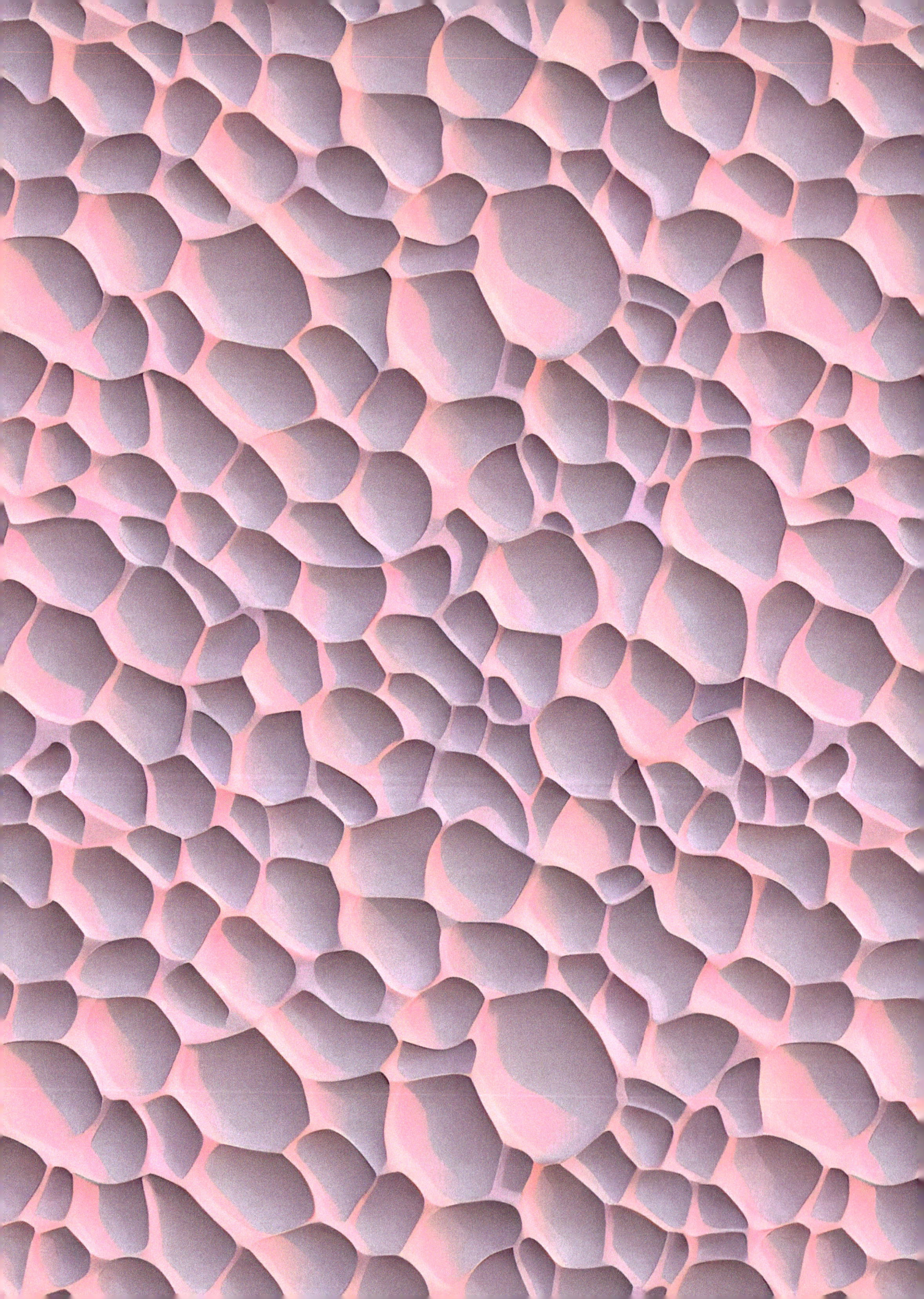

C
by
Sofs

p.4/4

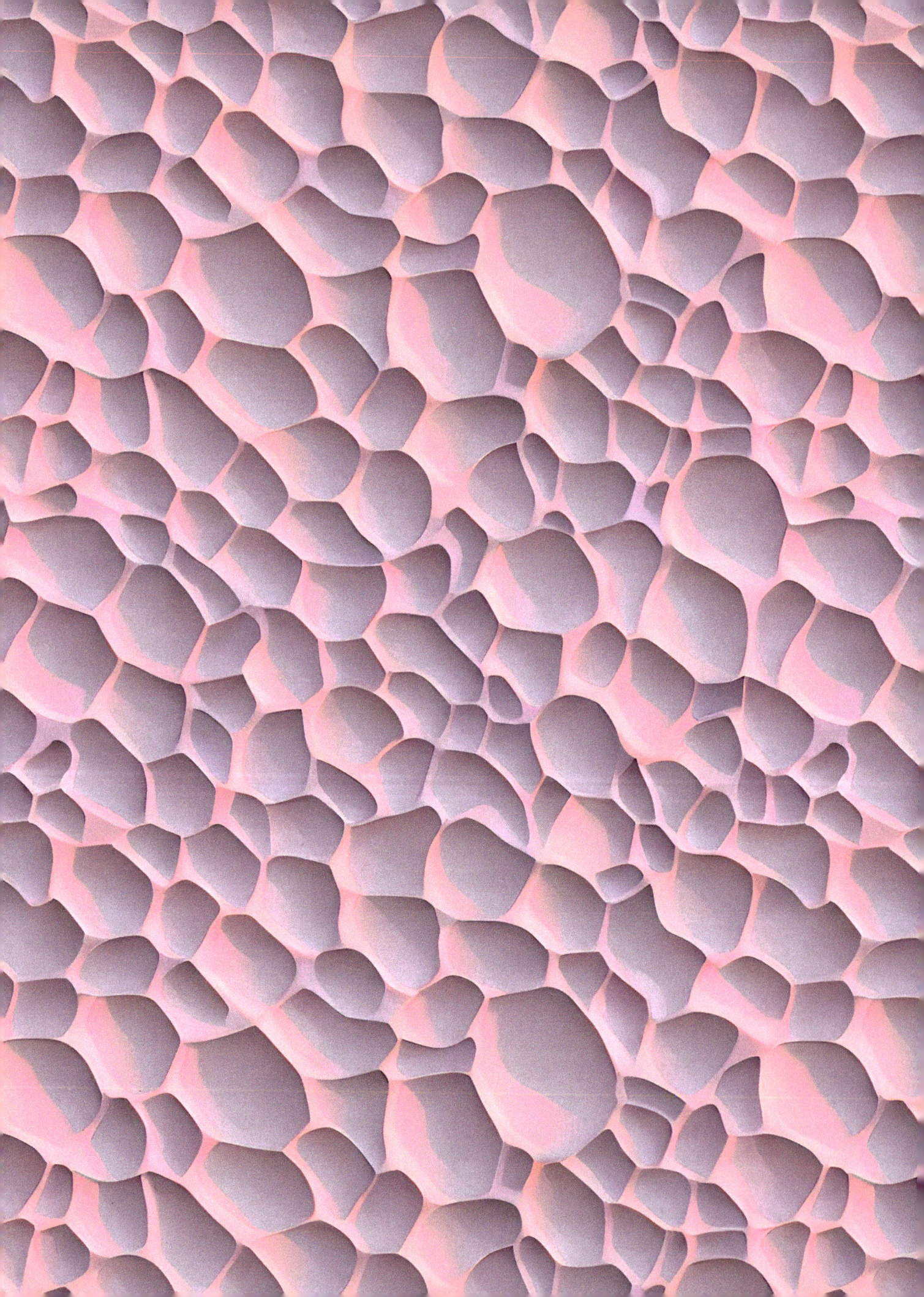

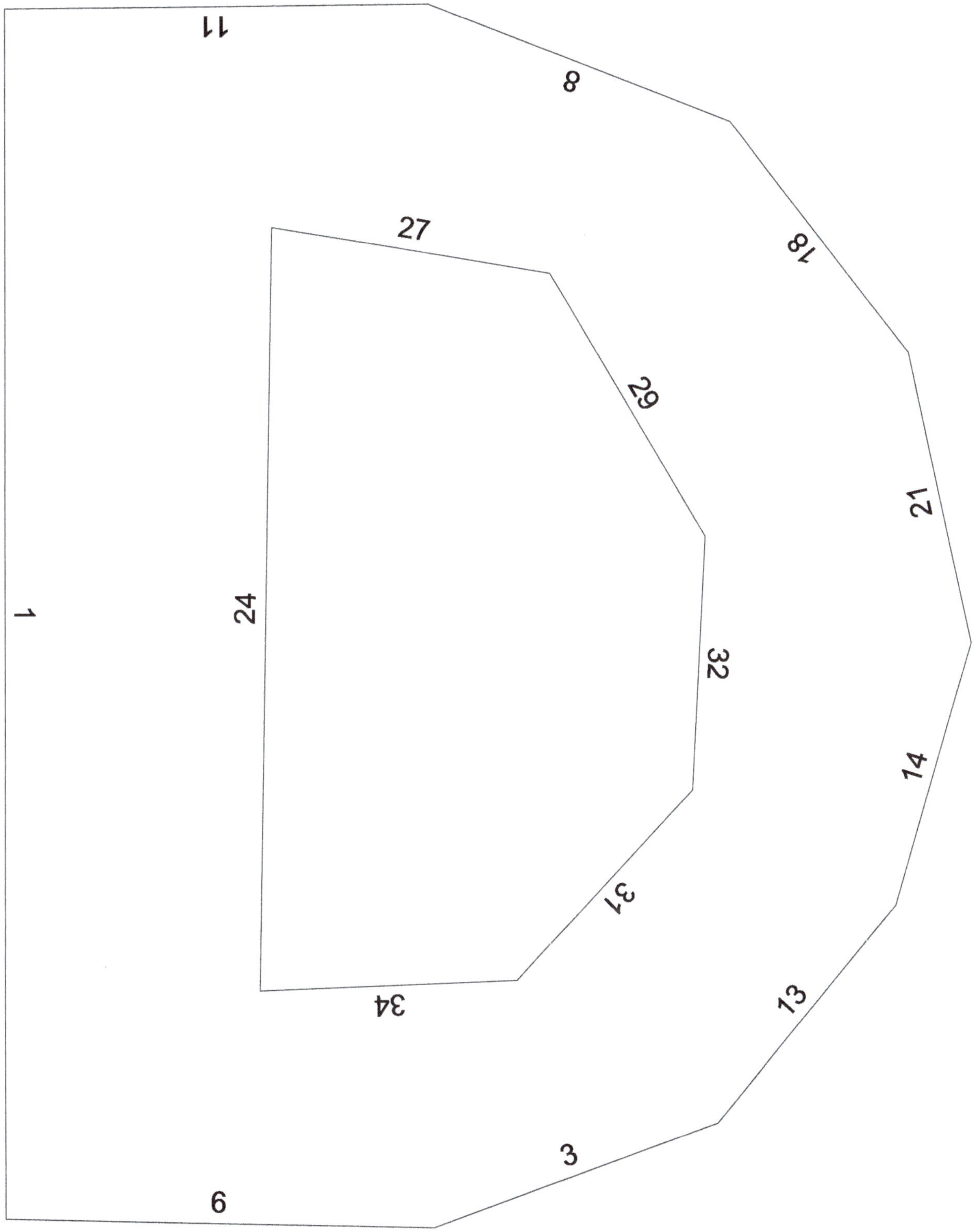

11

8

27

18

29

24

1

21

32

31

14

34

13

3

9

D  by Sofs

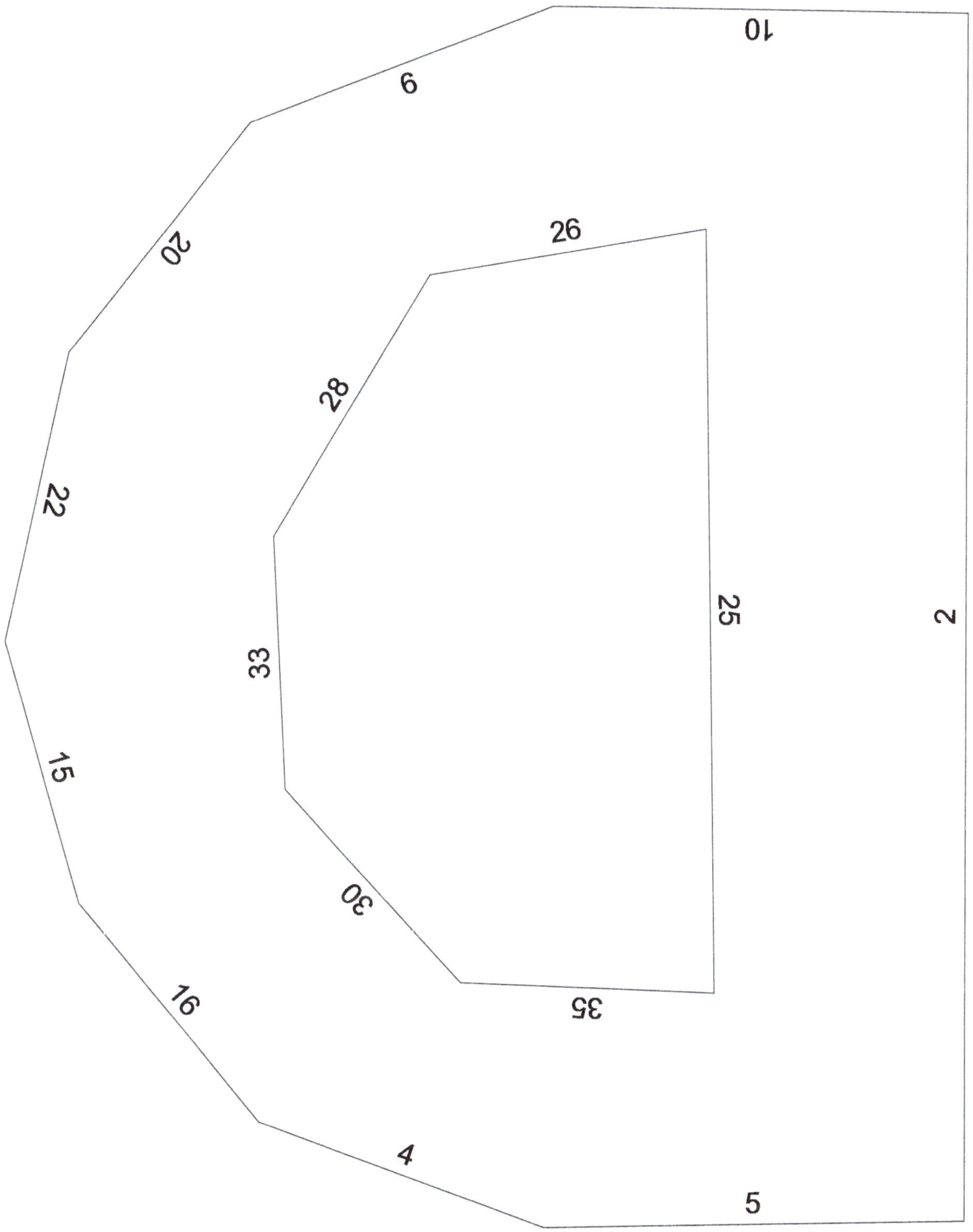

10

6

20

26

28

22

33

25

2

15

30

35

16

4

5

by

p.2/5

D by sofs

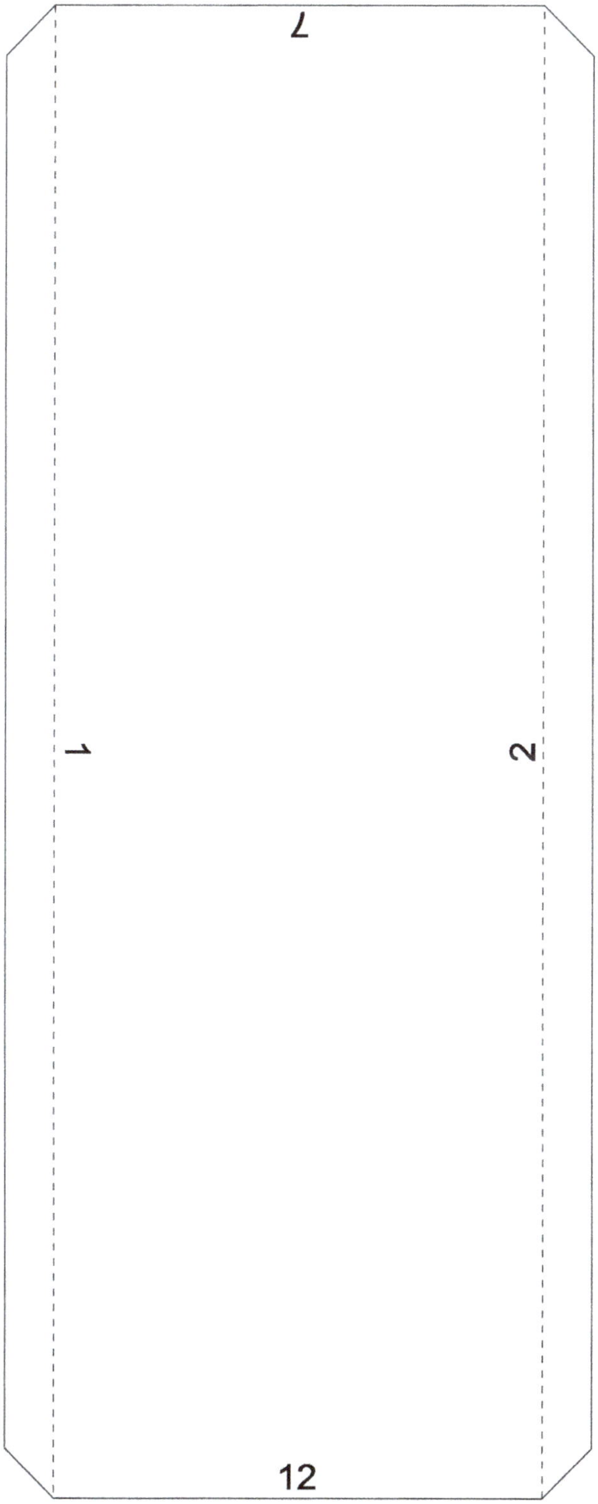
7
1
2
12

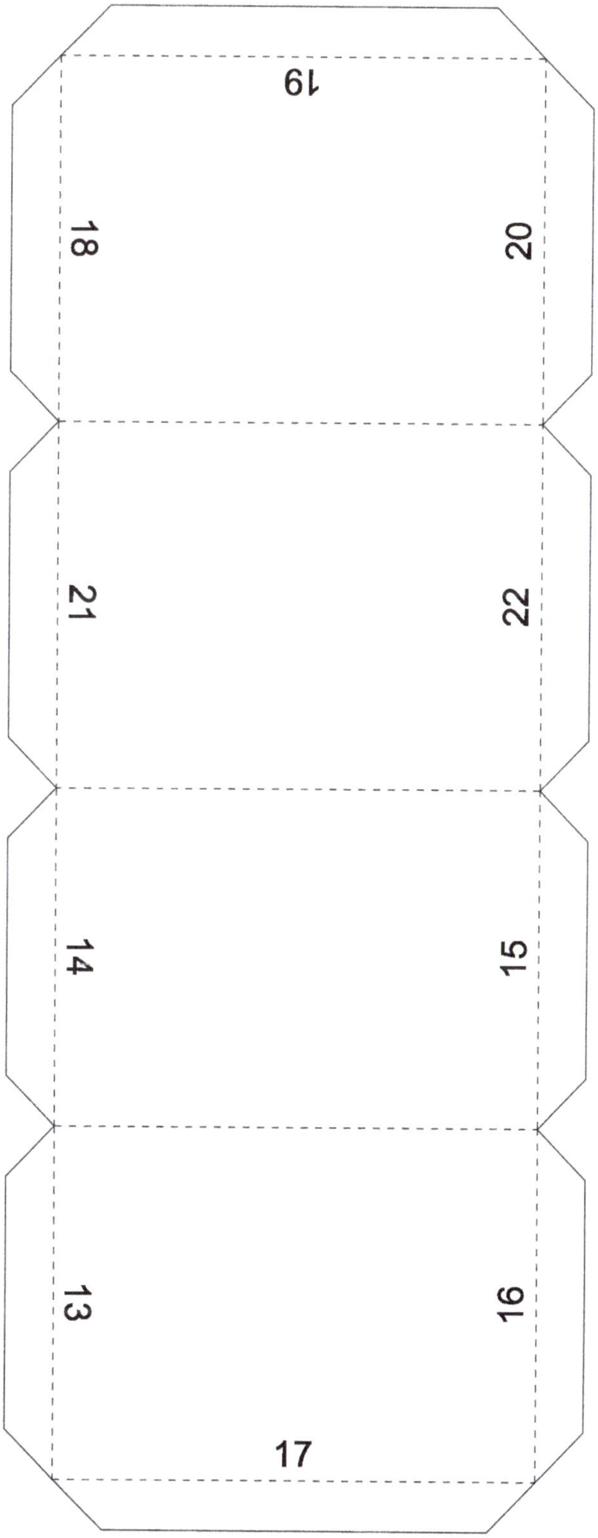
19
18
20
21
22
14
15
13
16
17

D by Sofs

17

3

4

6

5

7

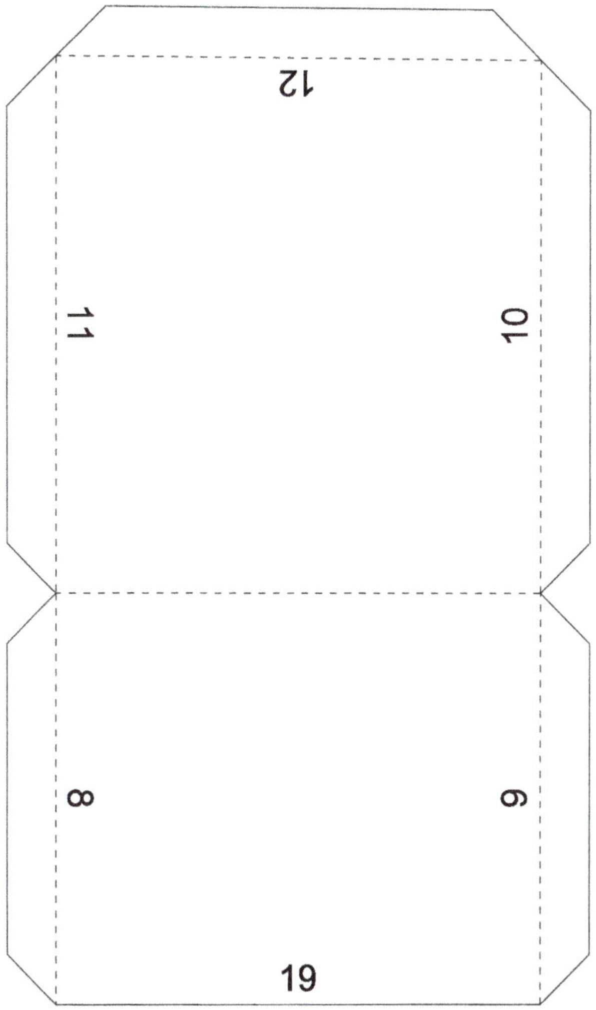

12

11

10

8

9

19

22

19

20

14

25

28

30

13

6

4

3

9

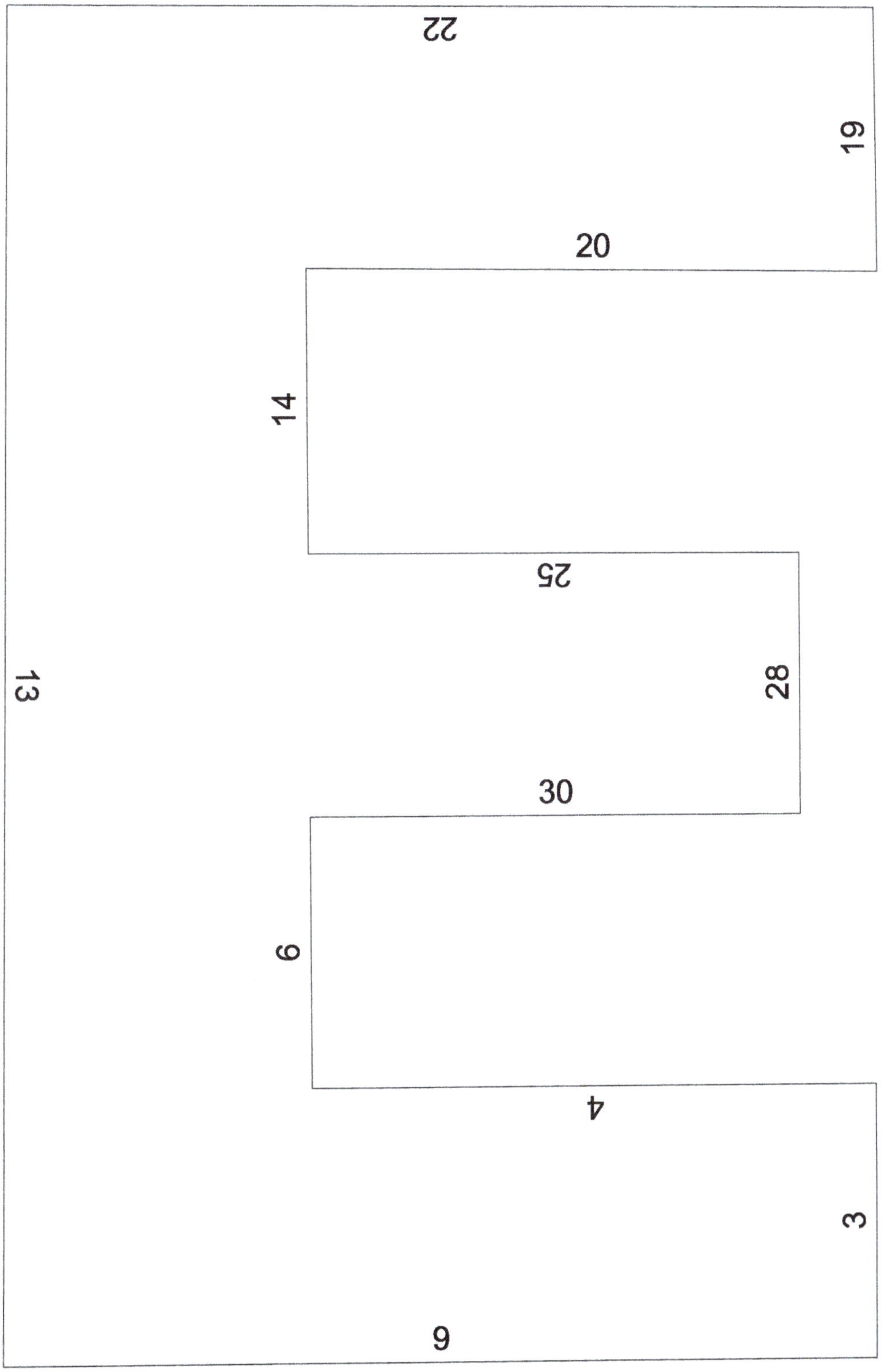

E by sofs

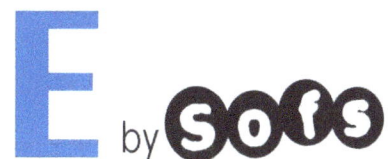

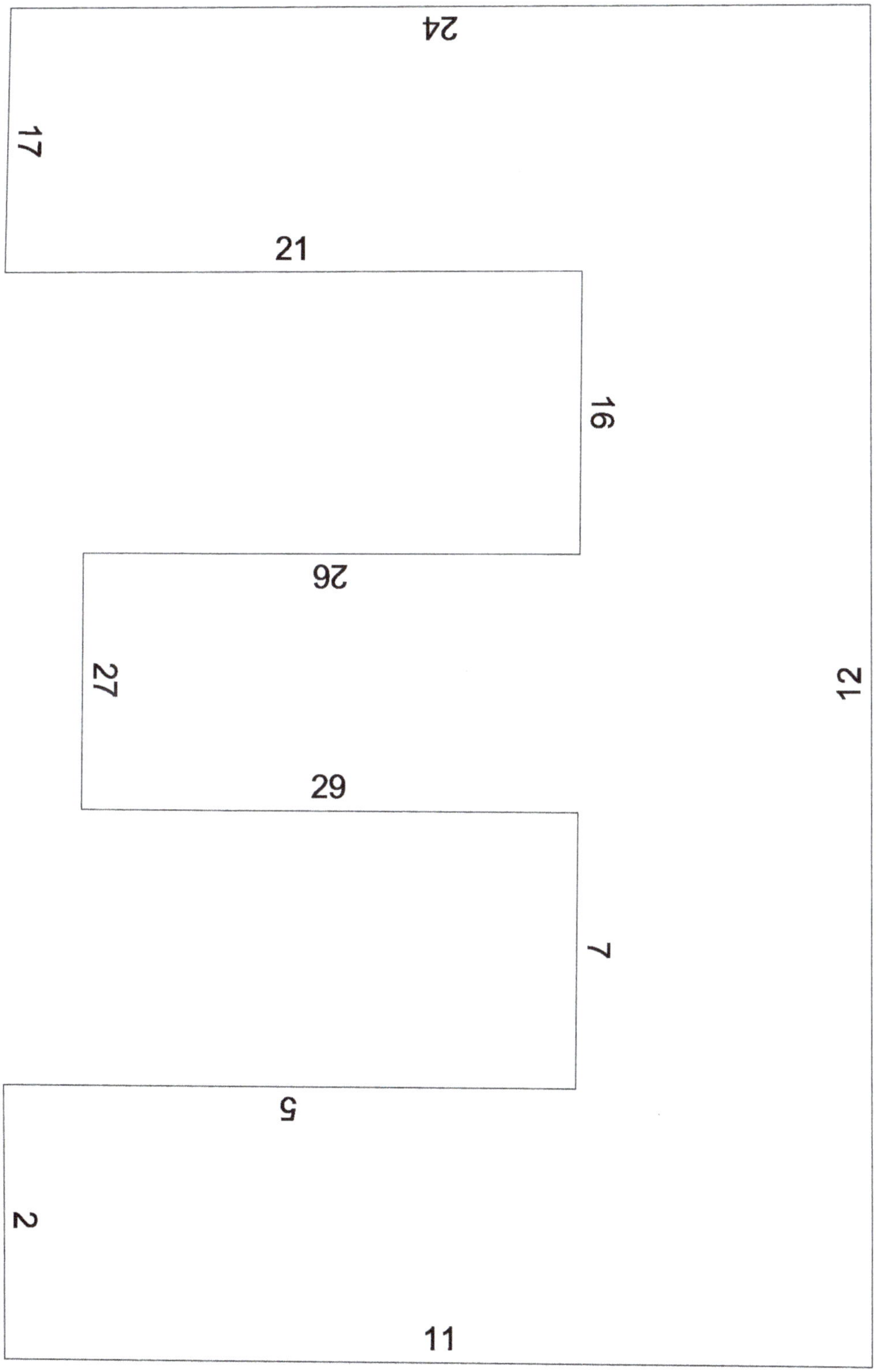
24
17
21
16
26
27
12
29
7
5
2
11

18

24

22

23

10

11

6

1

E by sofs

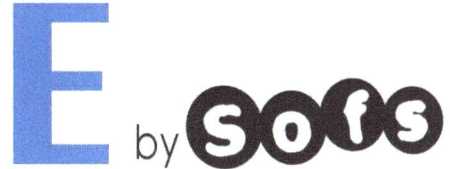

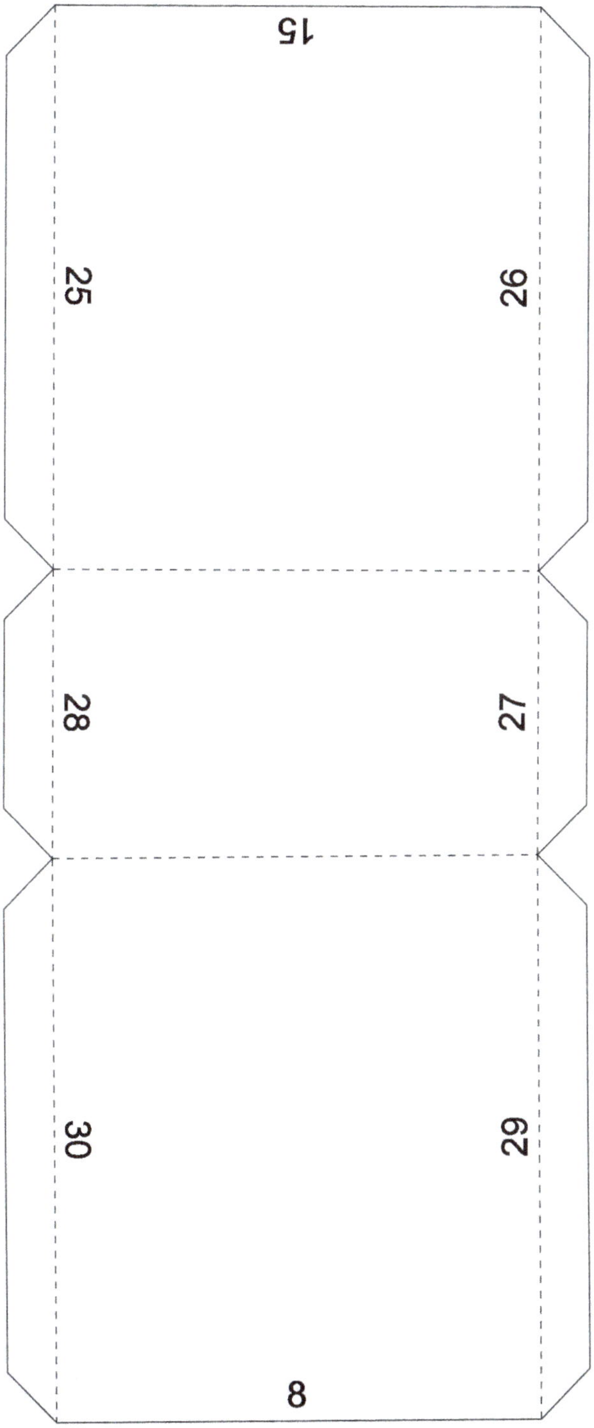
15
25
26
28
27
30
29
8

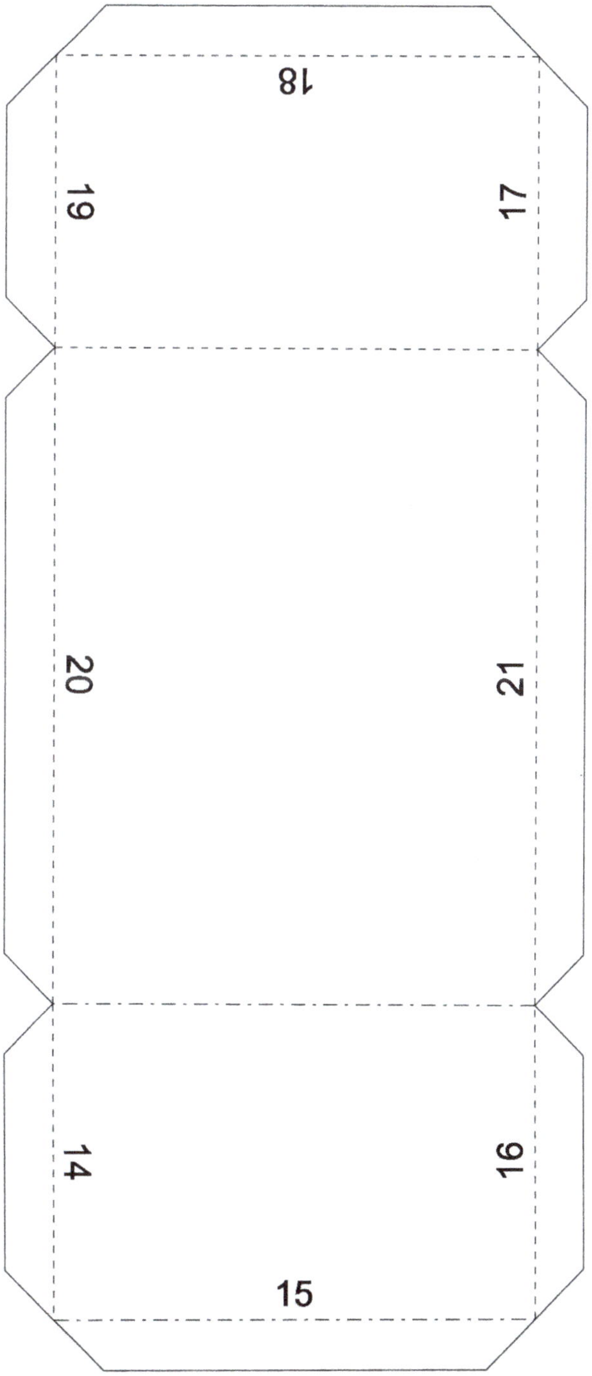
18
19
17
20
21
14
16
15

E by Sofs

23

12

13

10

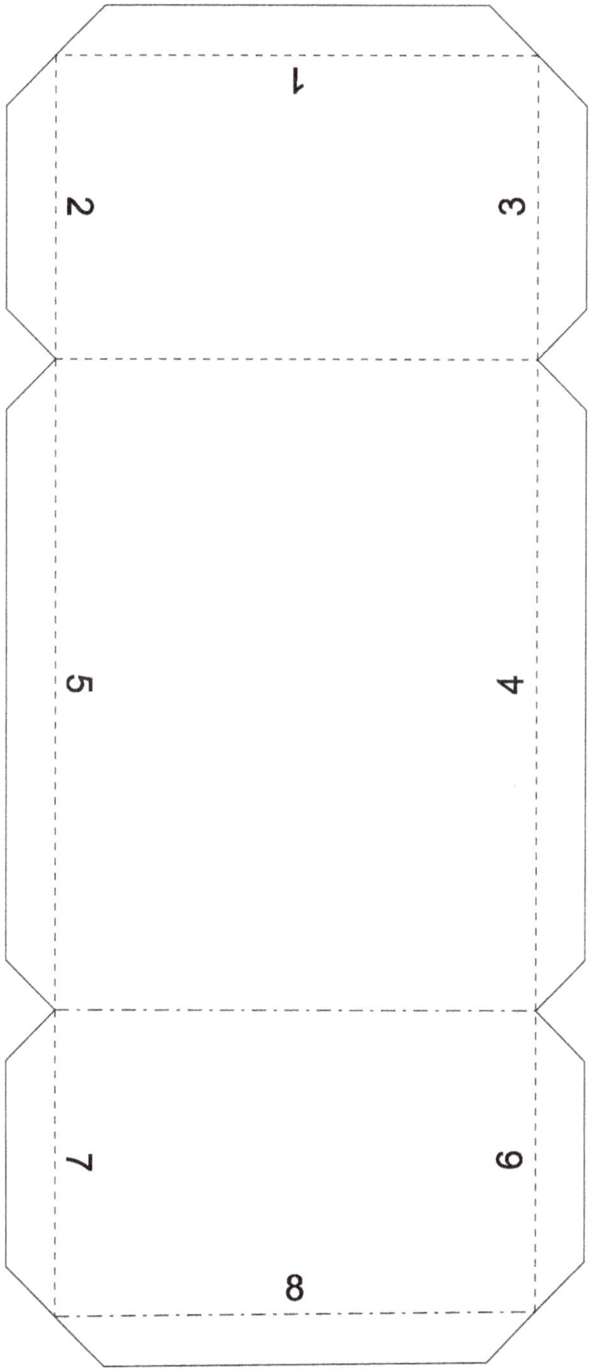

2

3

1

5

4

7

6

8

p.5/5

10

12

19

21

22

5

7

16

2

4

F by sofs

11

13

18

20

23

6

15

8

1

3

F by sofs

F by Sofs

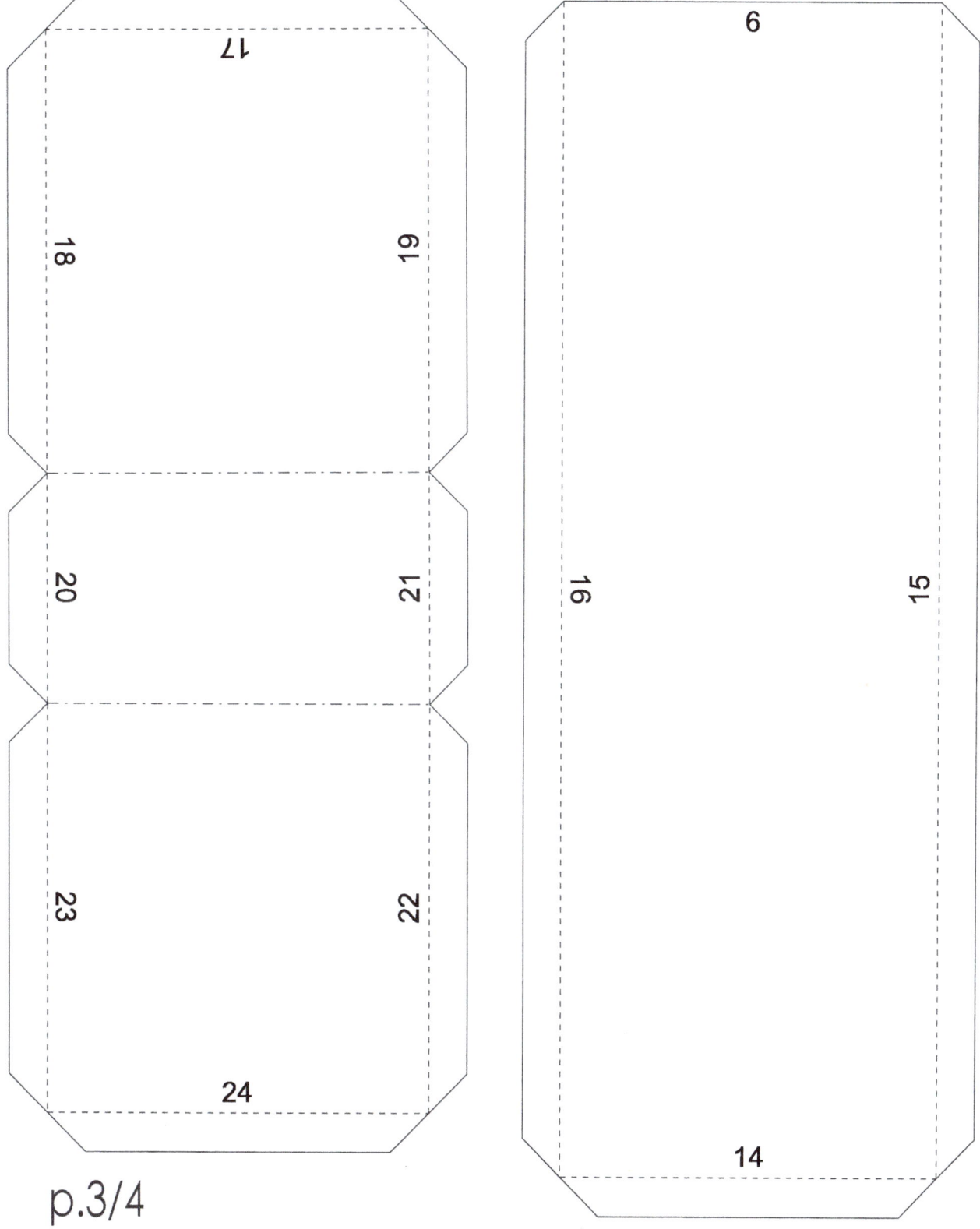

p.3/4

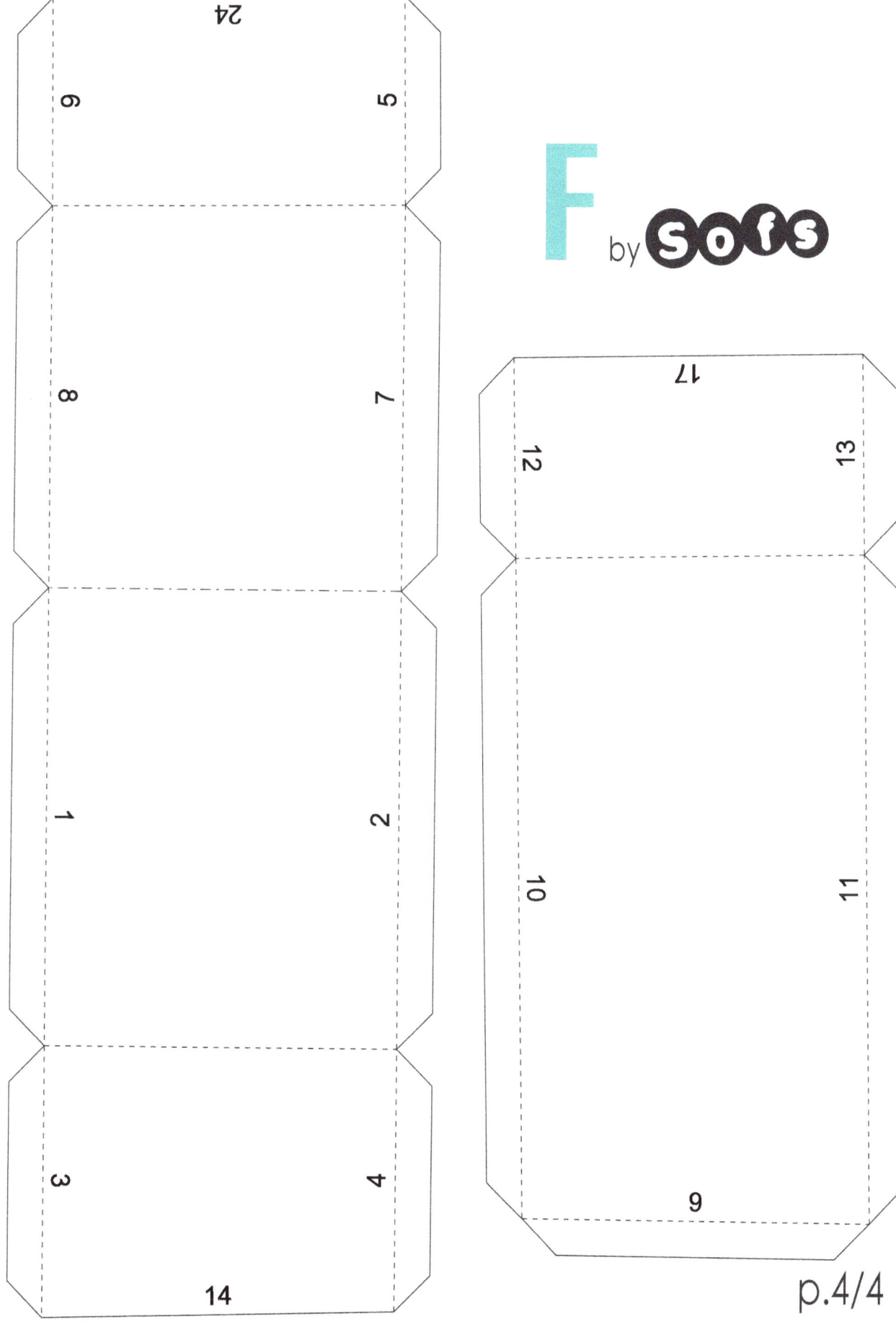

F by Sofs

p.4/4

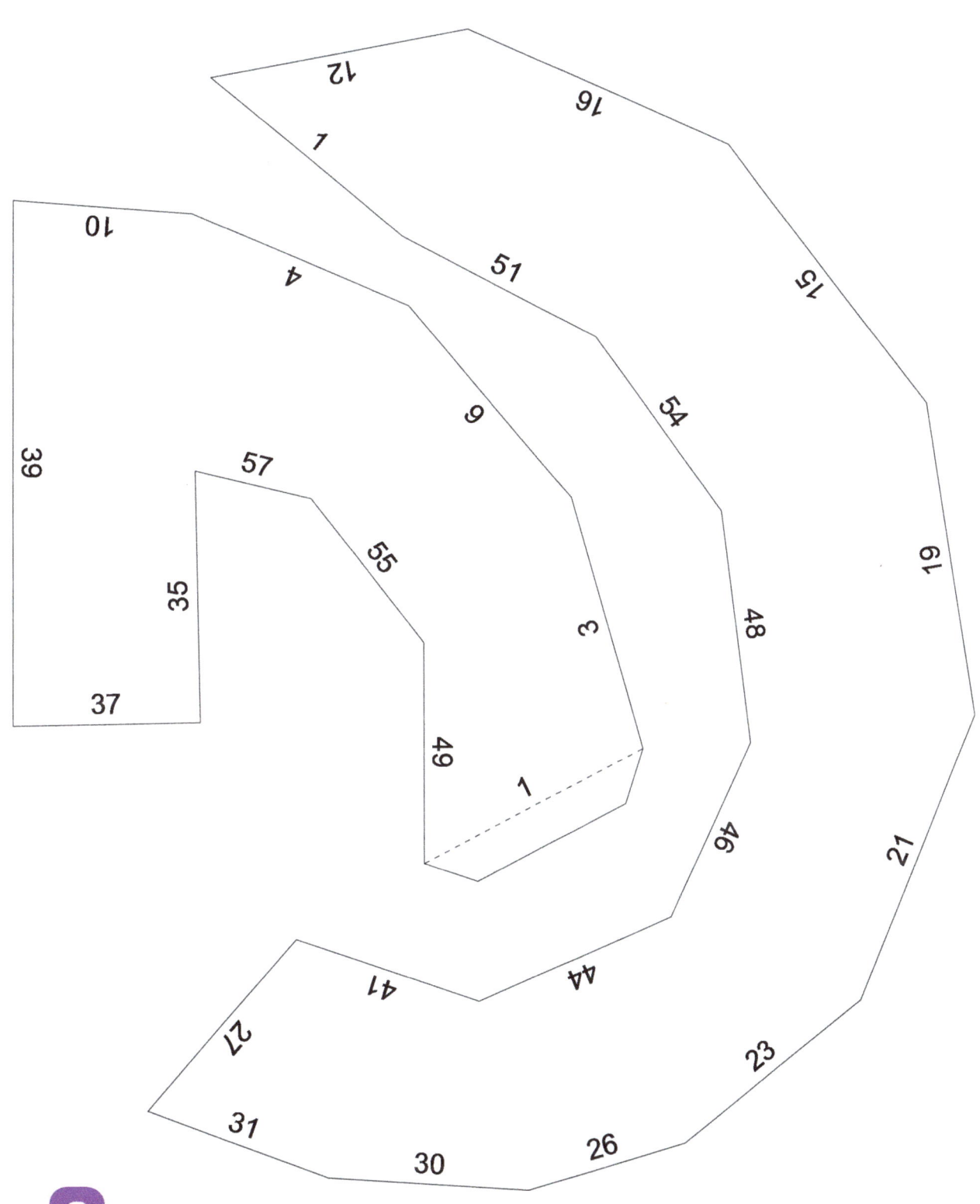

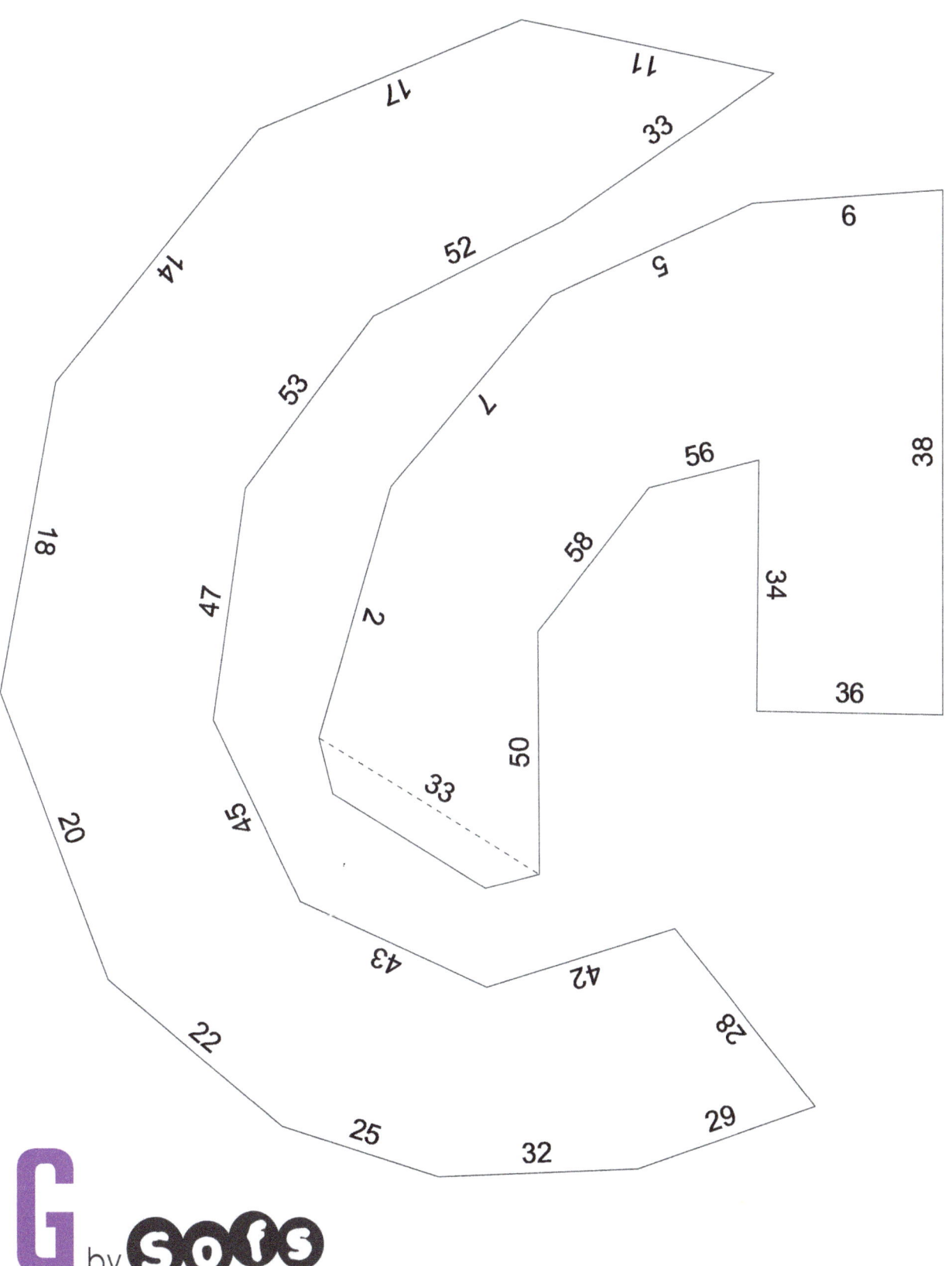

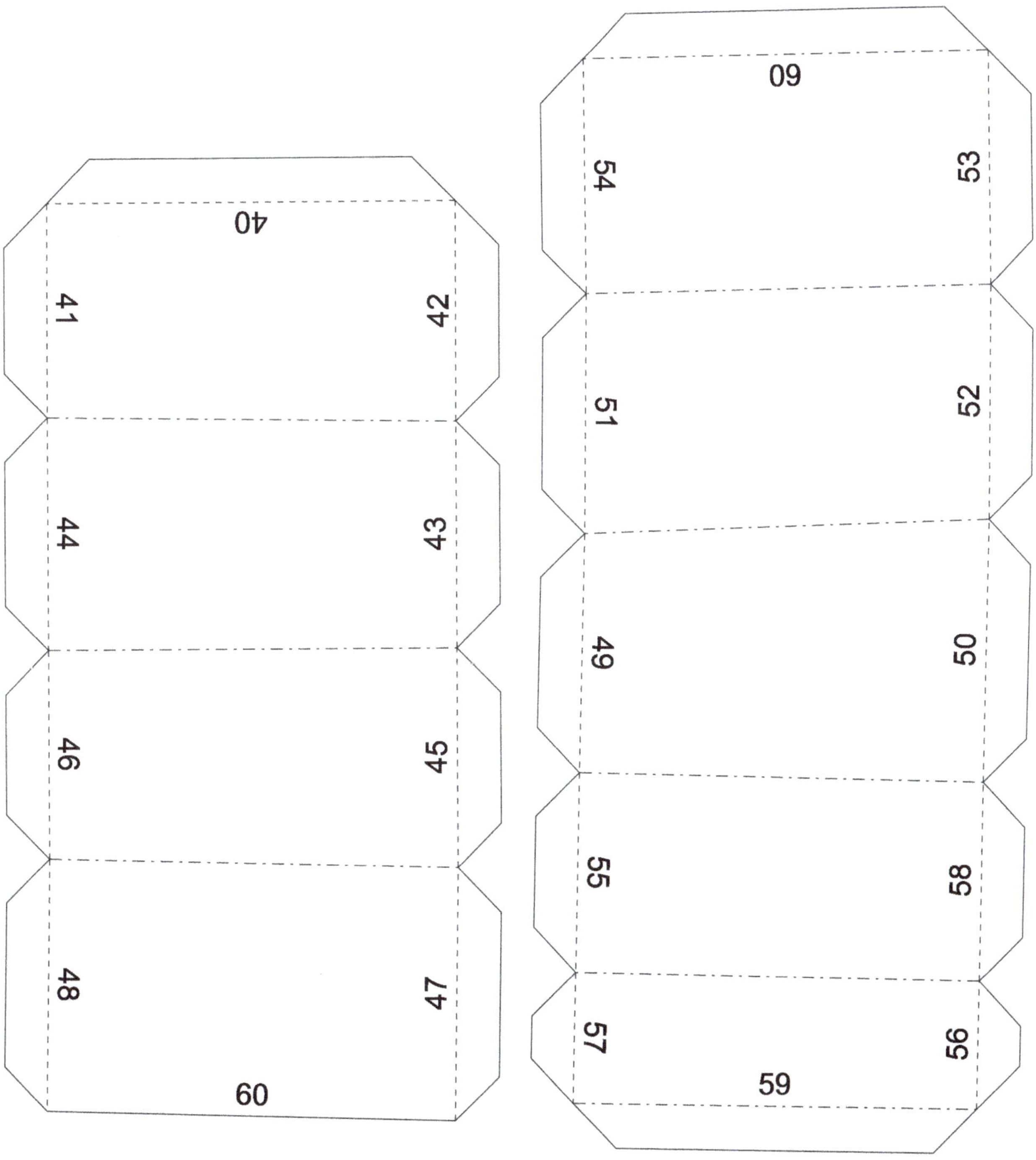

40

41

42

44

43

46

45

48

47

60

09

54

53

51

52

49

50

55

58

57

56

59

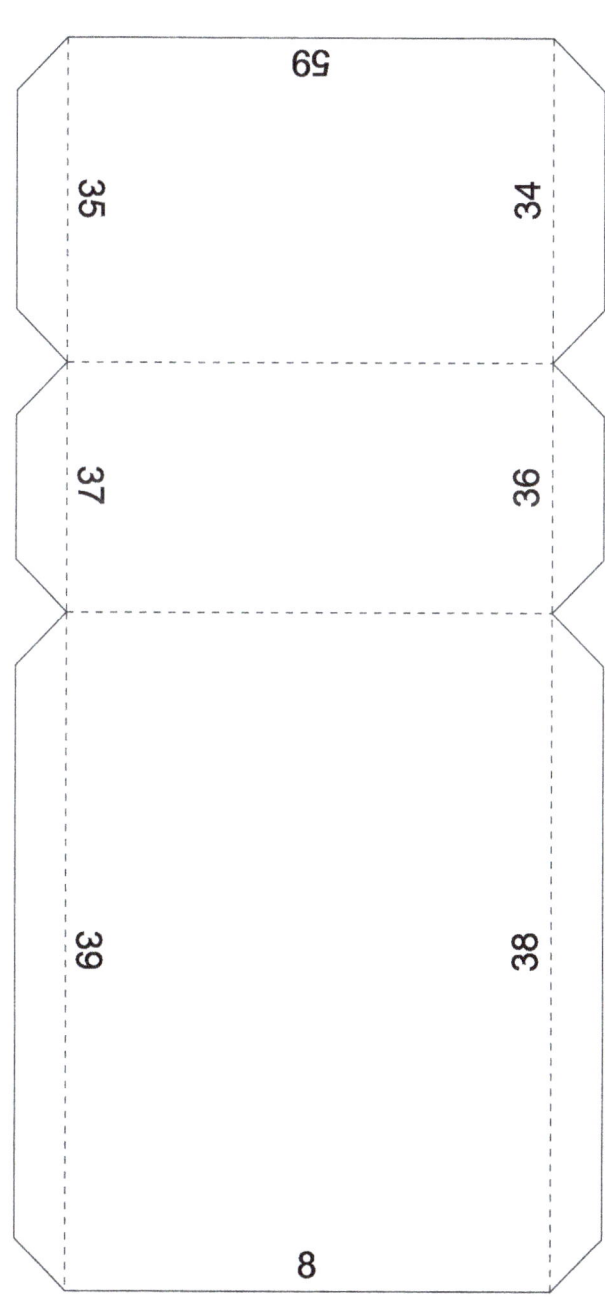

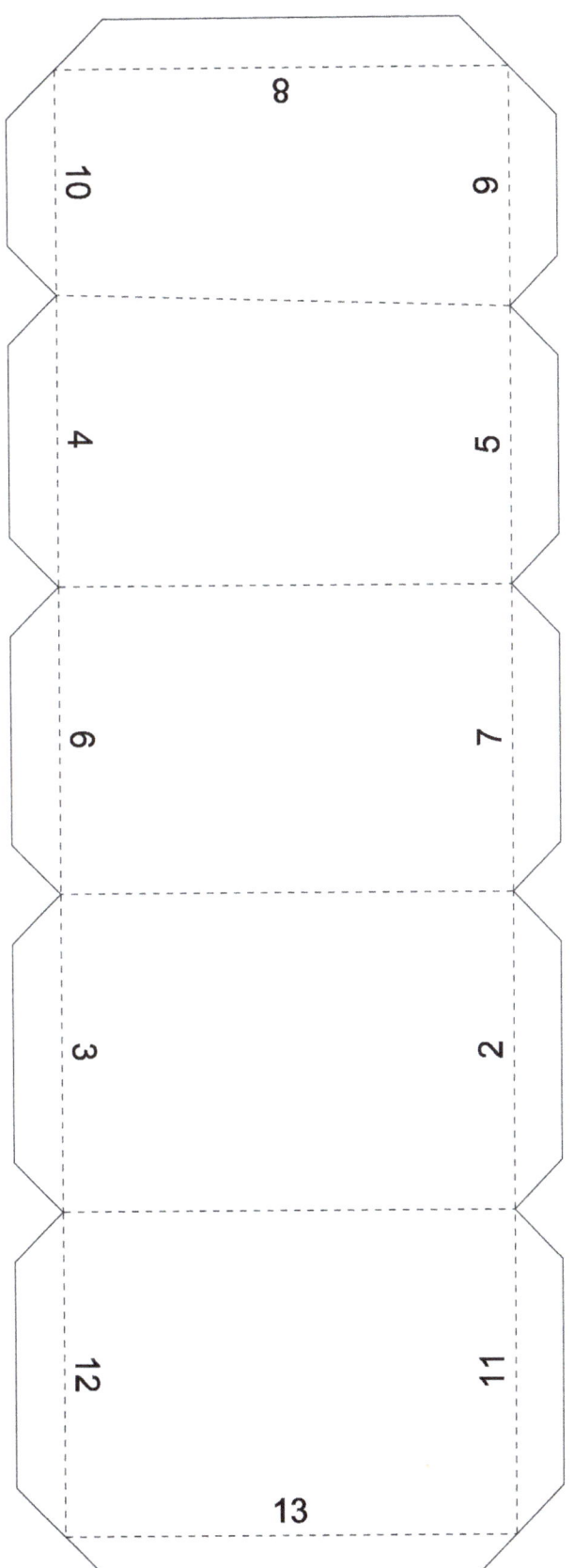

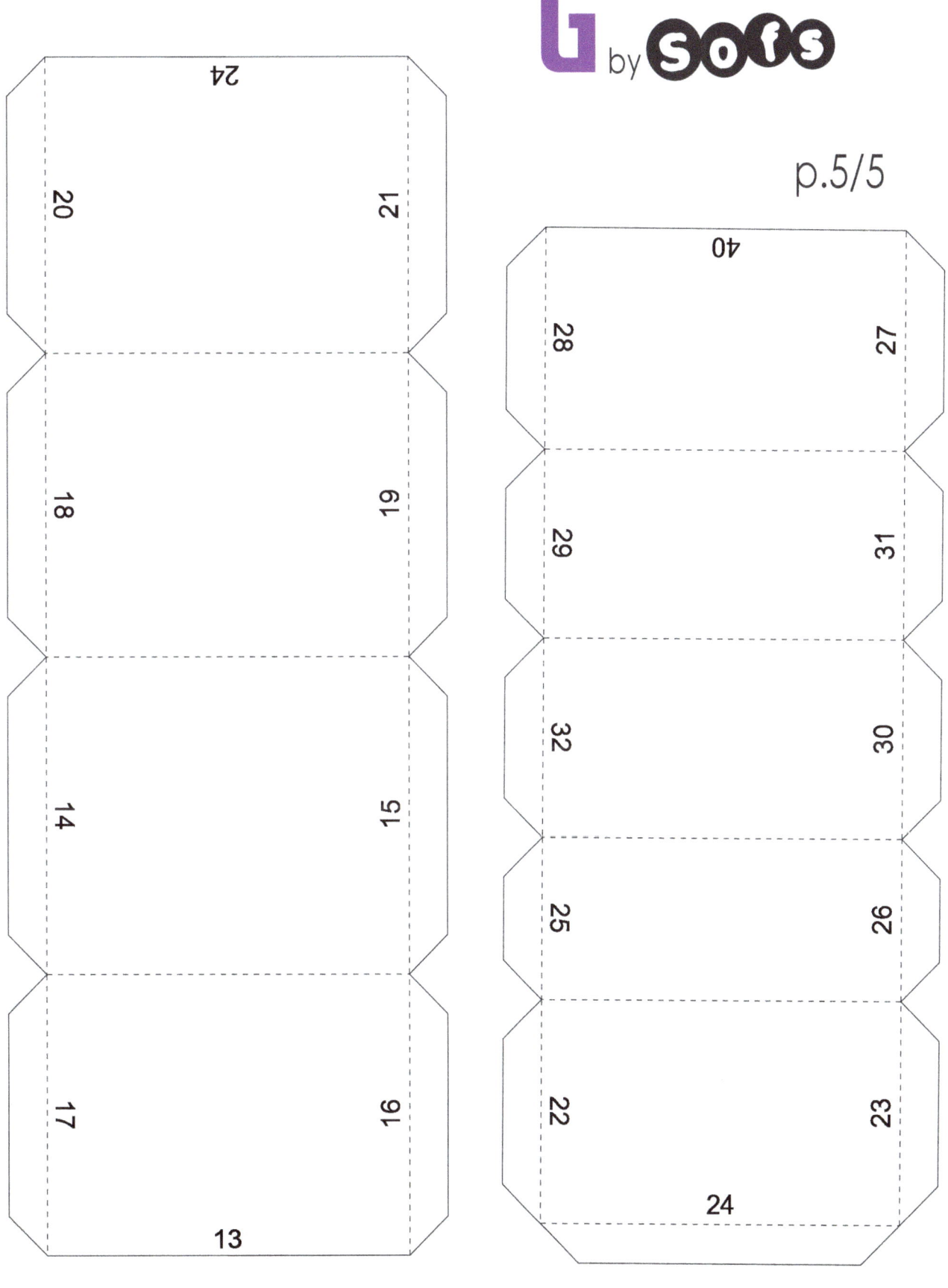

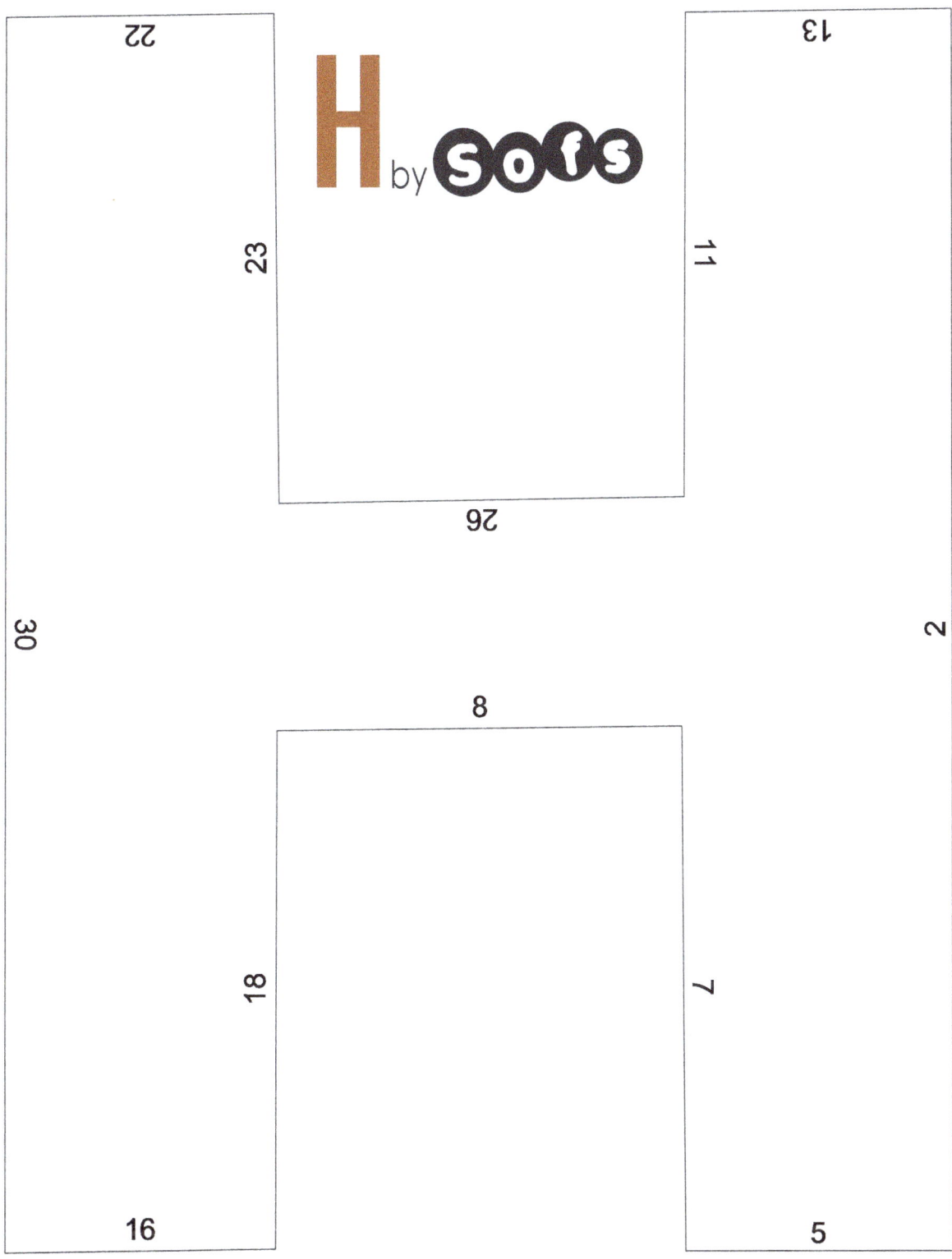

H by Sofs

p.1/5

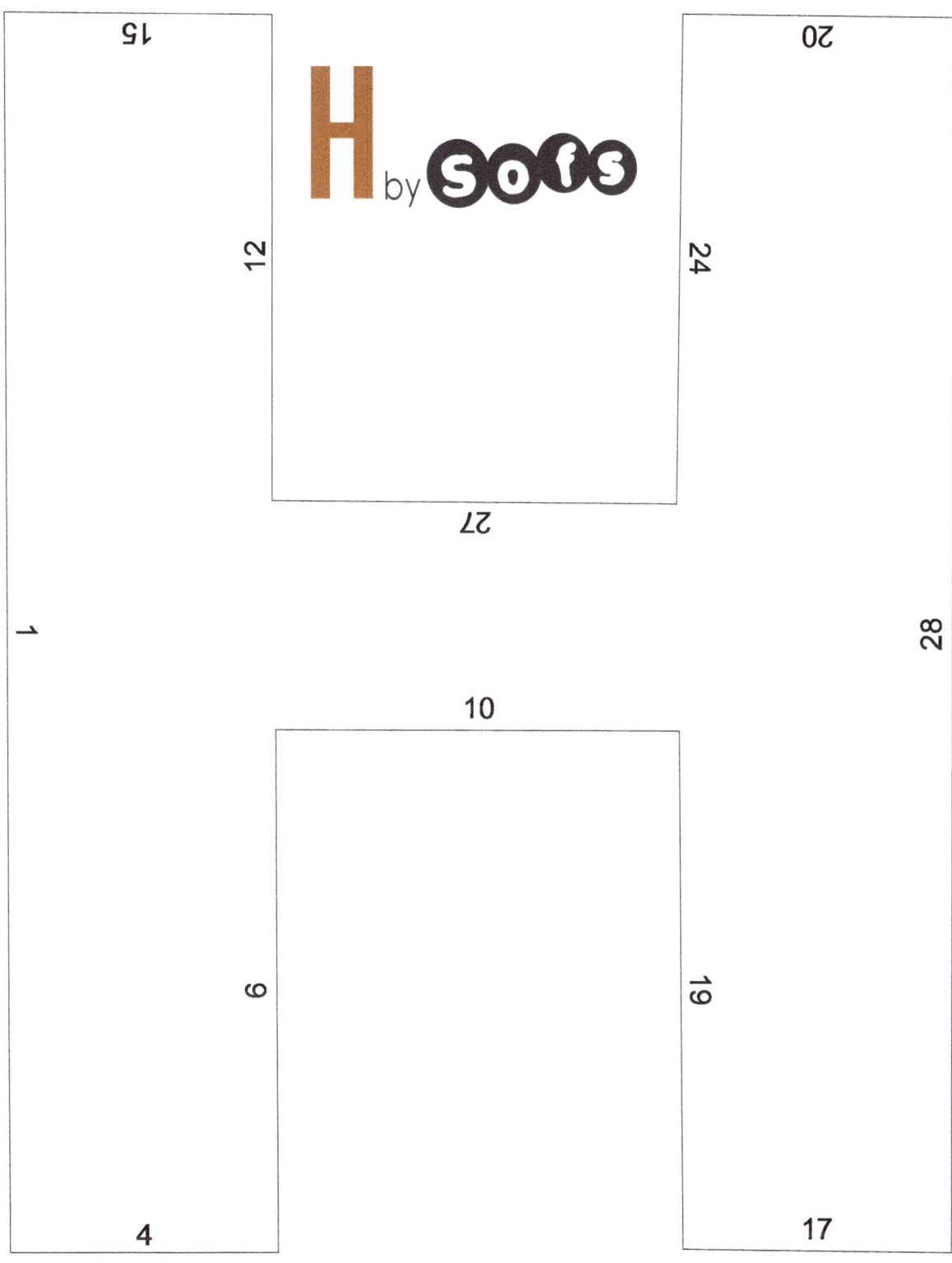

15

20

12

24

27

1

28

10

9

19

4

17

H by Sofs

21

28

30

29

14

2

1

3

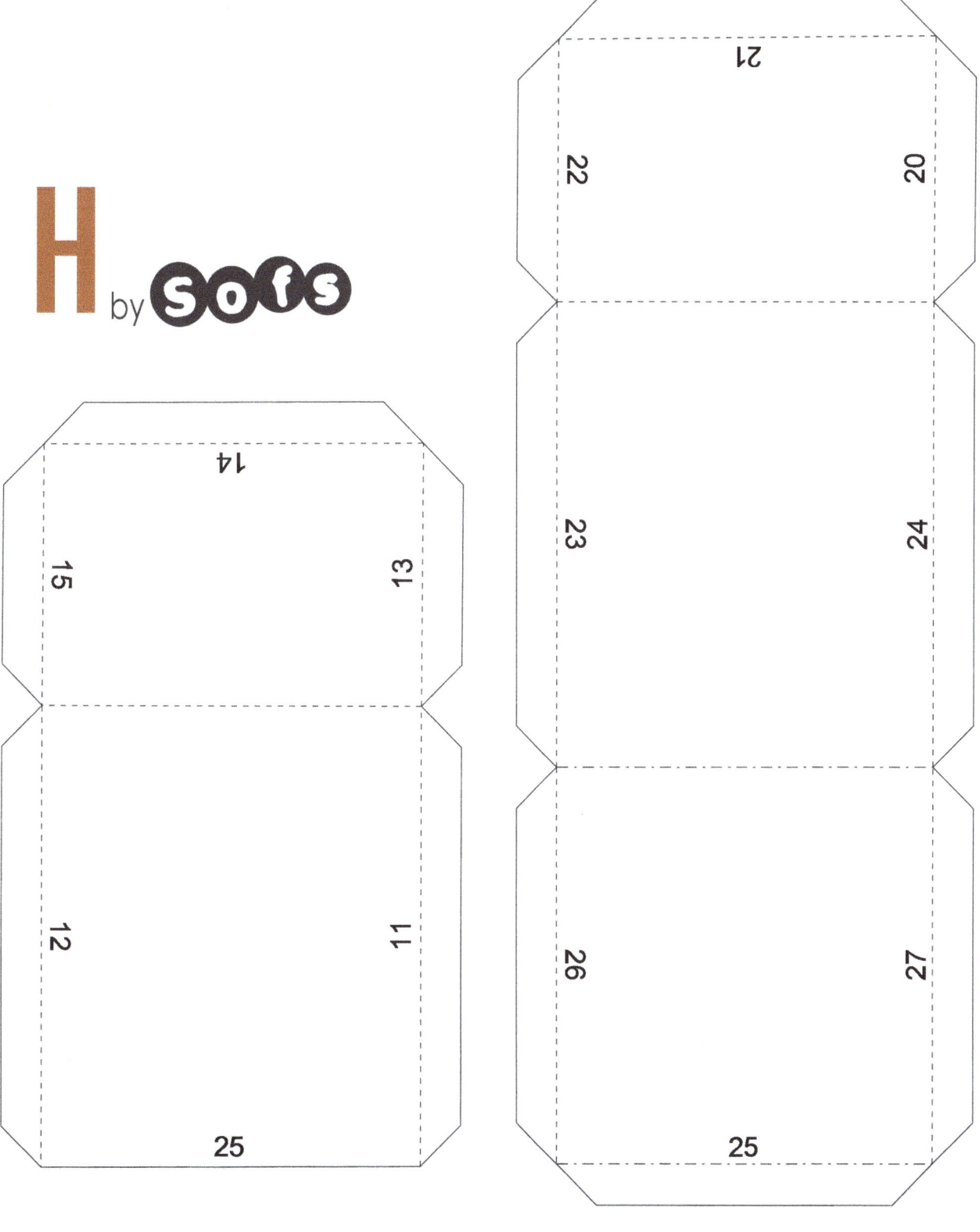

H by **Sofs**

p.4/5

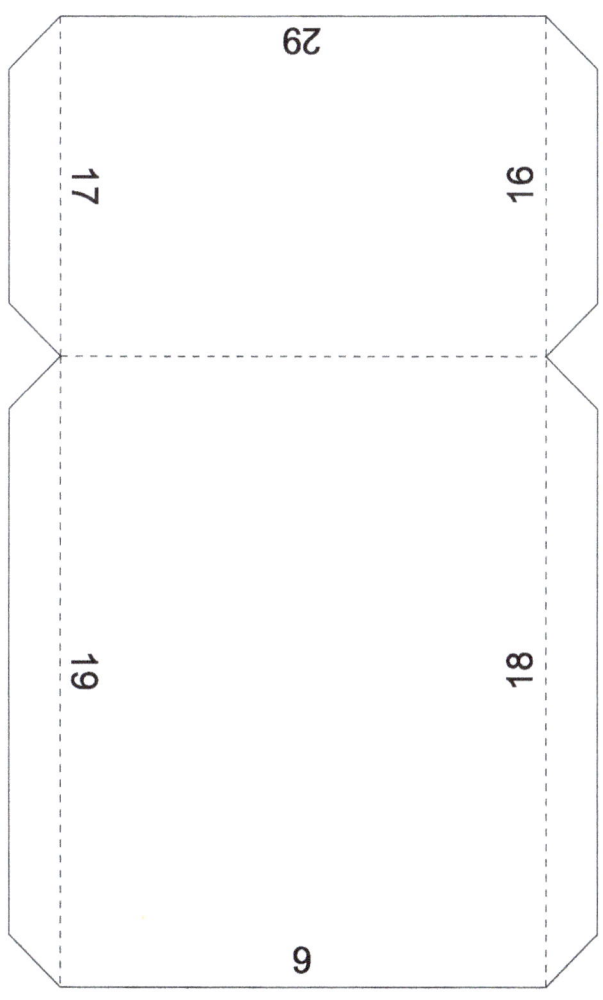

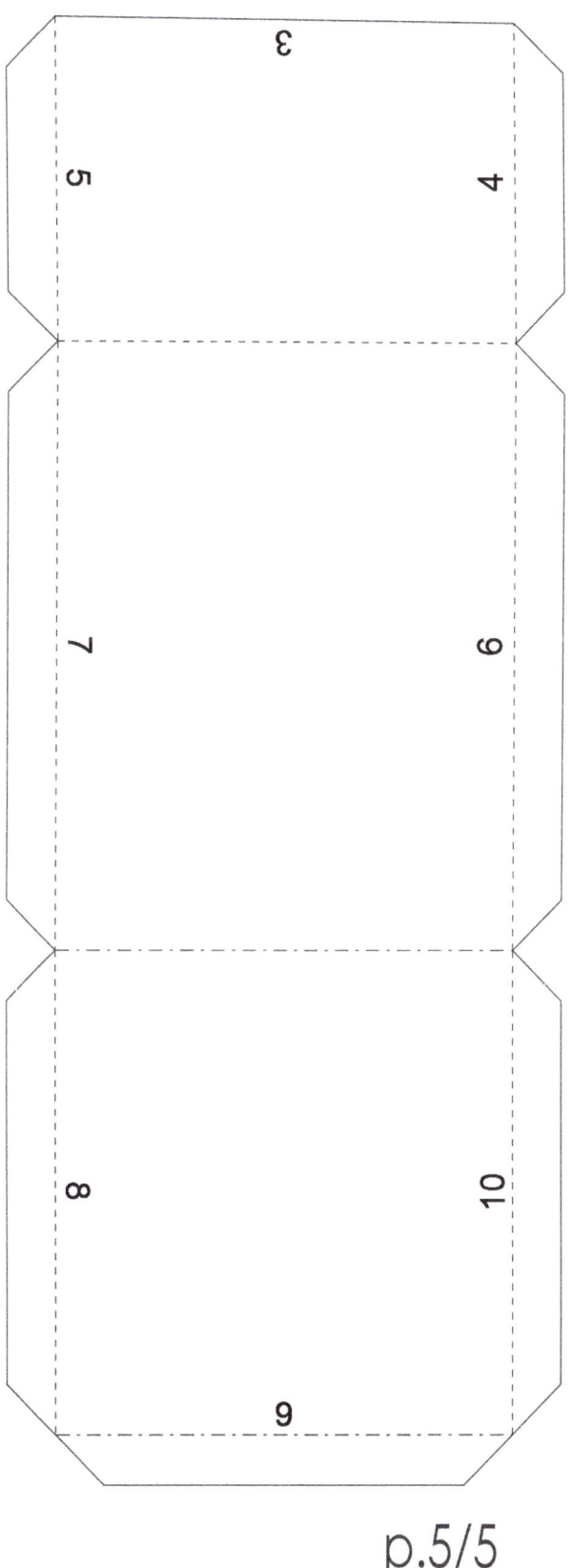

p.5/5

3

1

9

8

7

5

12

10

2

5

6

9

4

7

8

11

by **sofs**

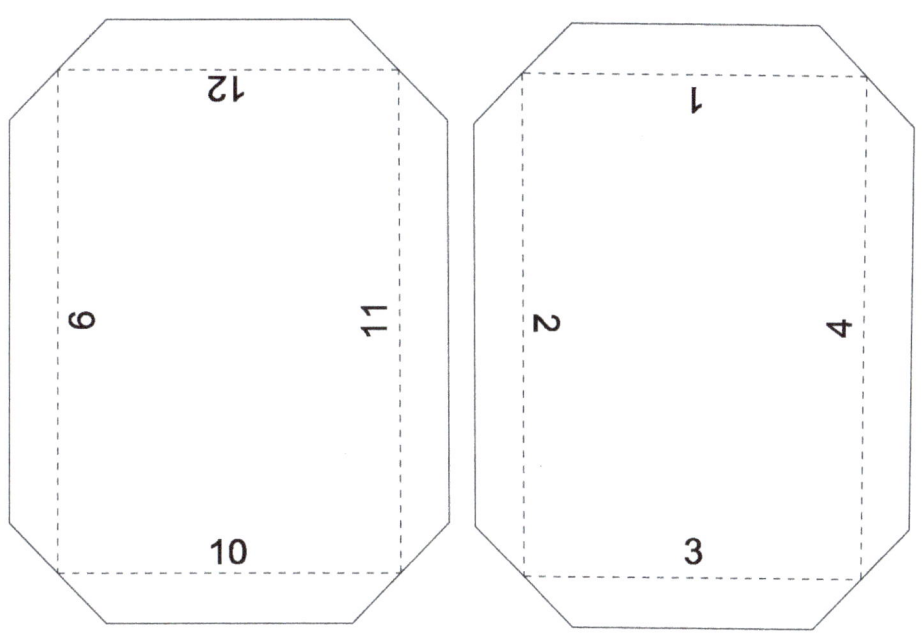

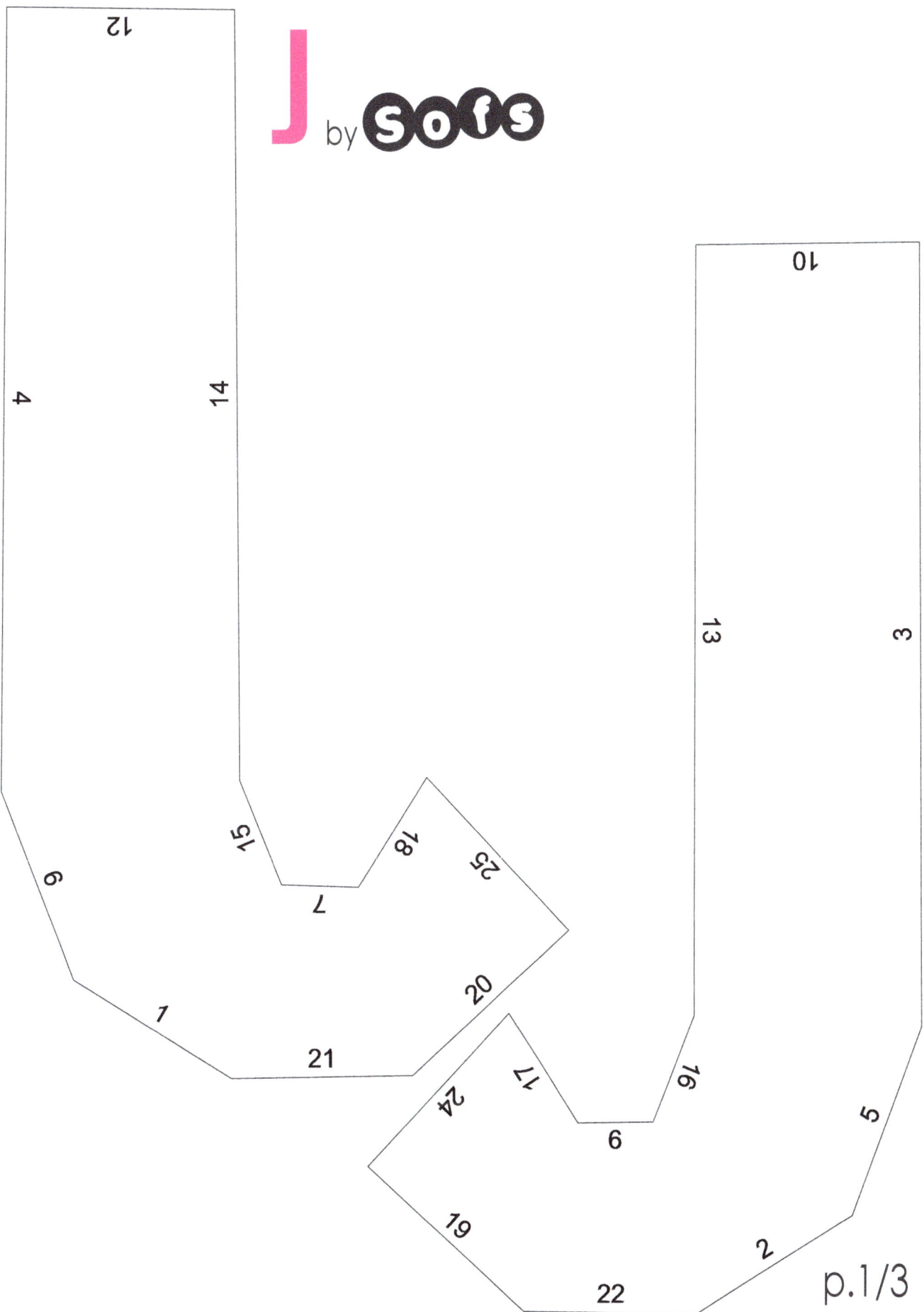

J by Sofs

p.1/3

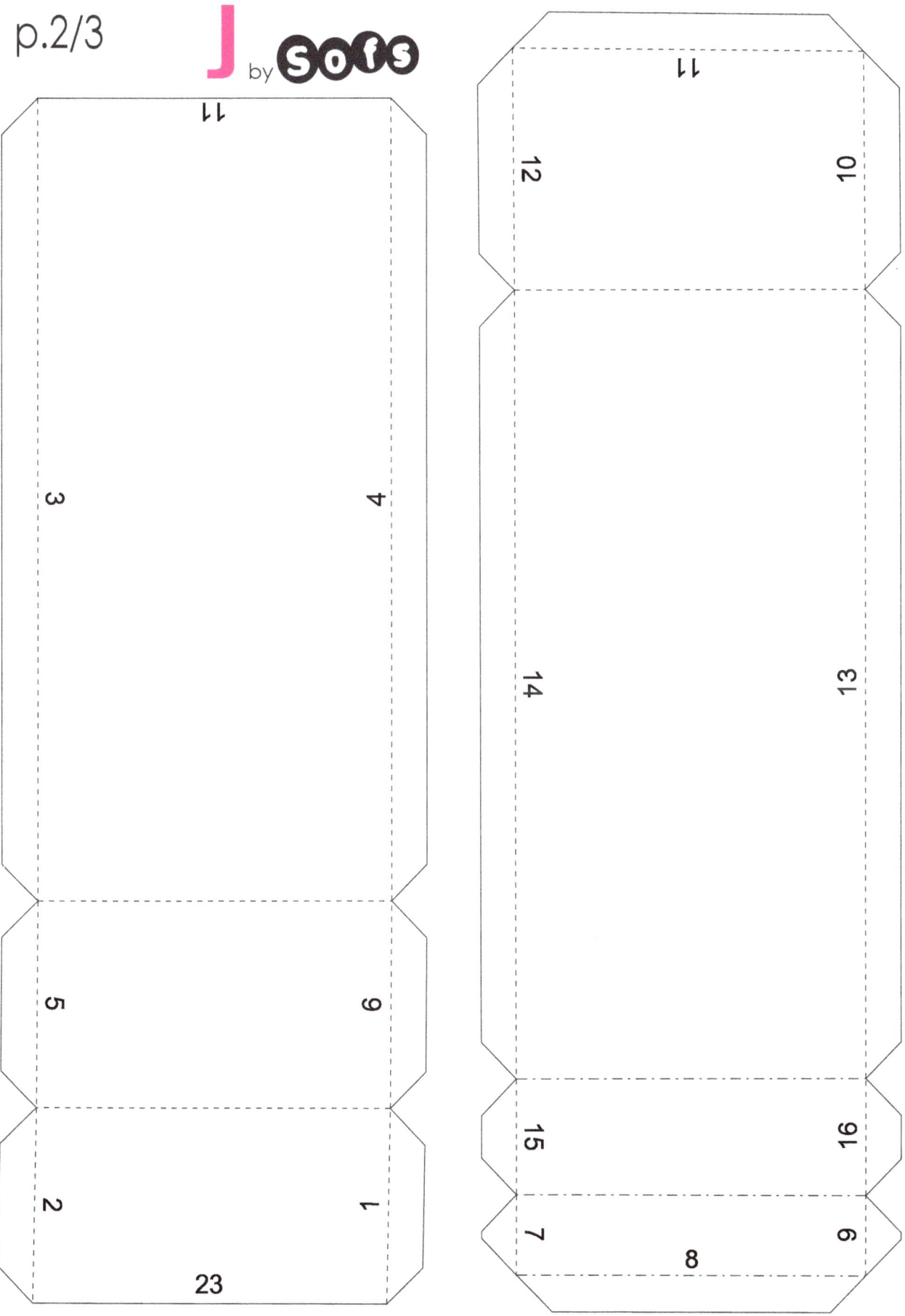

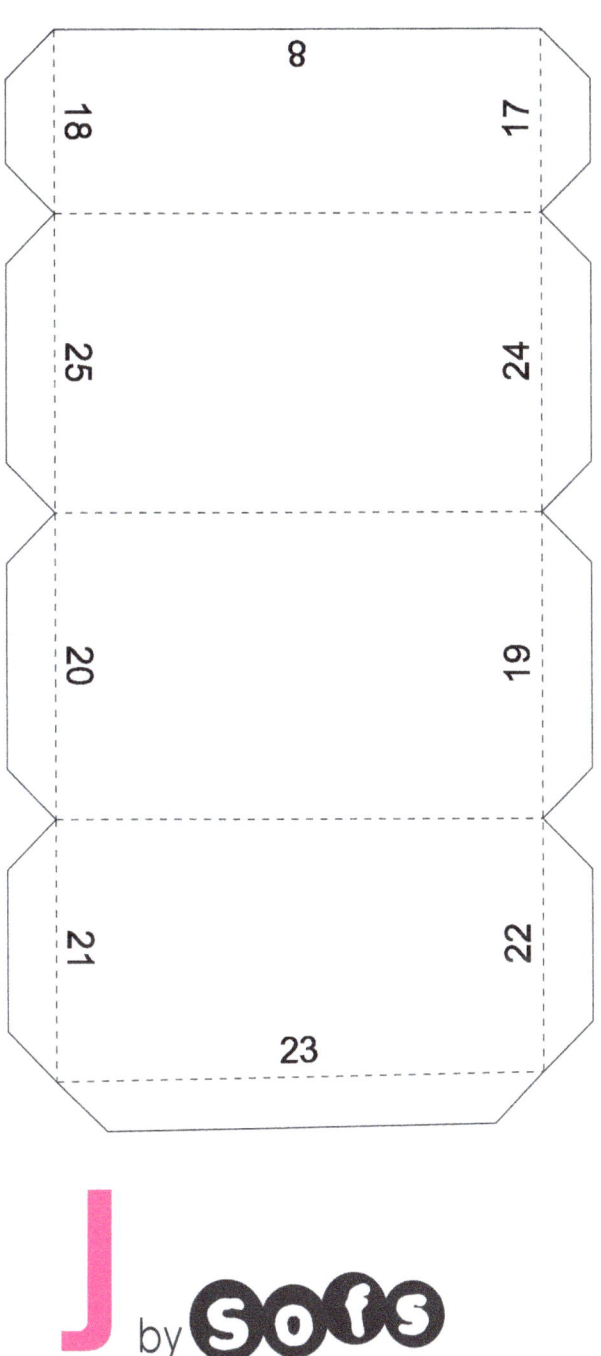

J by sofs

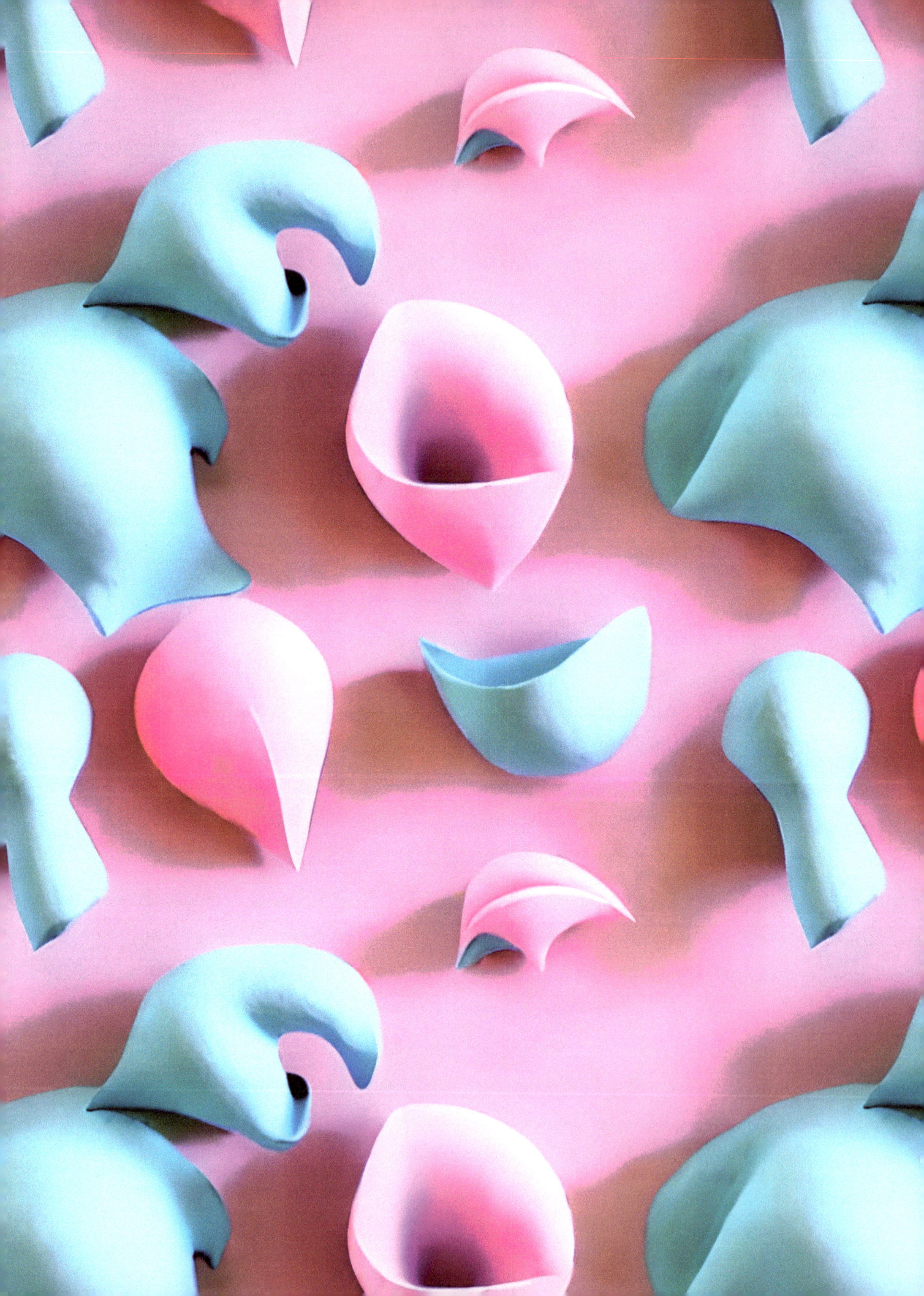

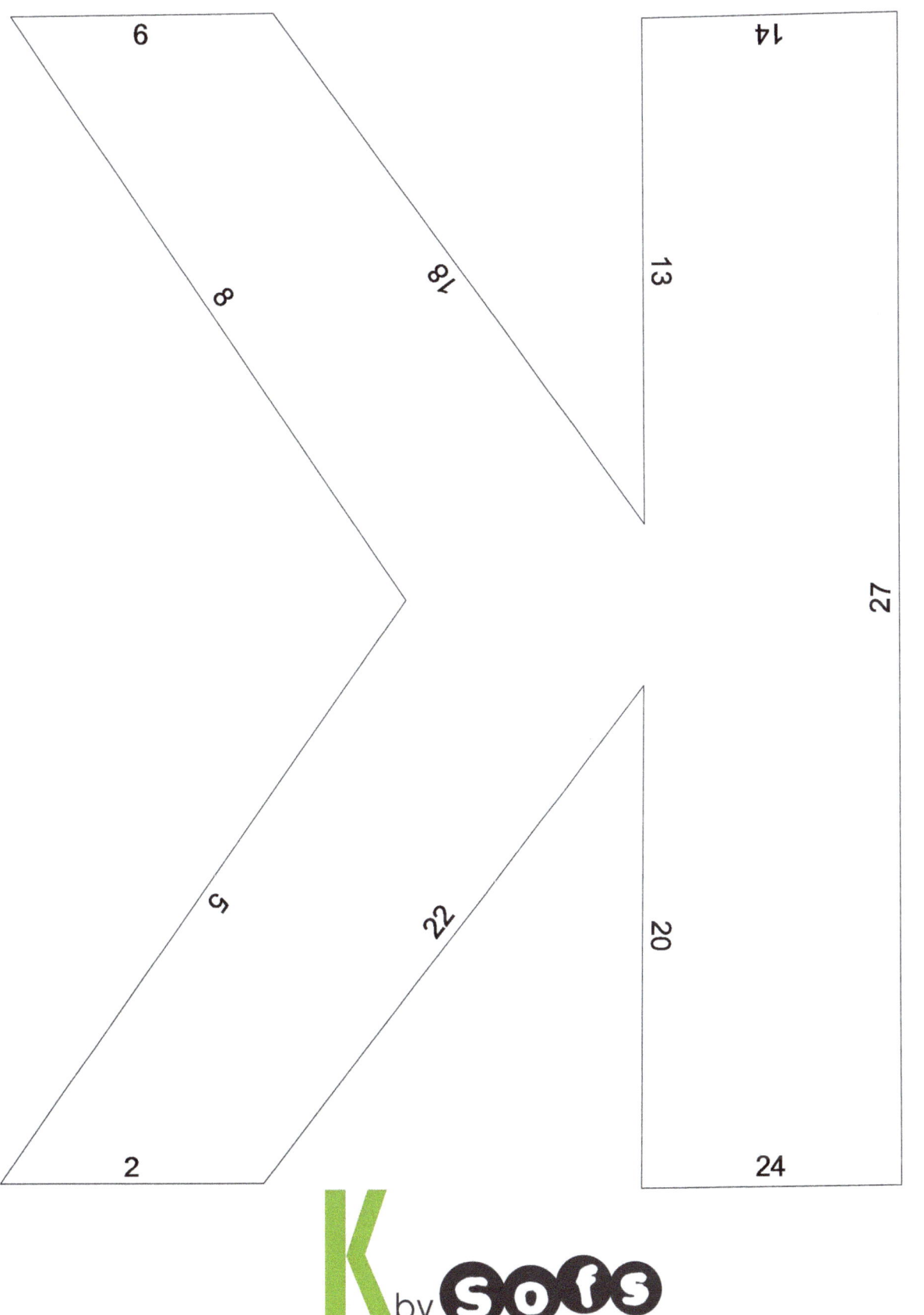

6

8

18

5

22

2

13

27

20

14

24

K by Sofs

p.1/5

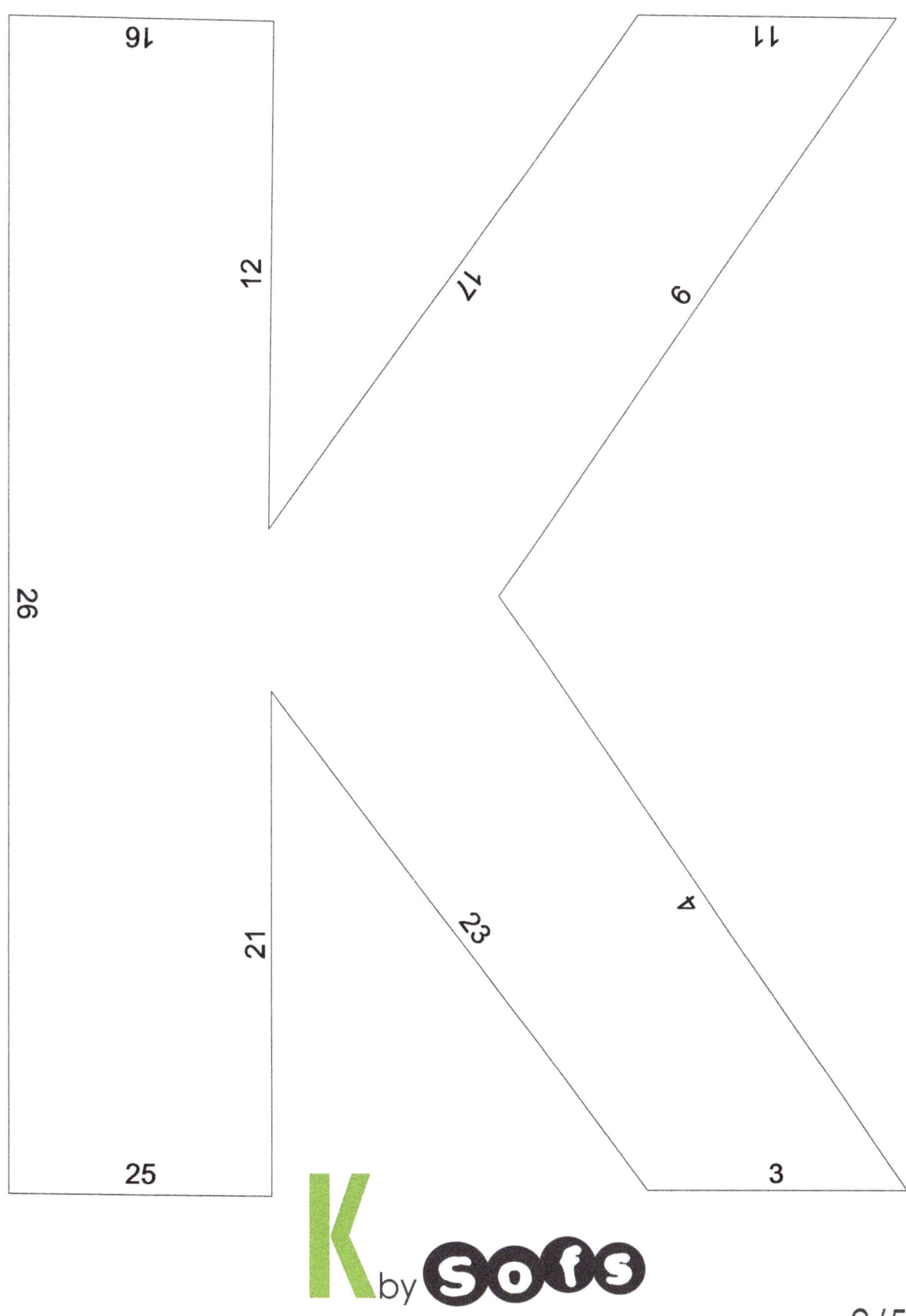

16

12

11

17

9

26

23

4

21

25

3

K by Sofs

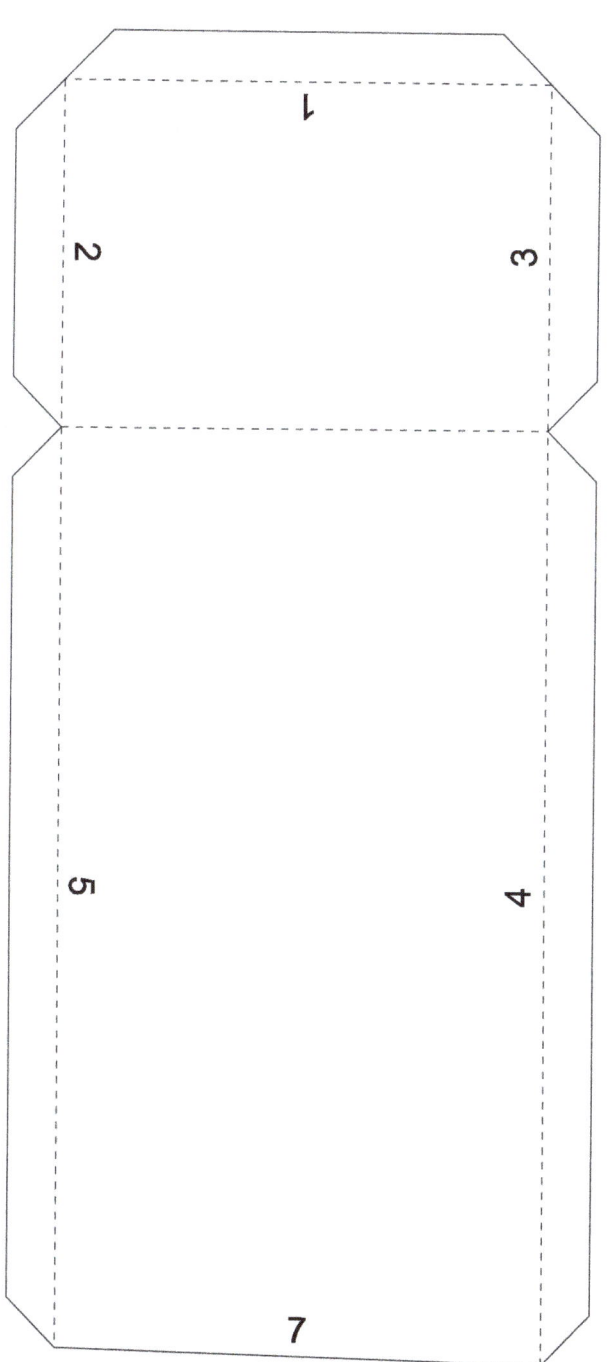

p.4/5

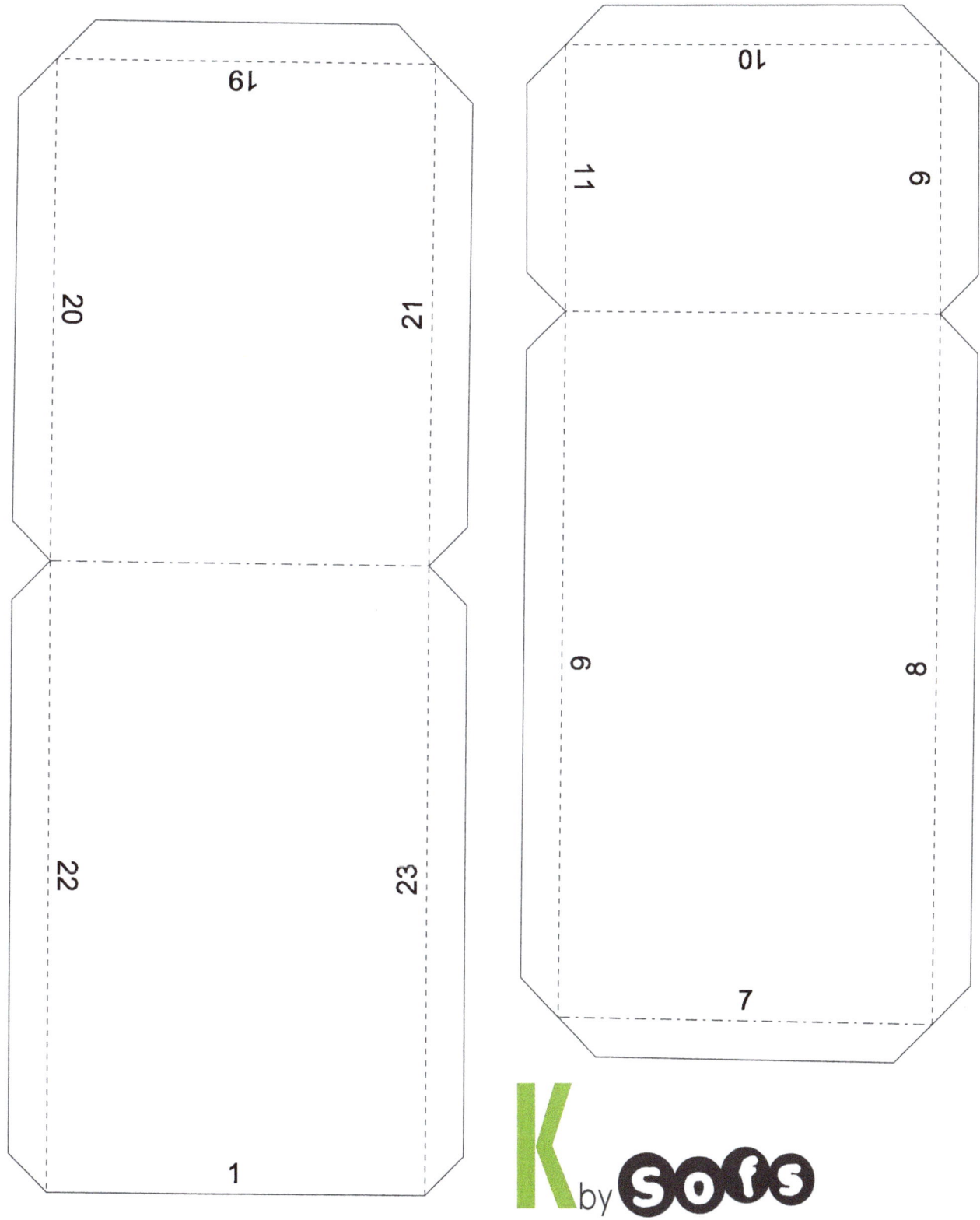

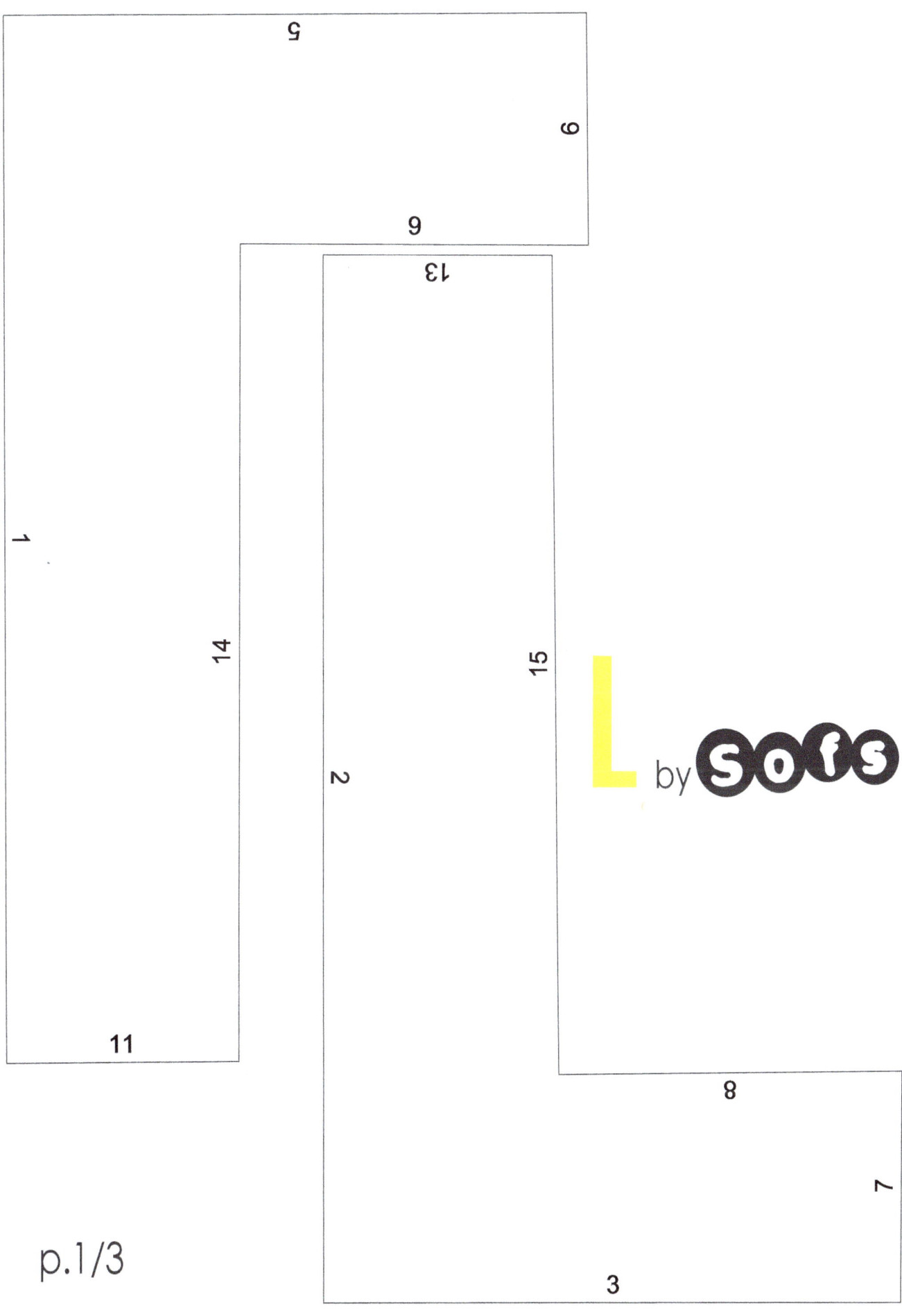

p.1/3

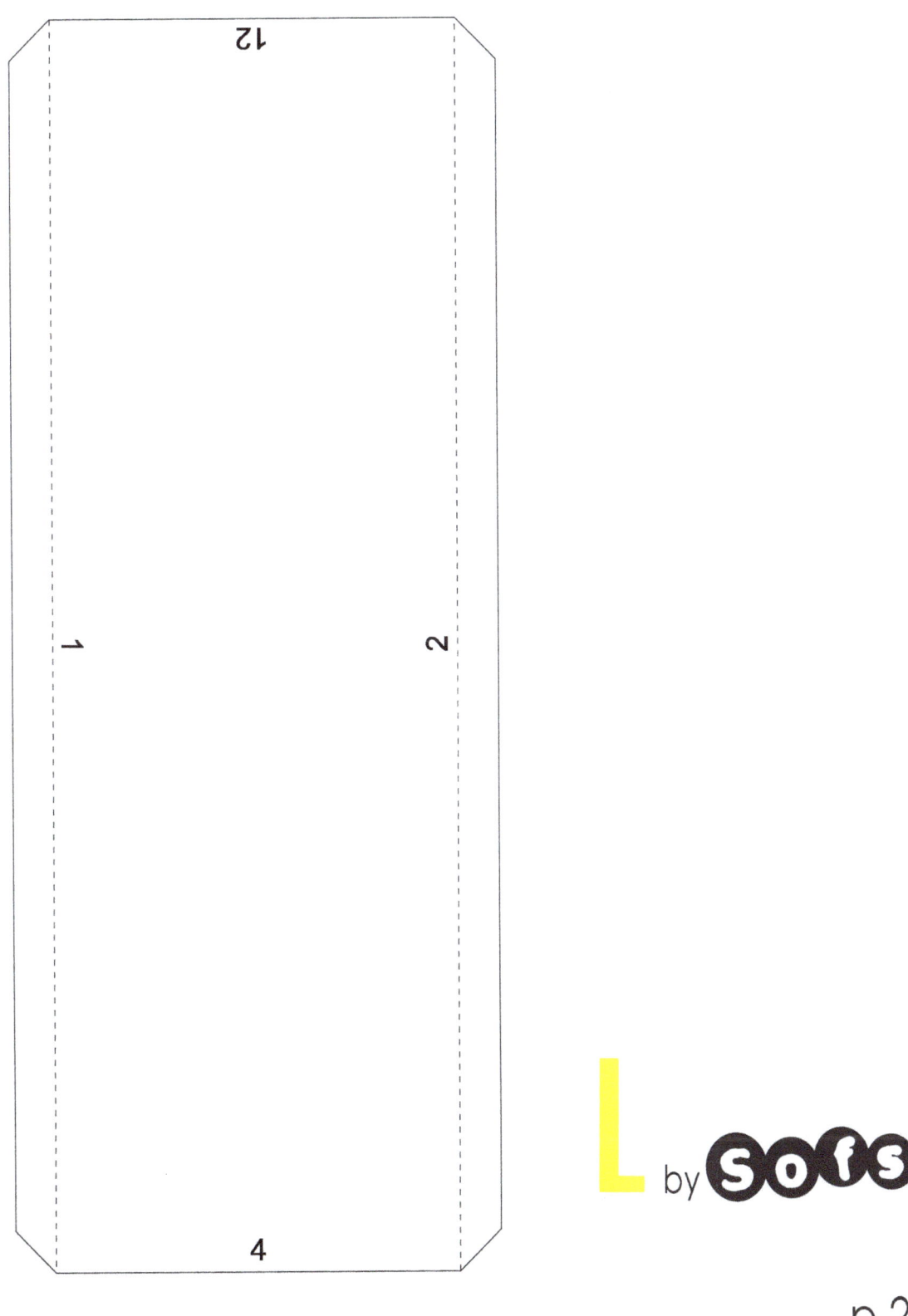

L by sofs

p.2/3

by **Sofs** p.3/3

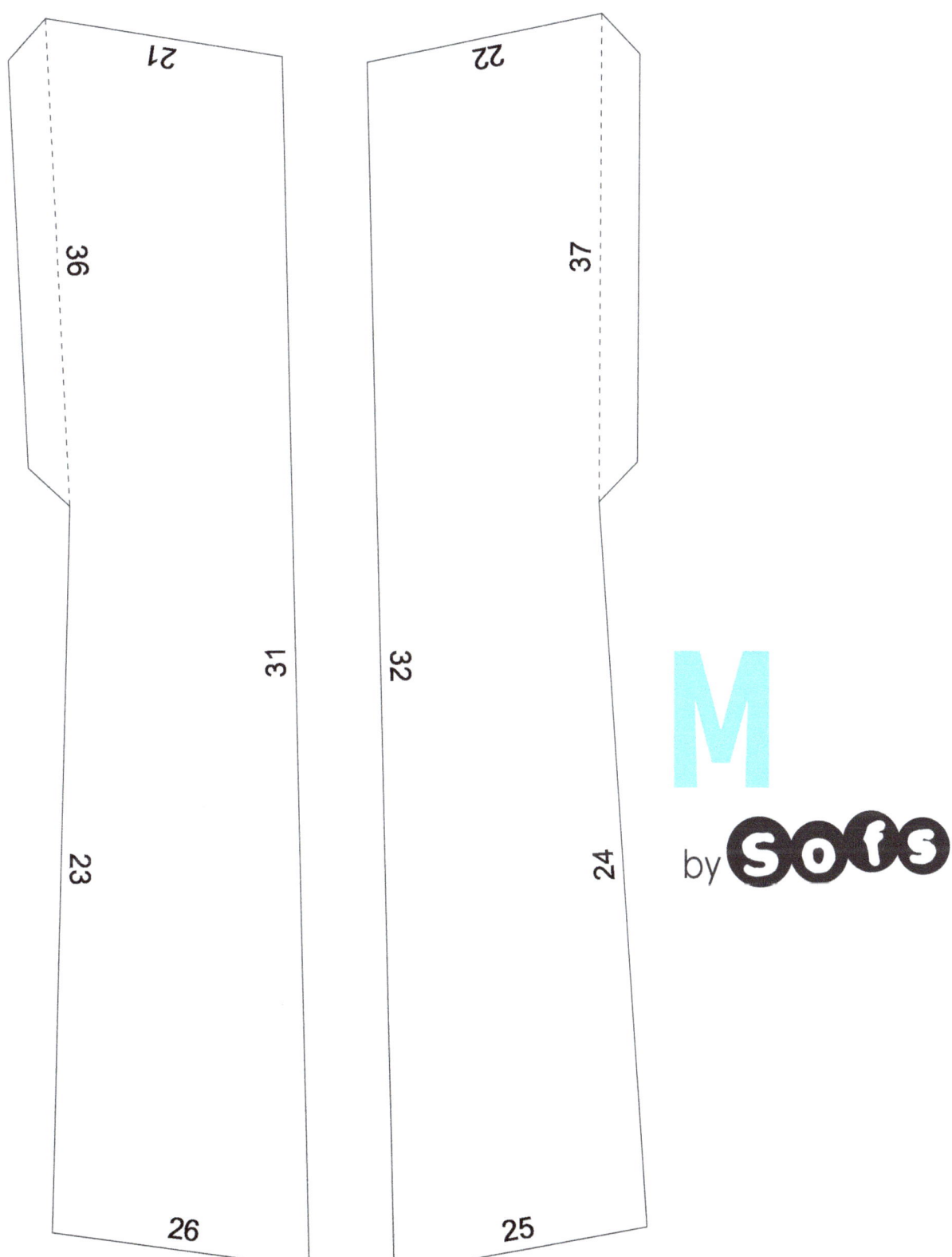

M
by Sofs

p.1/5

8

35

1

35

7

36

19

28

16

14

30

10

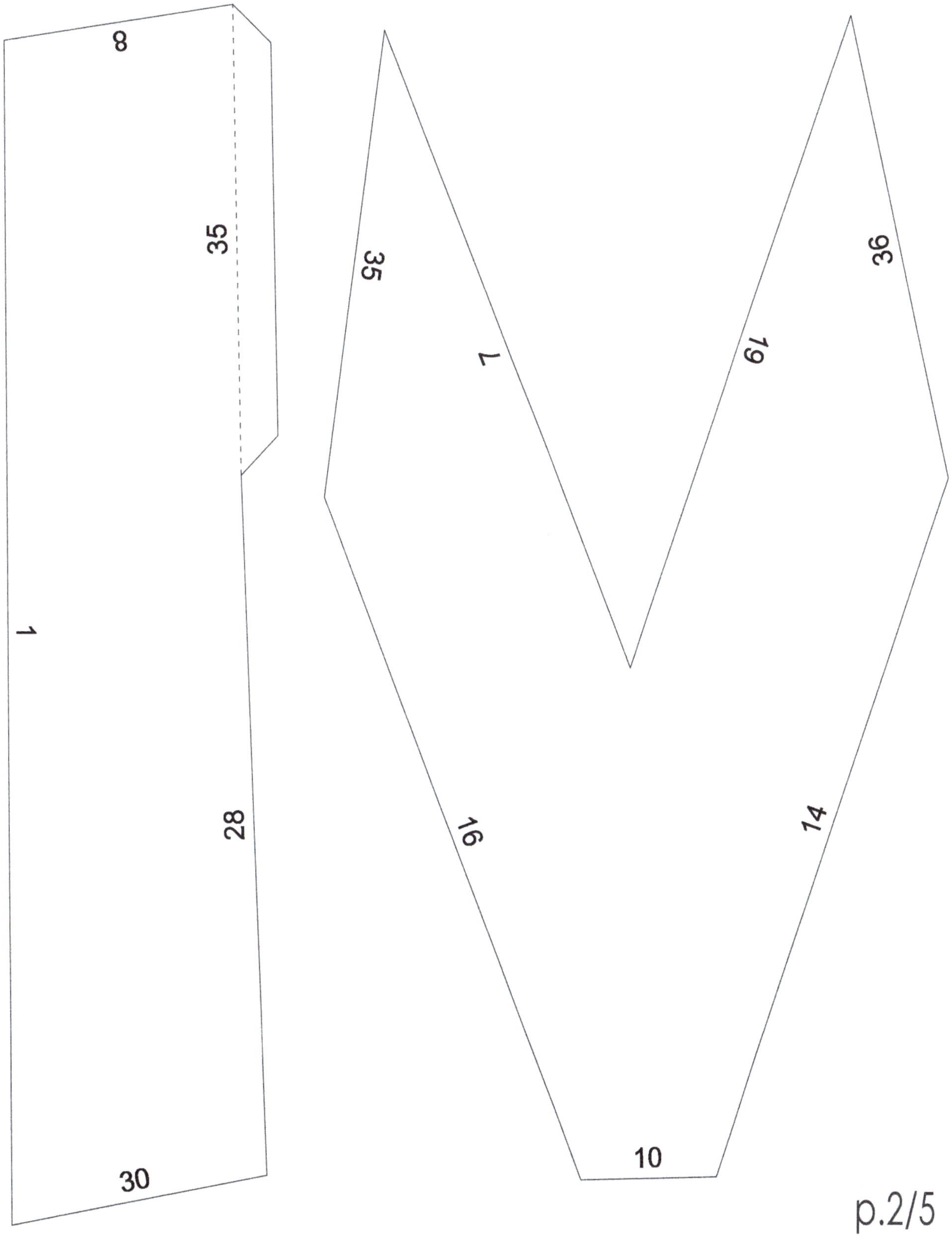

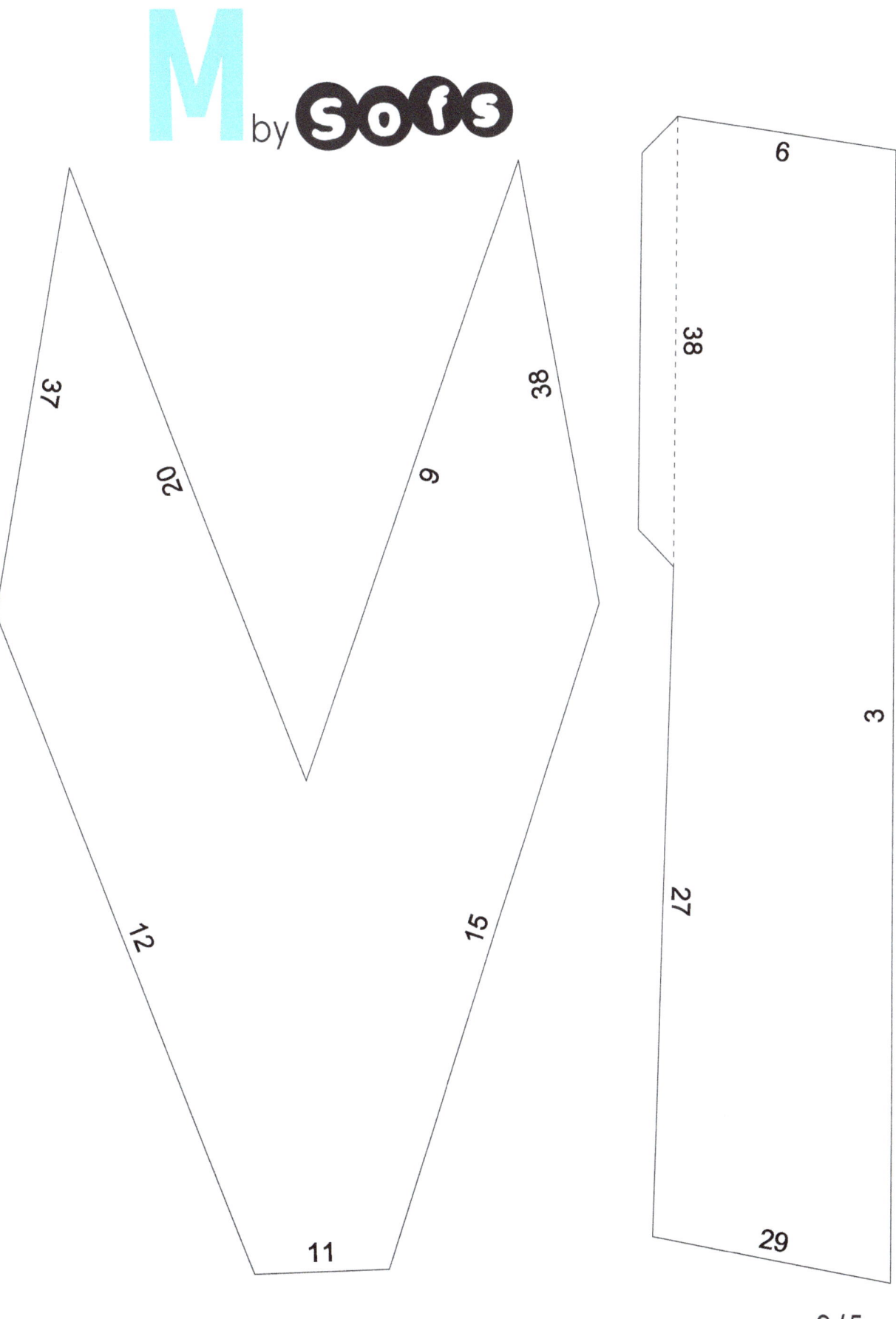

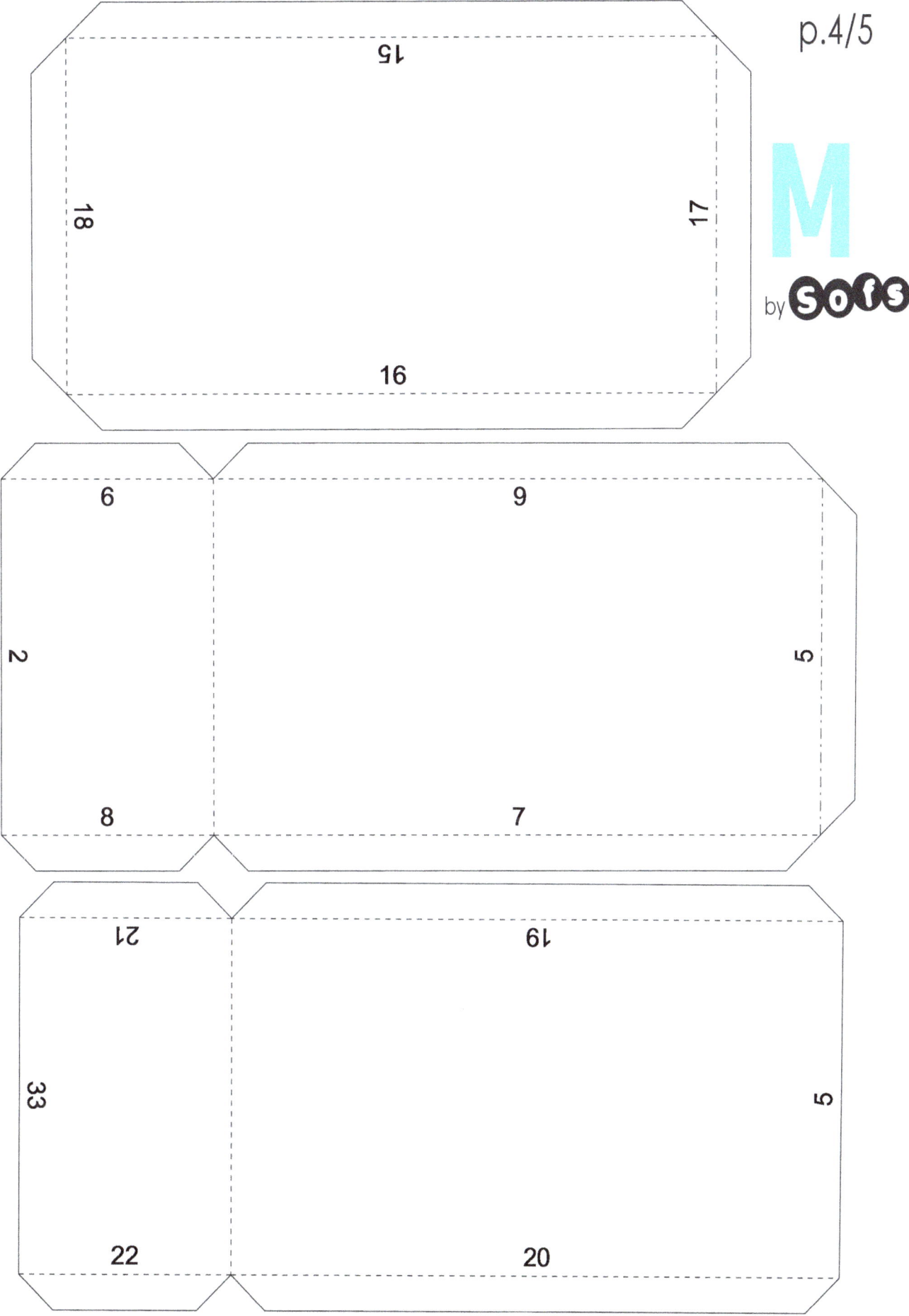

M by Sofs

33

31

32

3

2

1

34

4

p.4/5

p.5/5

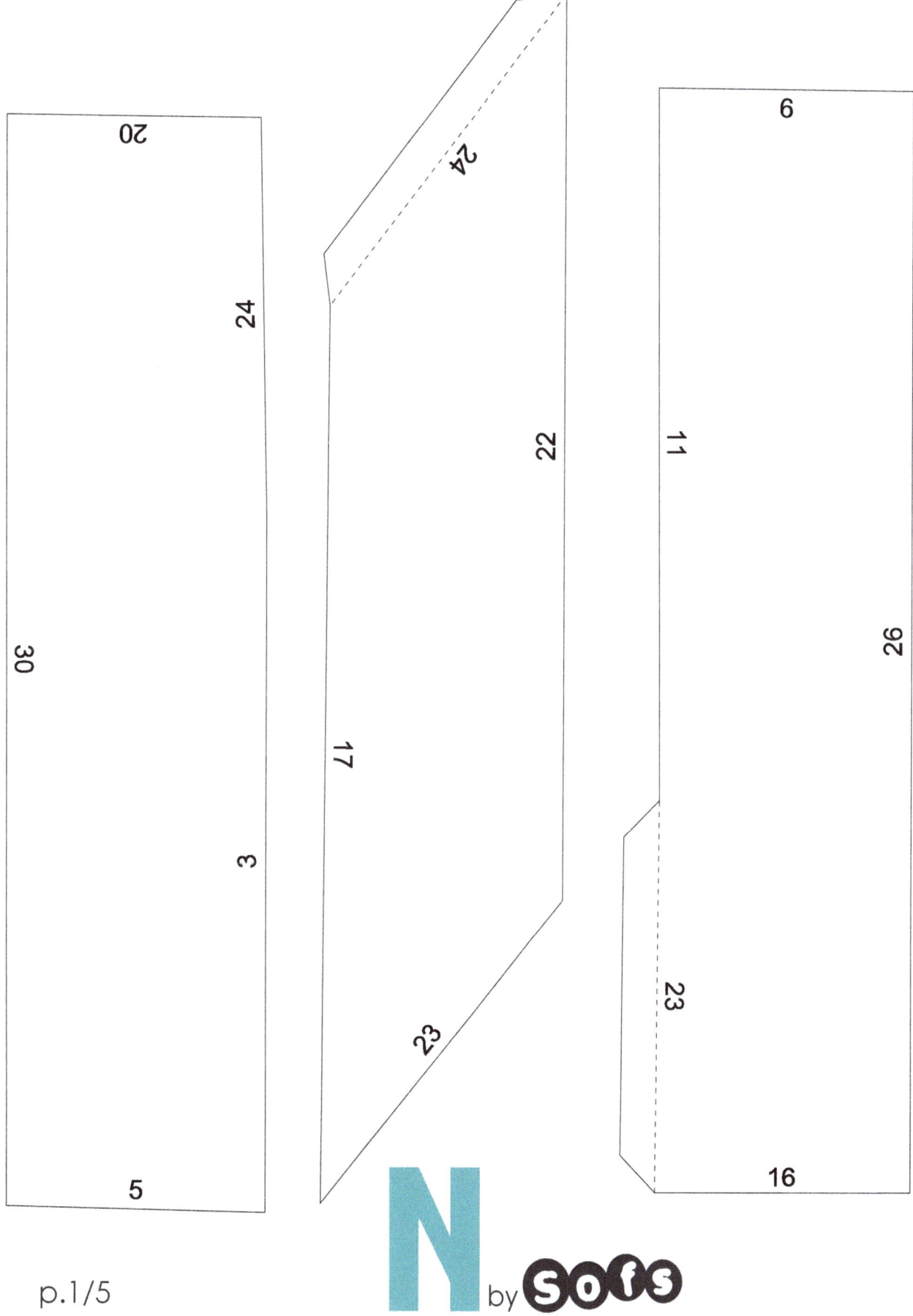

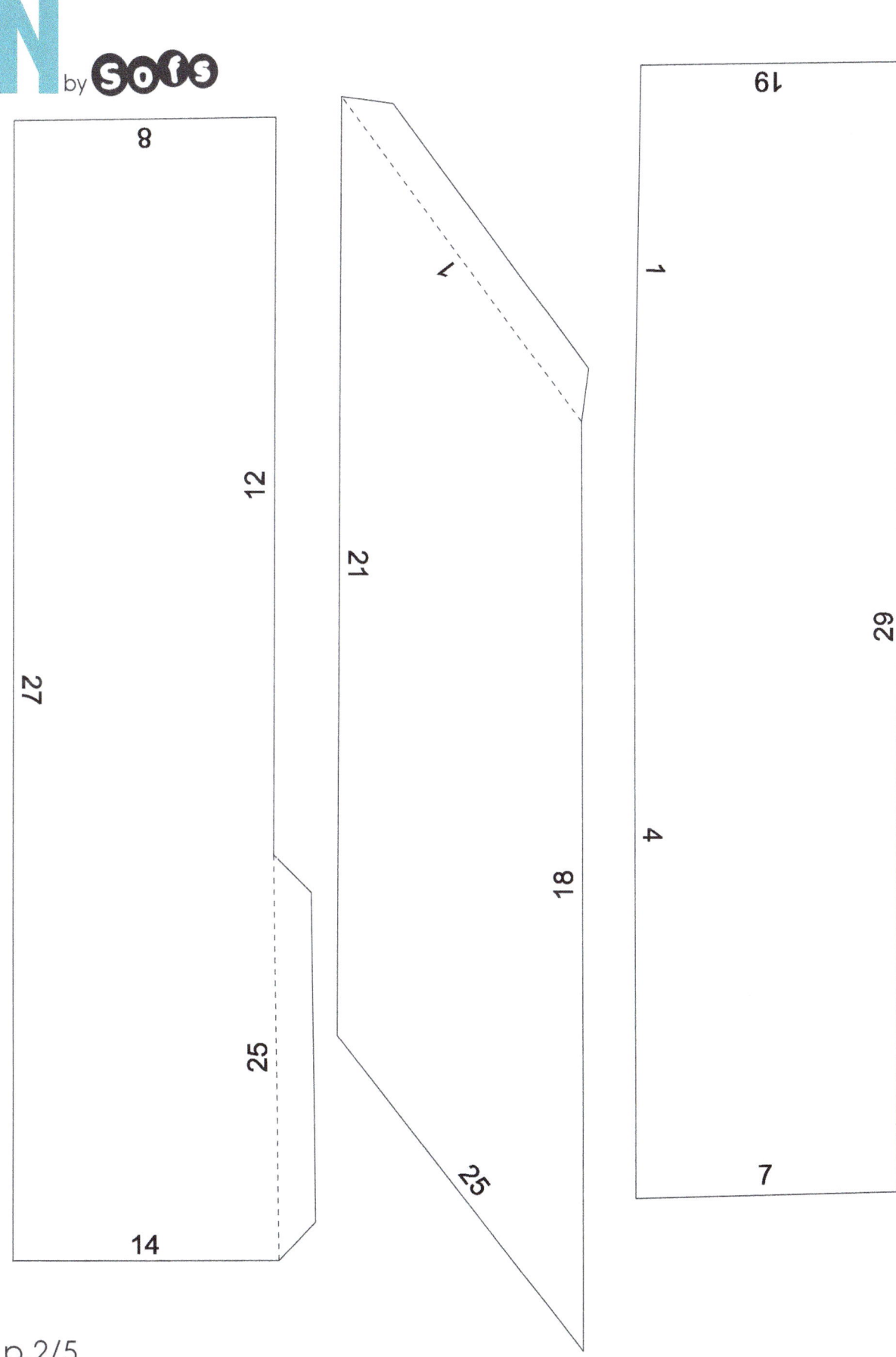

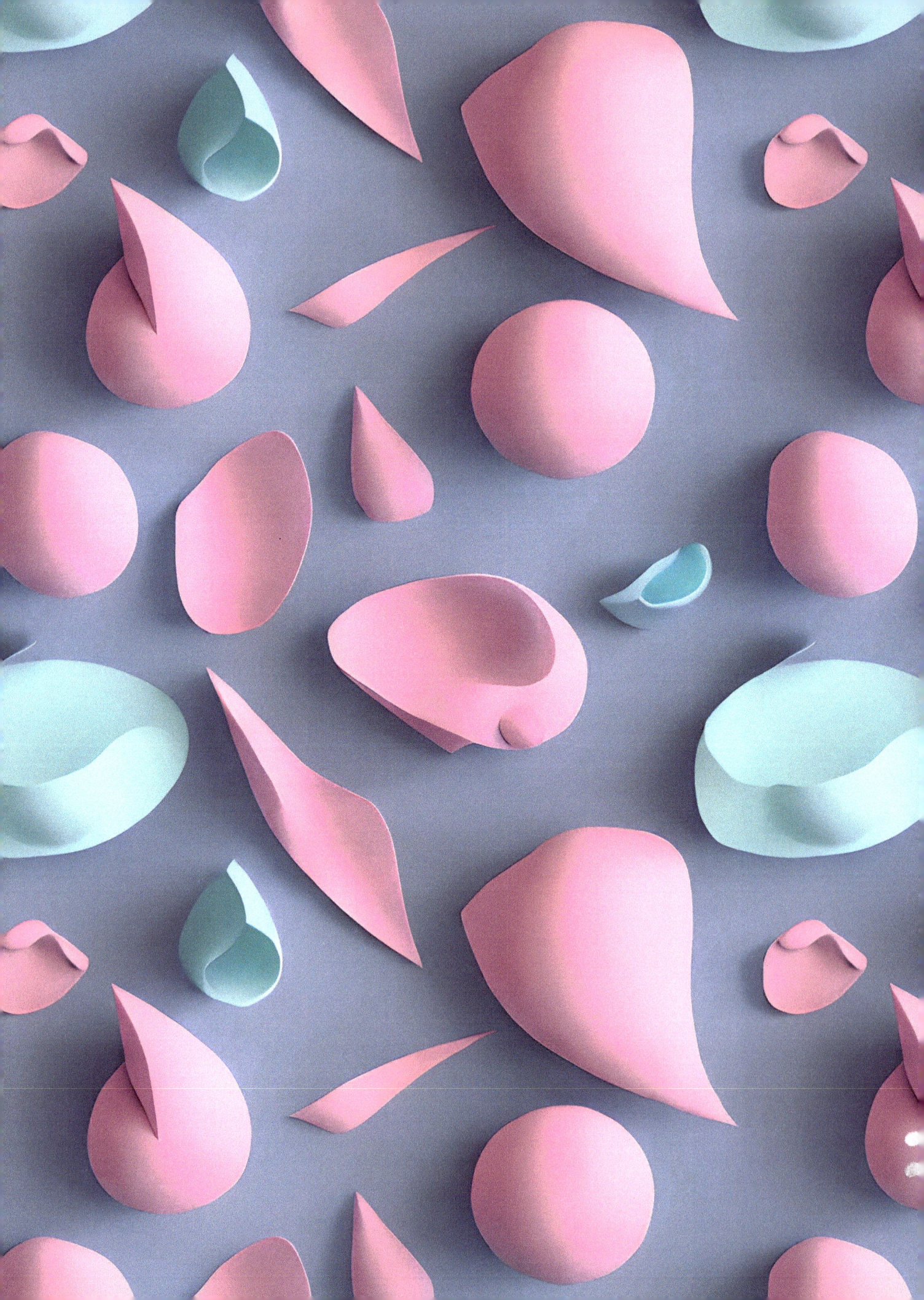

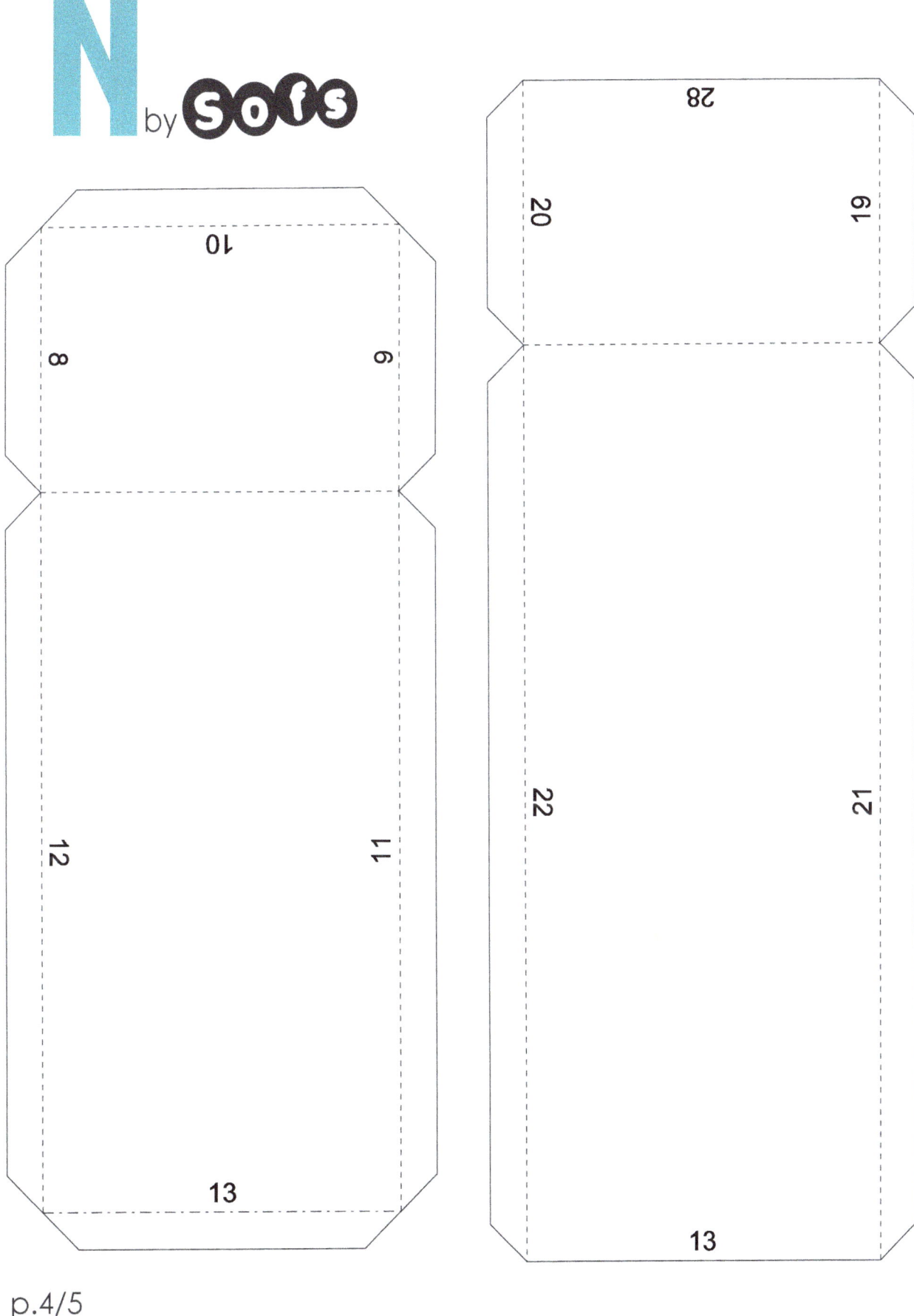

p.4/5

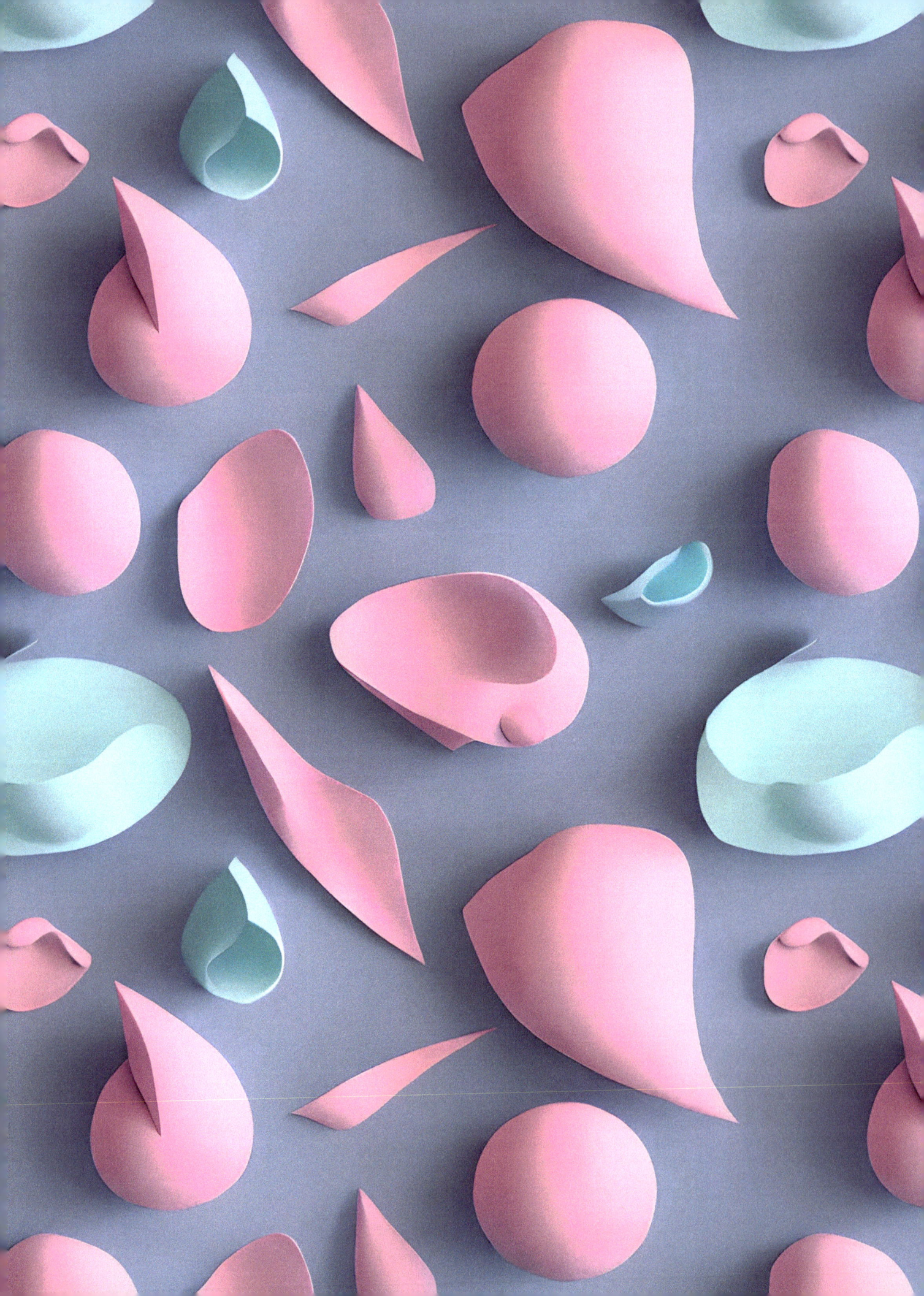

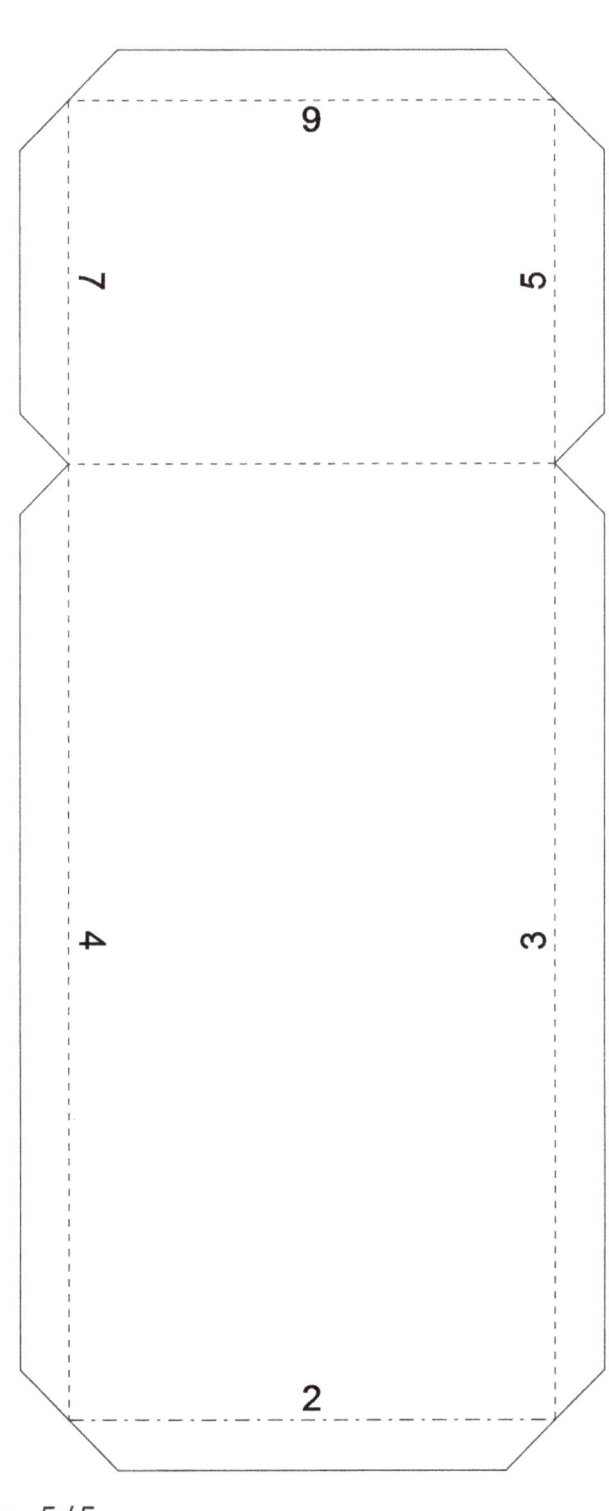

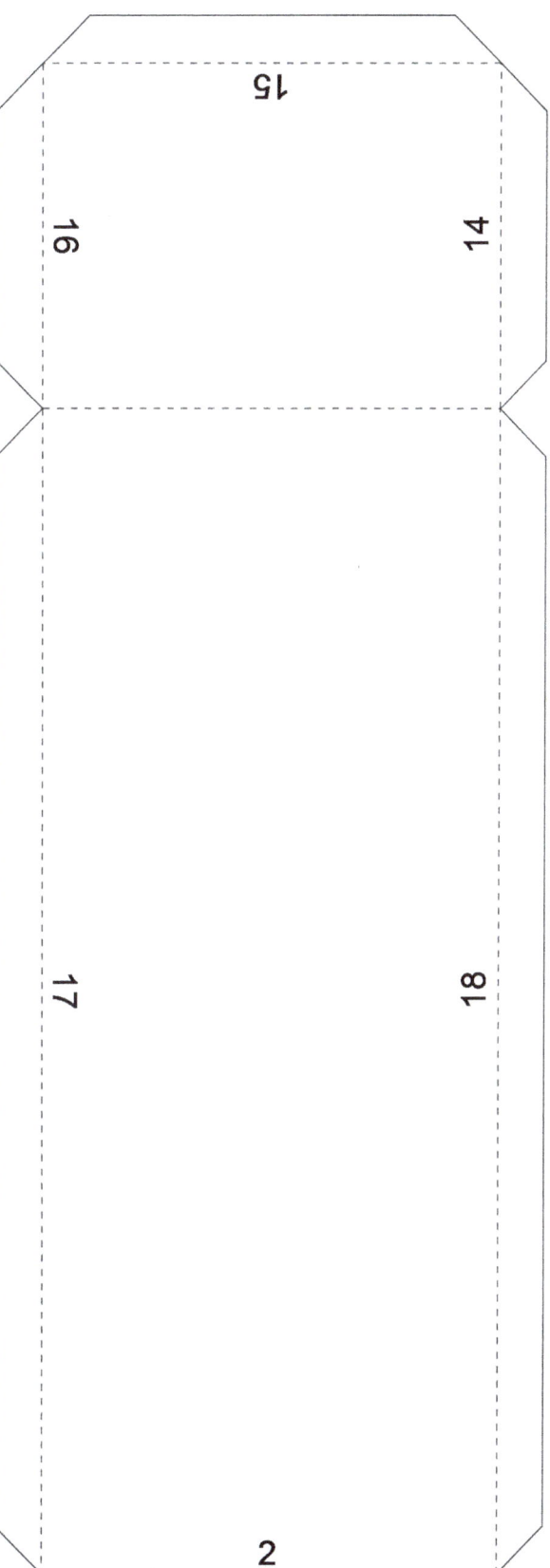

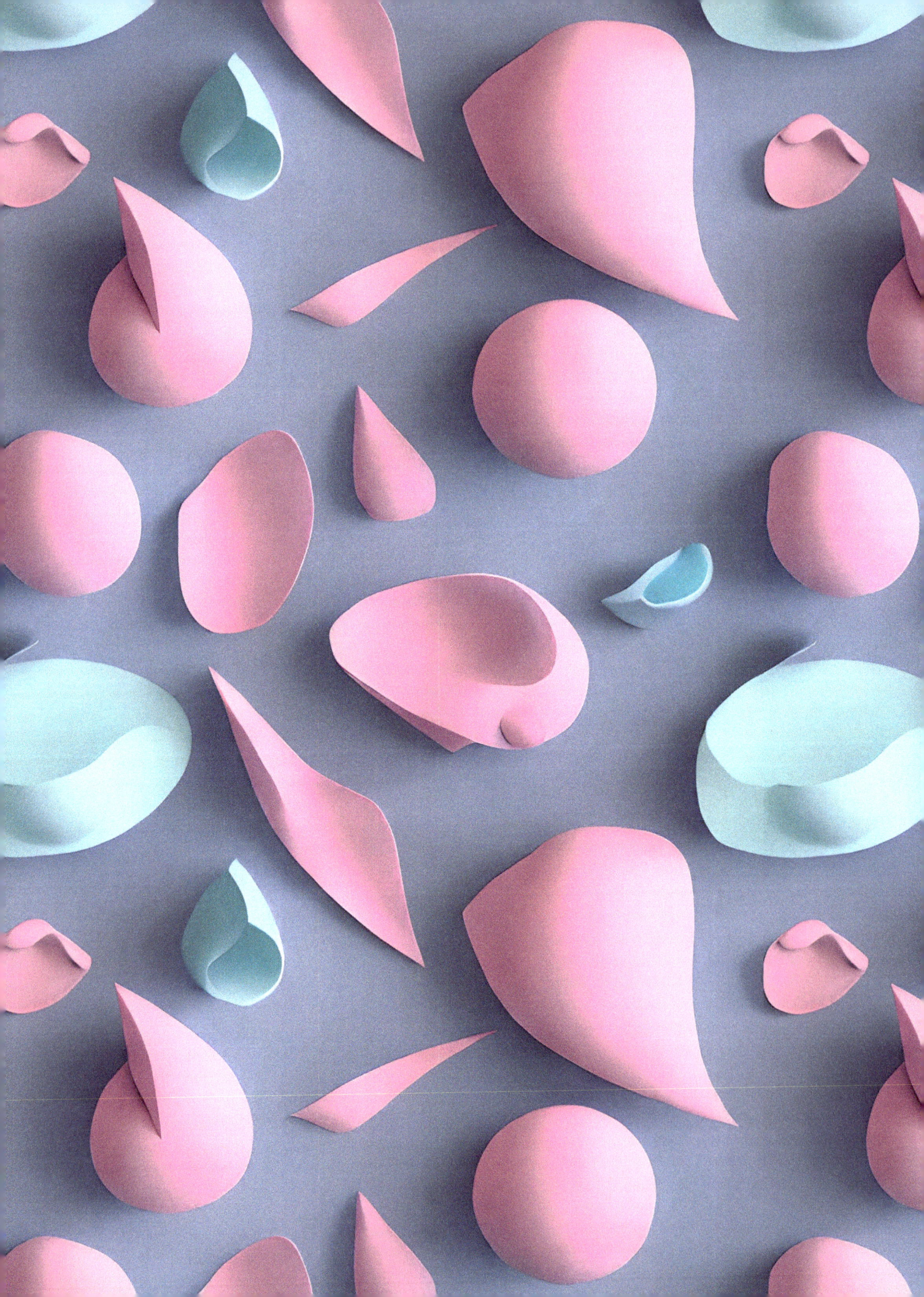

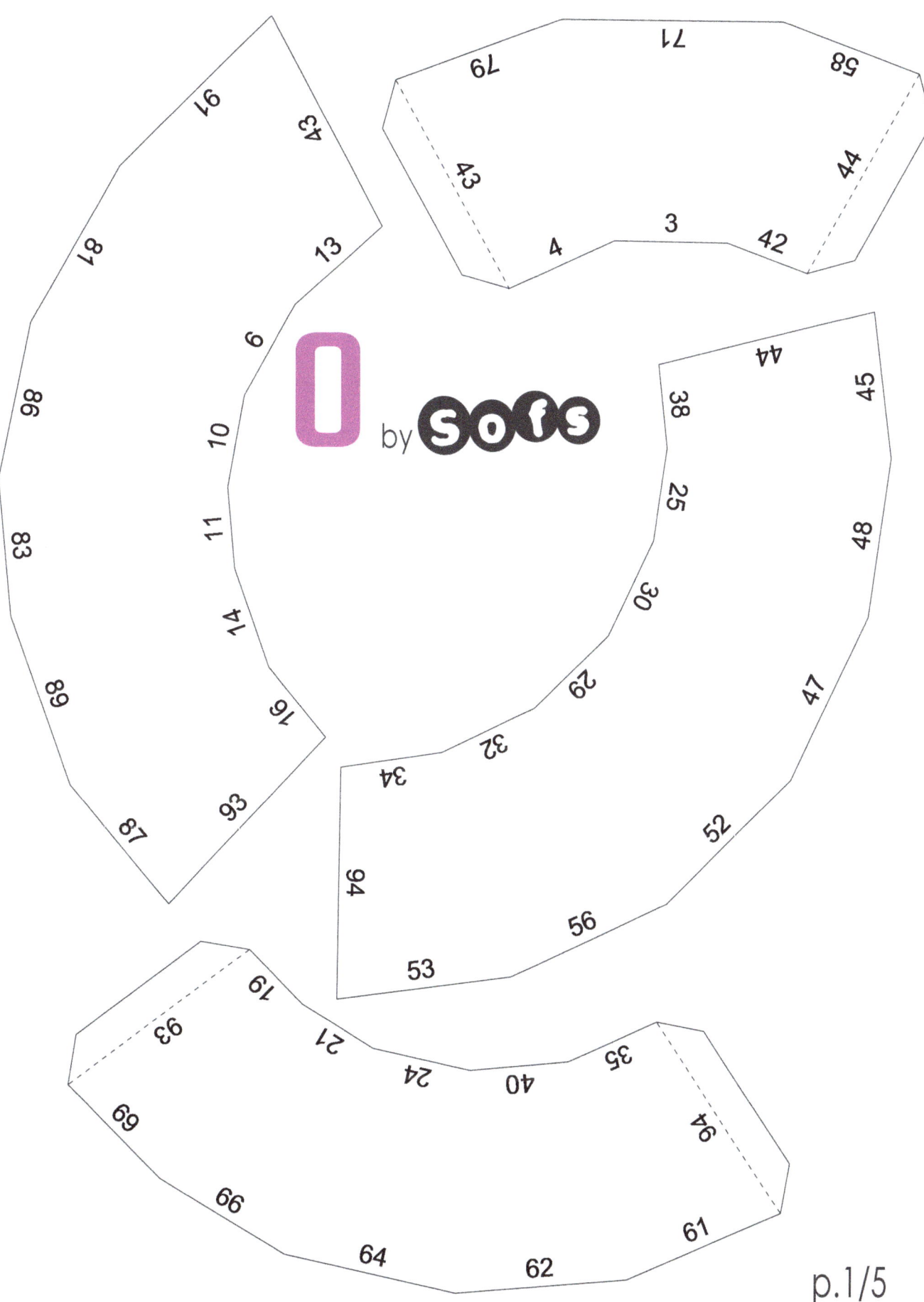

p.1/5

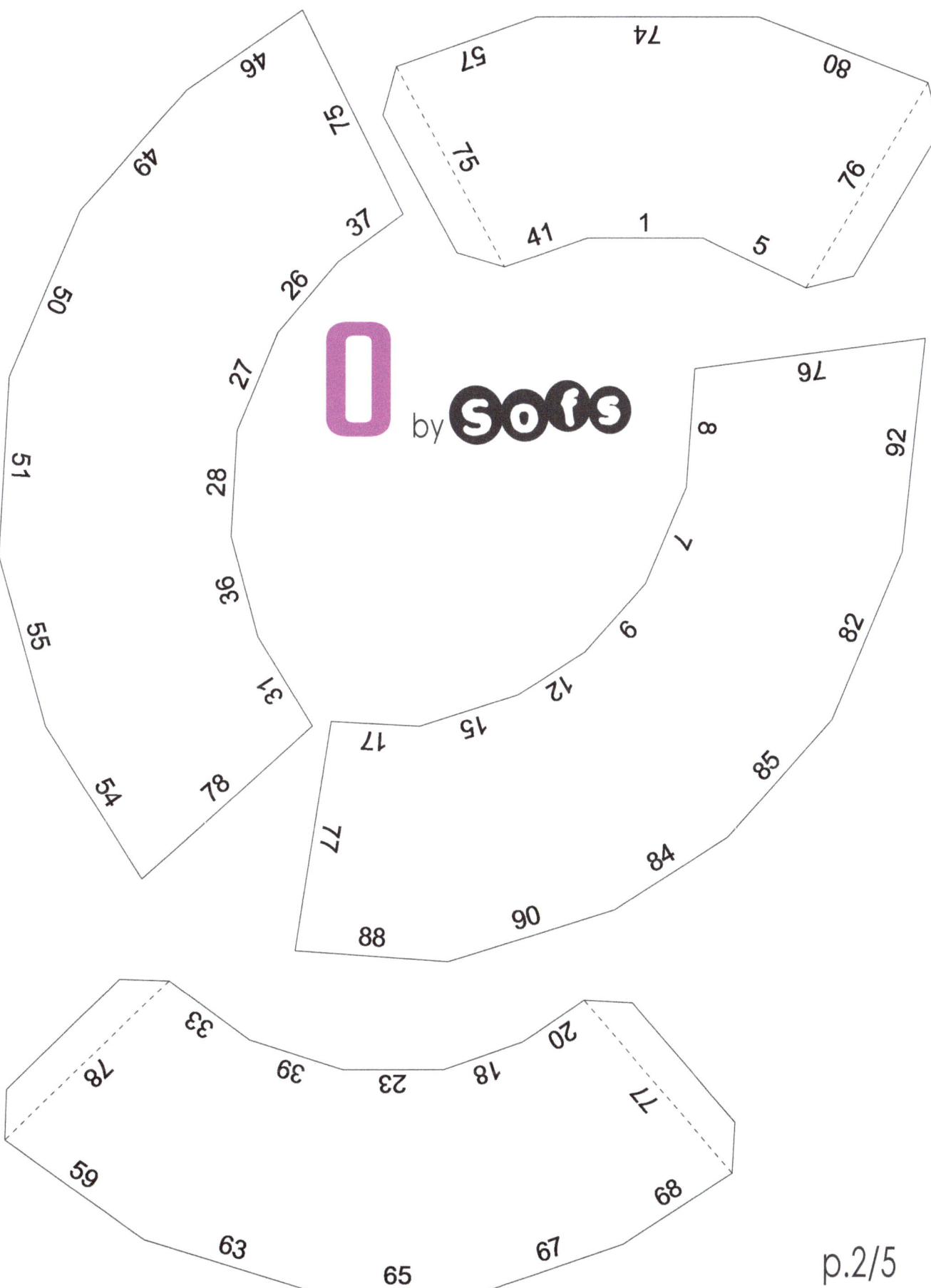

p.2/5

0 by Sofs

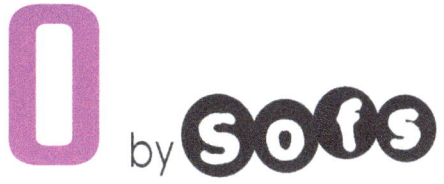

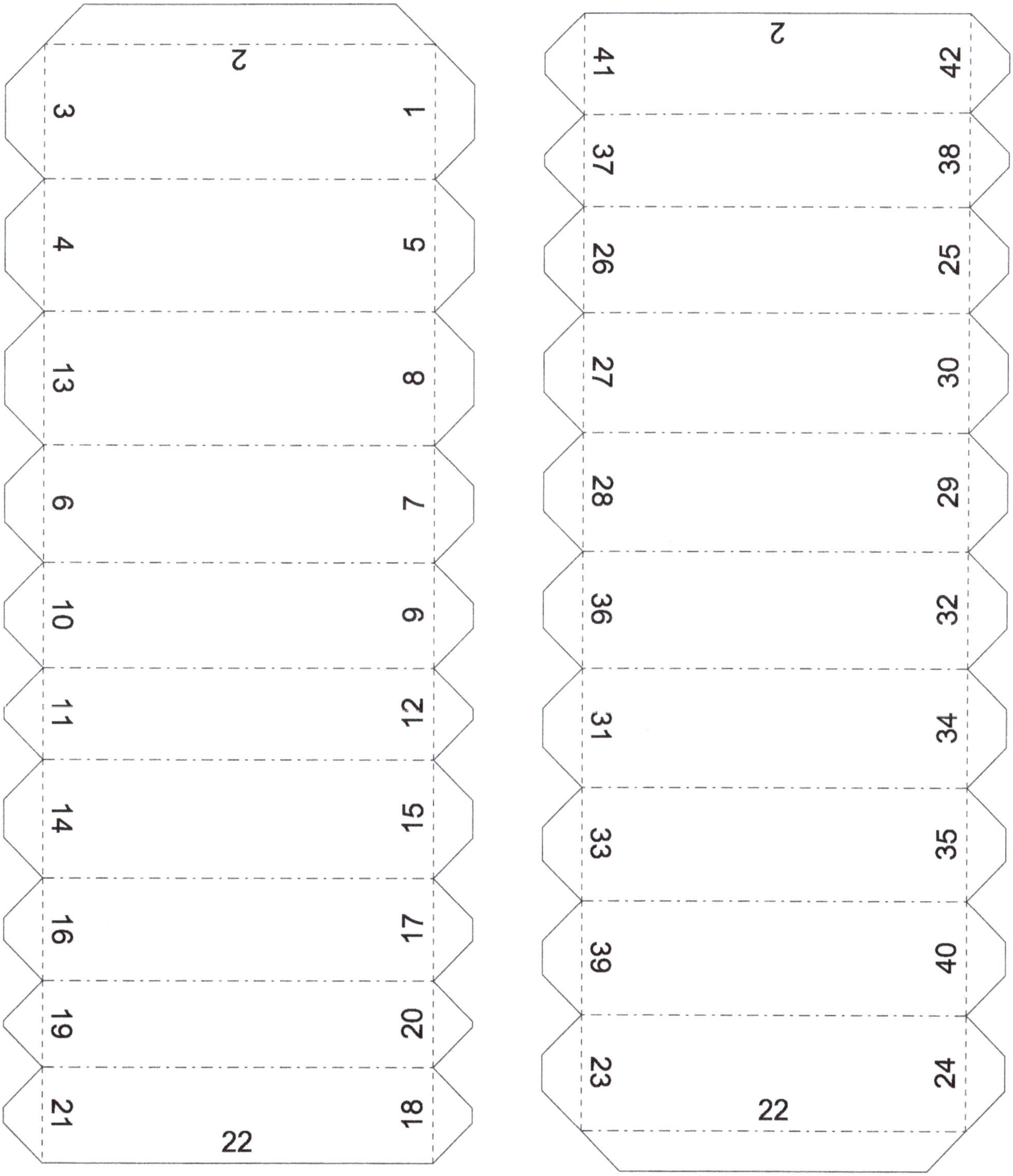
2
3
1
4
5
13
8
6
7
10
9
11
12
14
15
16
17
19
20
21
18
22
2
41
42
37
38
26
25
27
30
28
29
36
32
31
34
33
35
39
40
23
24
22

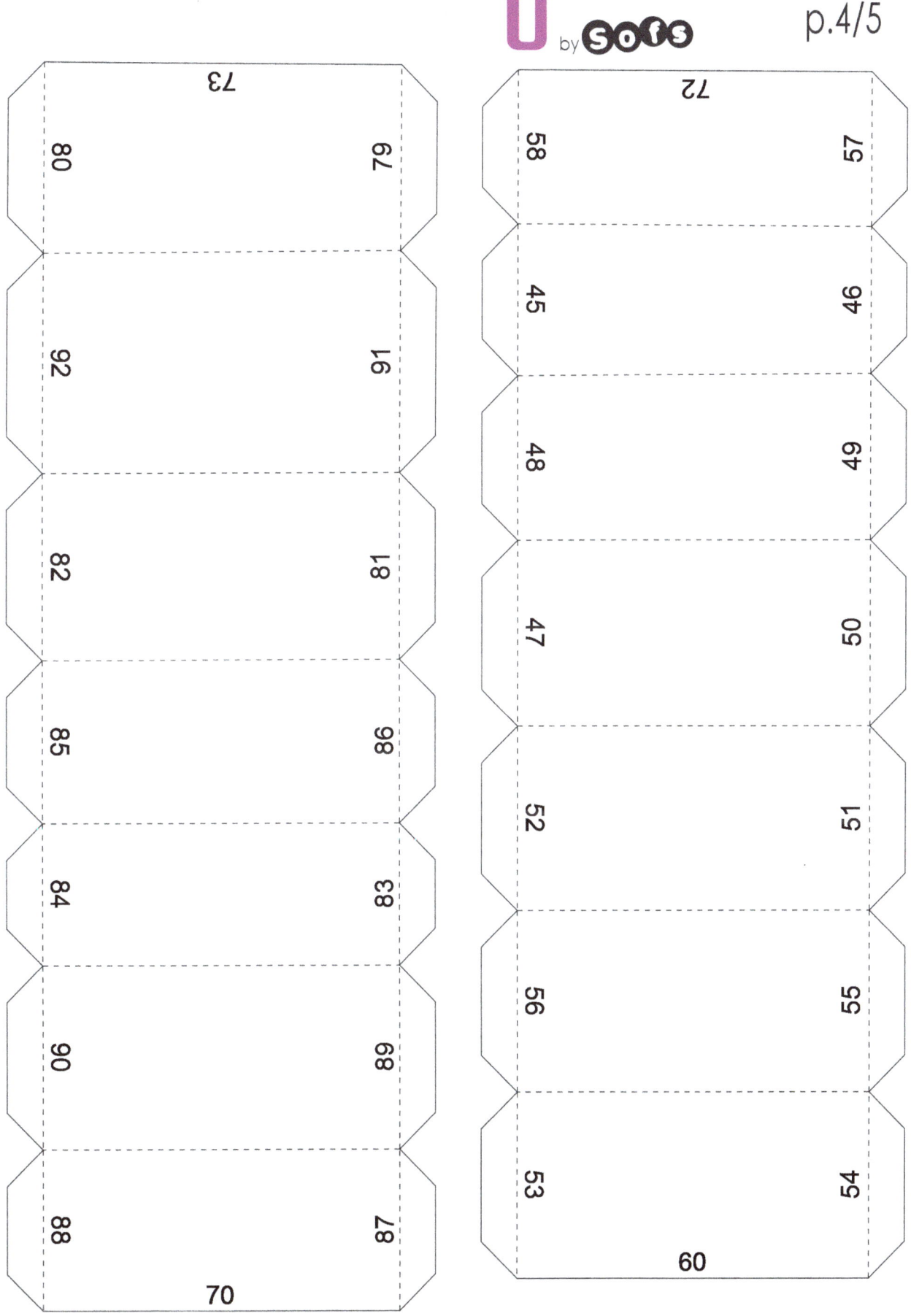

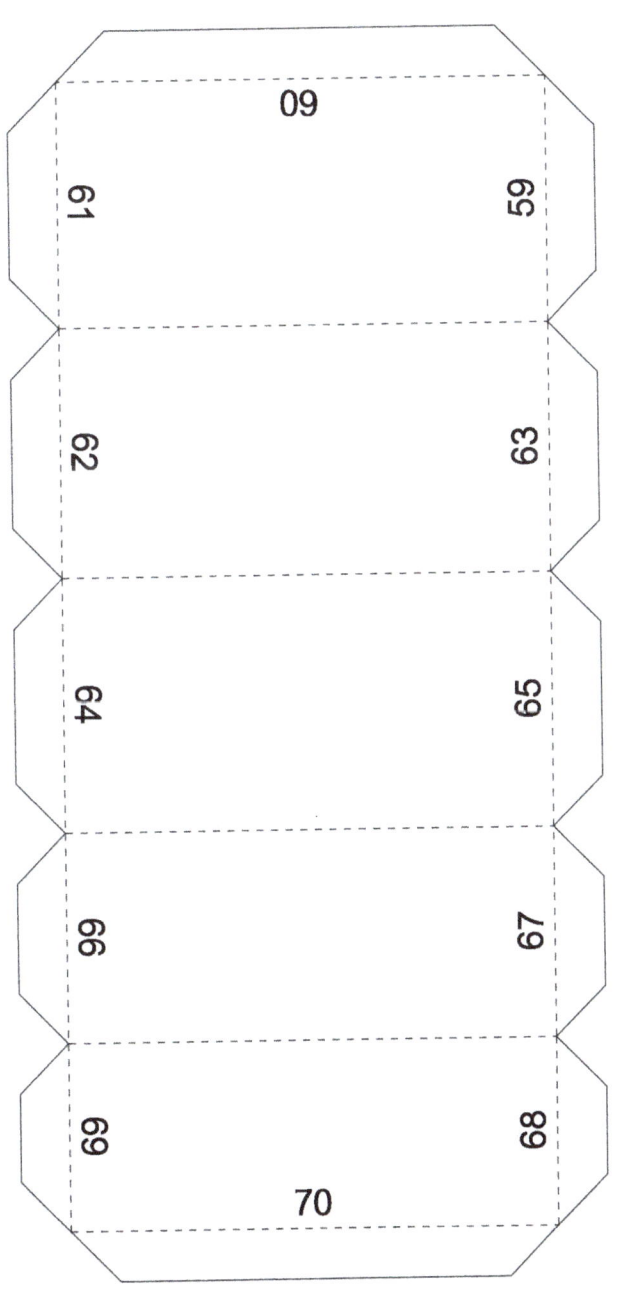

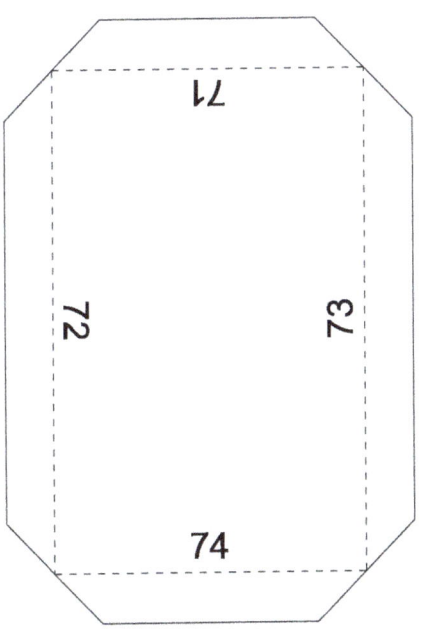

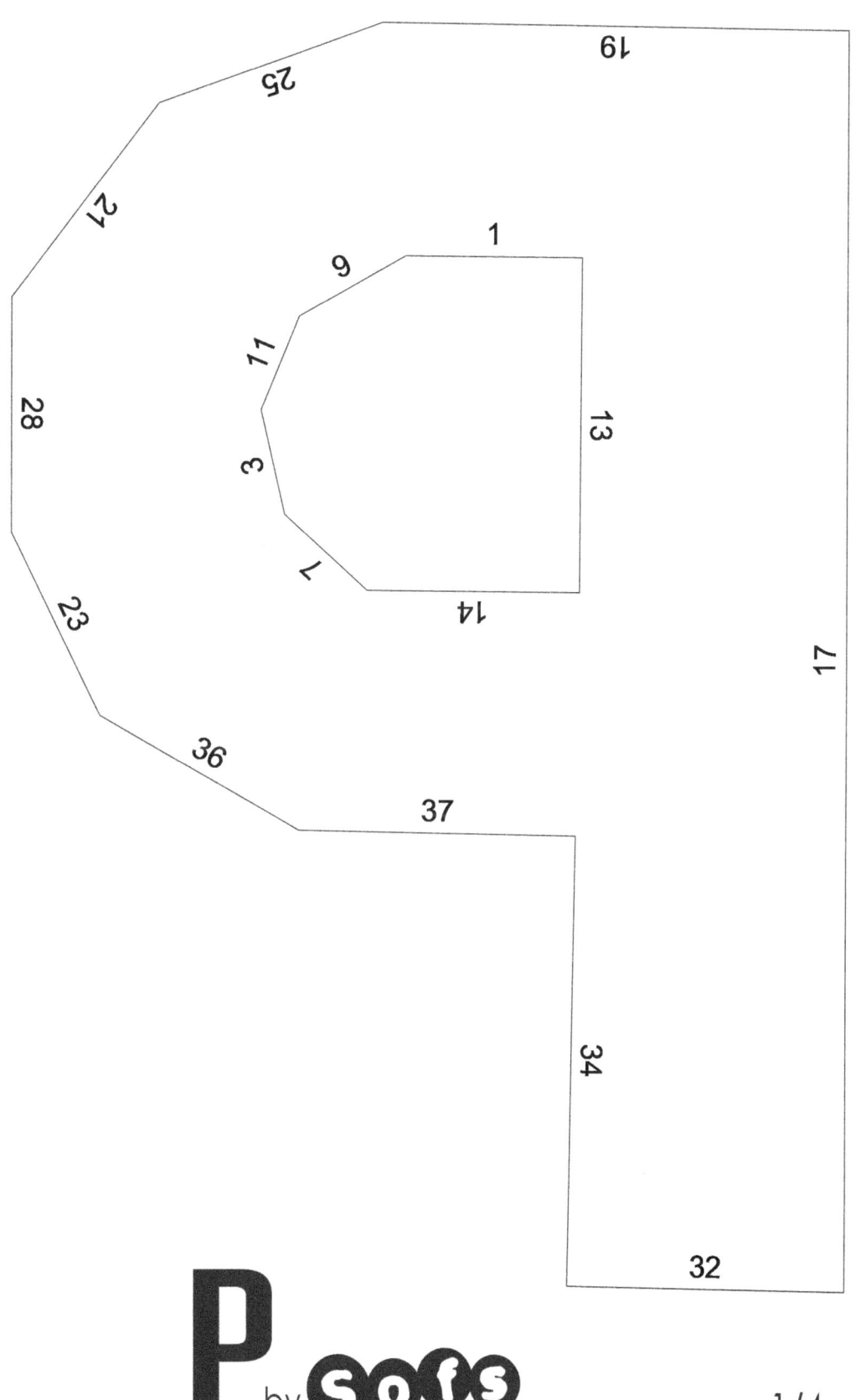

1

6

11

25

19

21

3

13

28

7

14

23

17

36

37

34

32

32

P by **sofs**

p.1/4

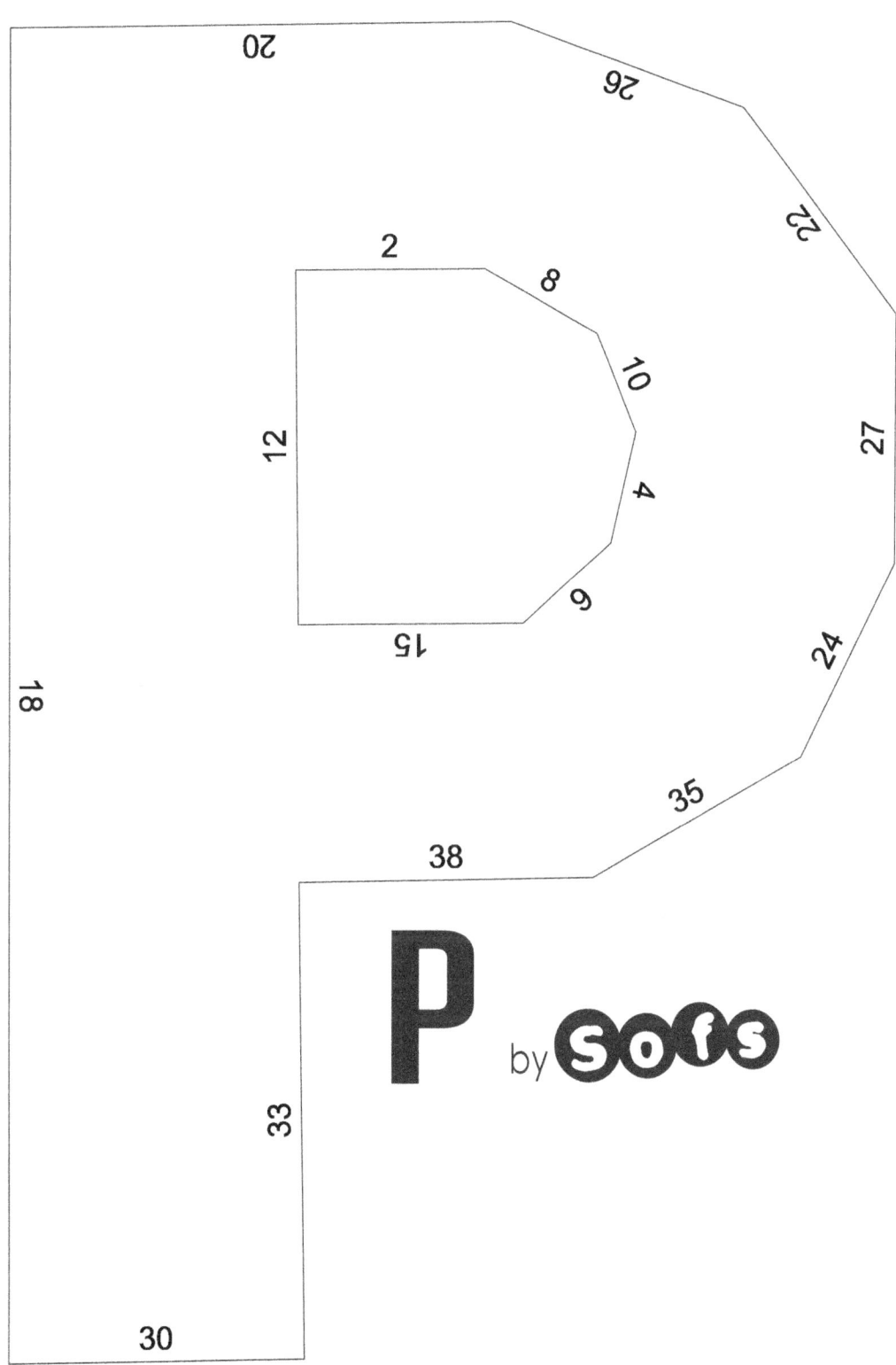

P by Sofs

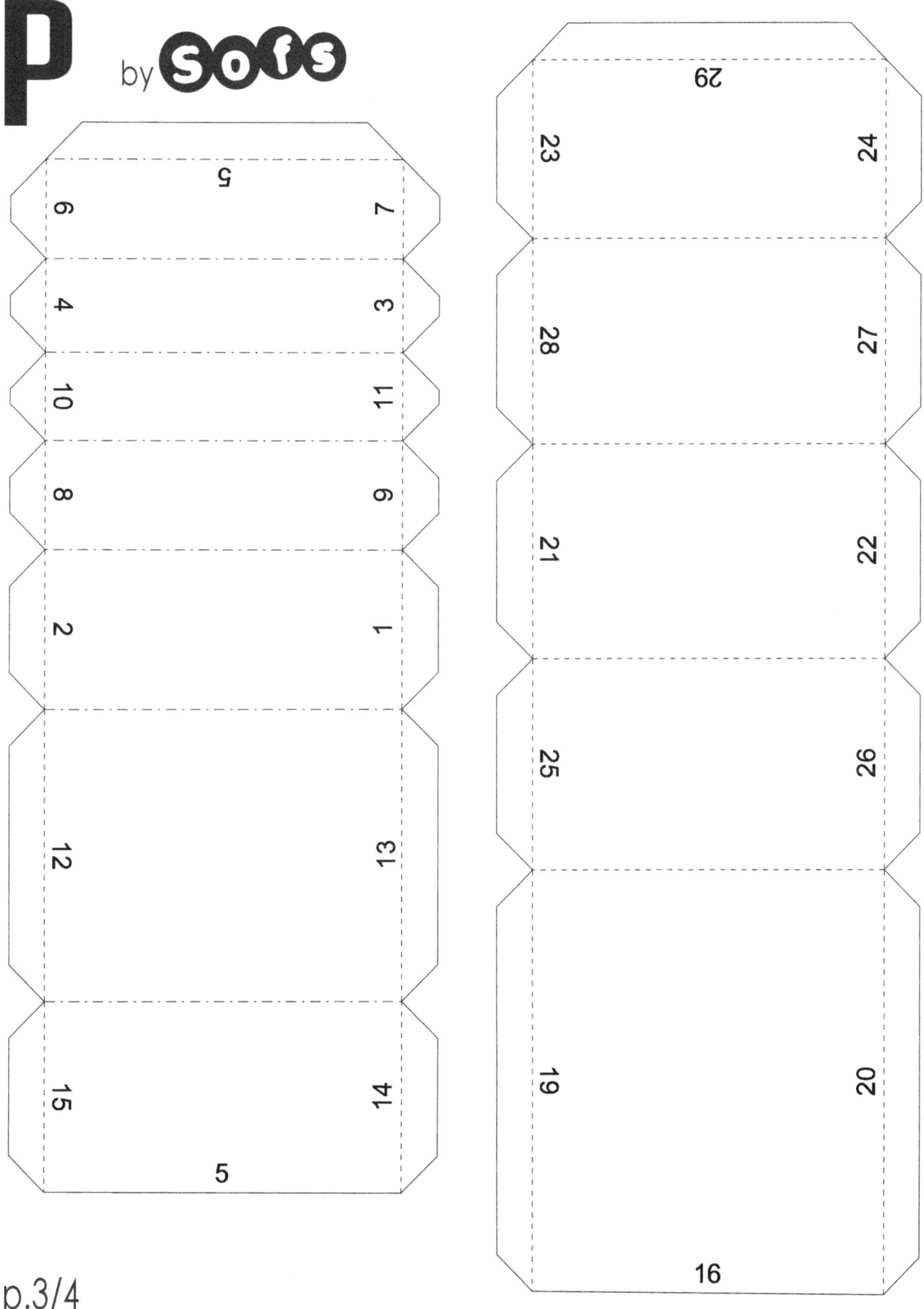

P by Sofs

p.3/4

P by Sofs

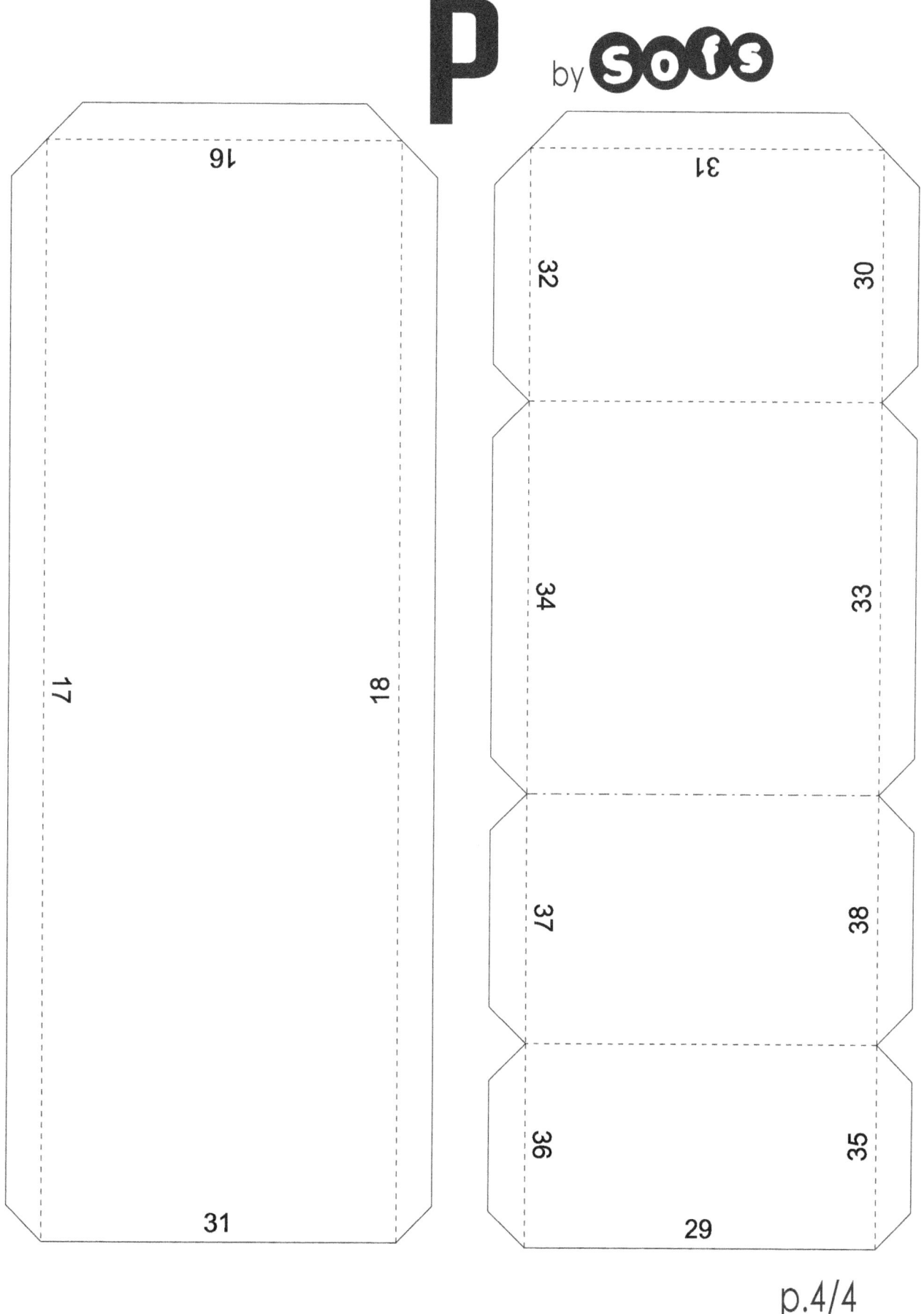

p.4/4

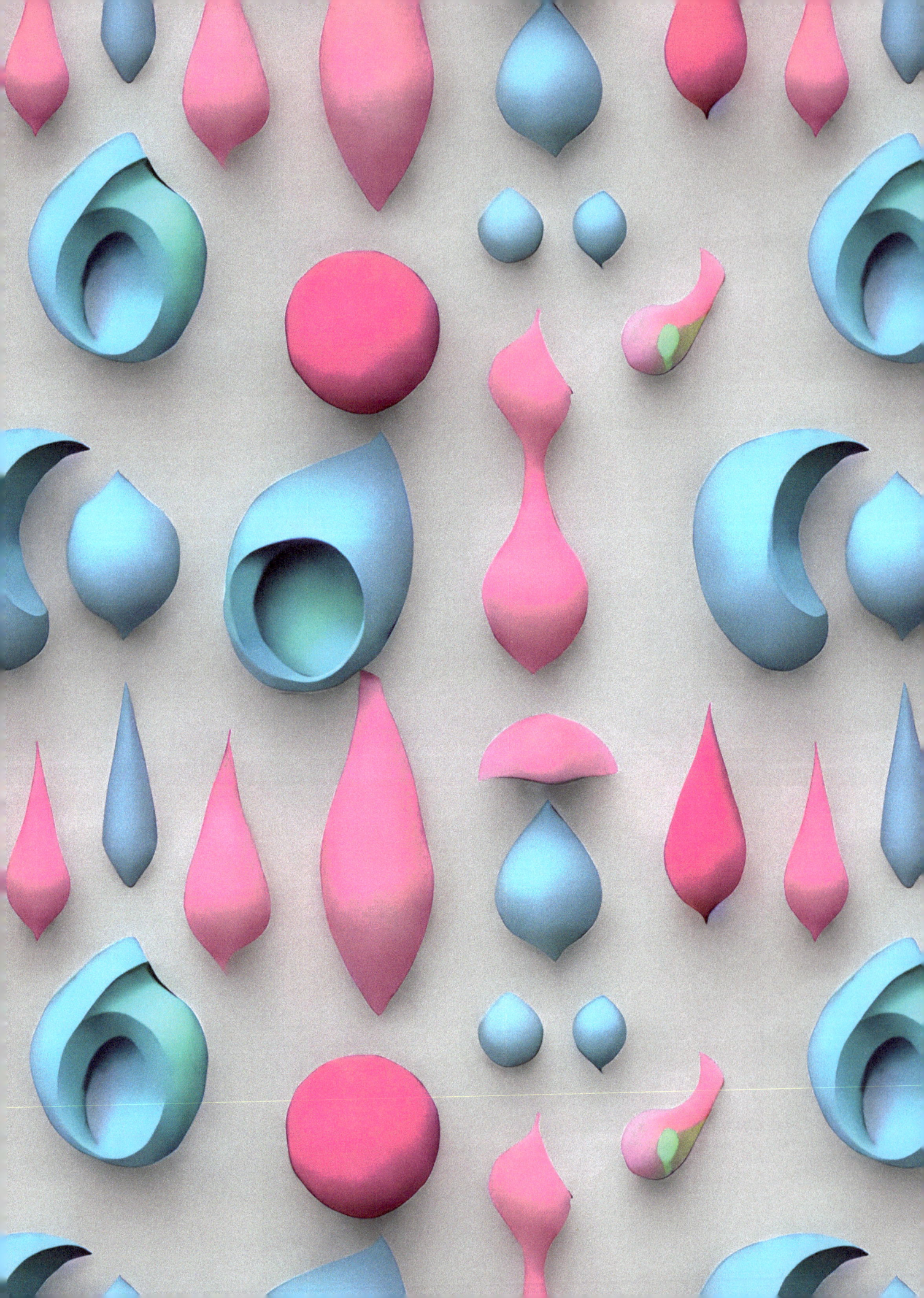

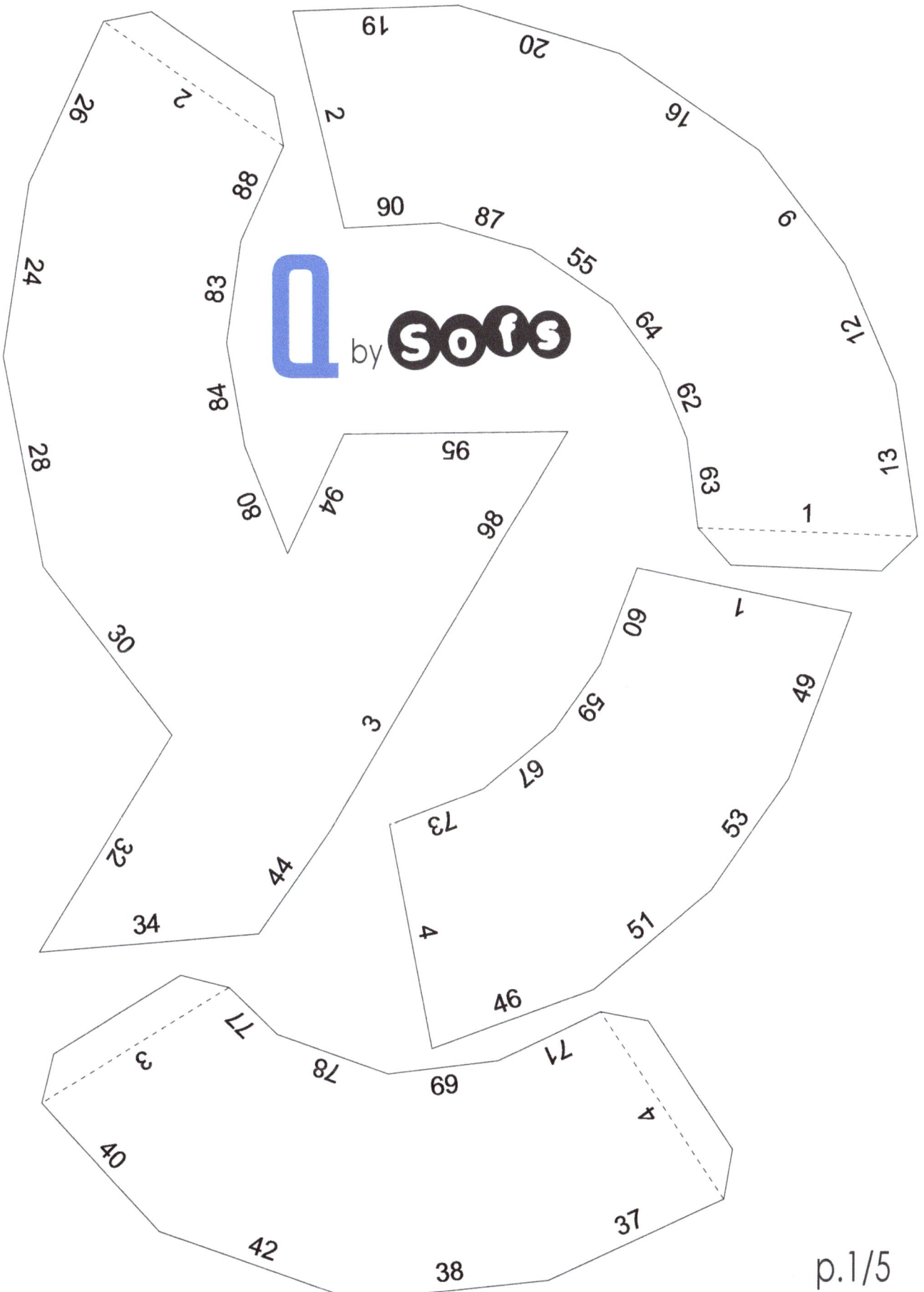

p.1/5

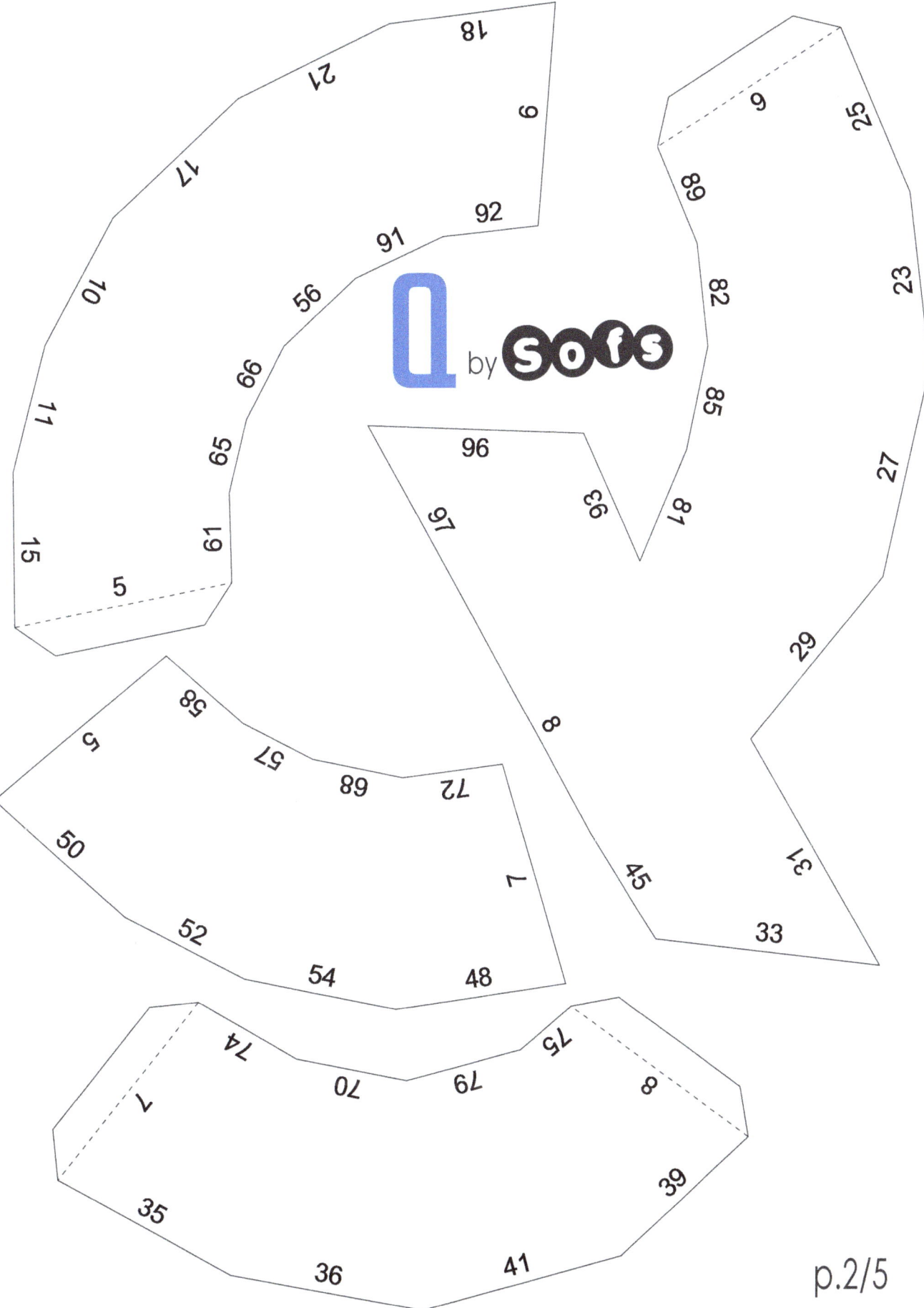

p.2/5

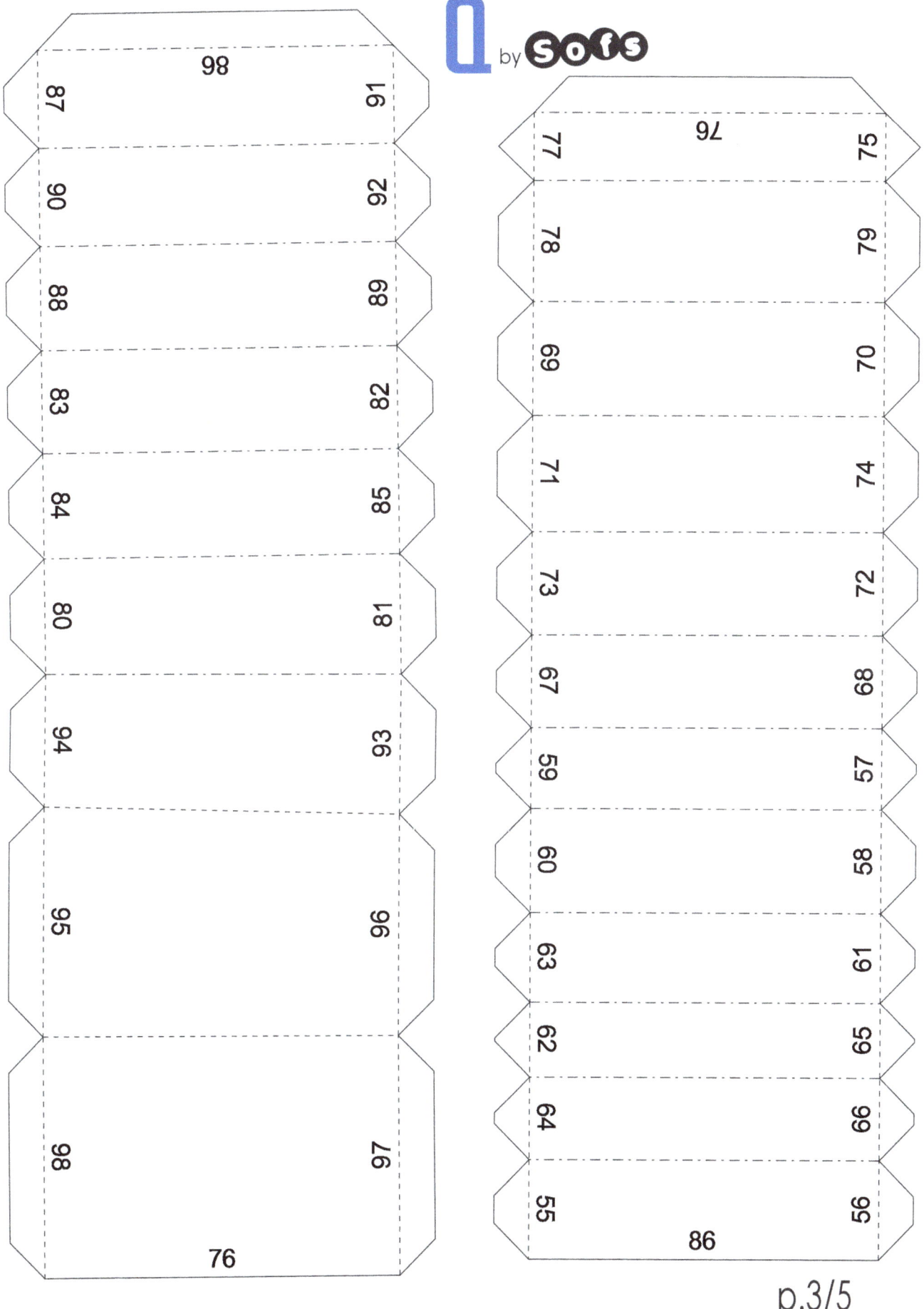

p.3/5

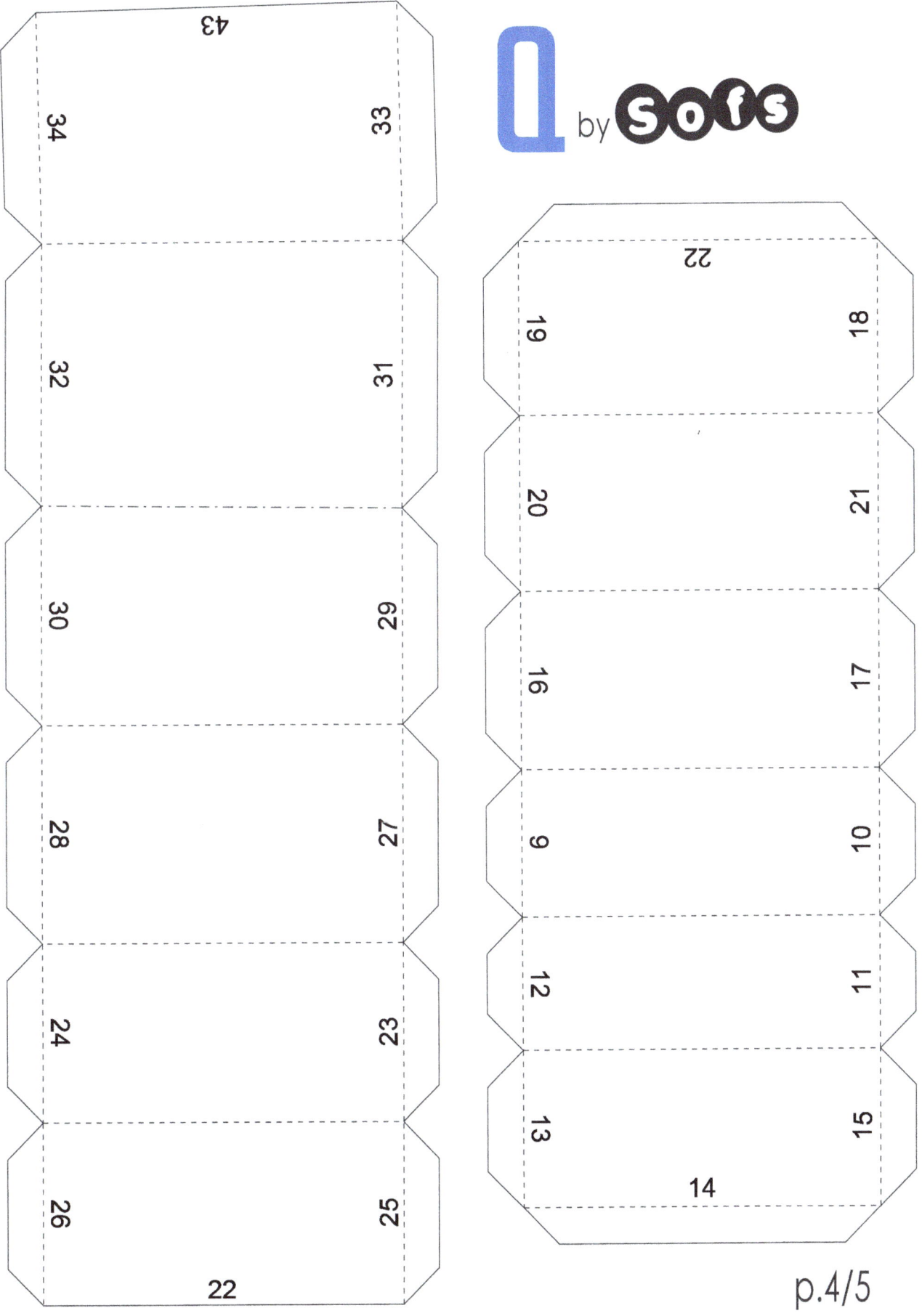

by sofs

p.4/5

by Sofs

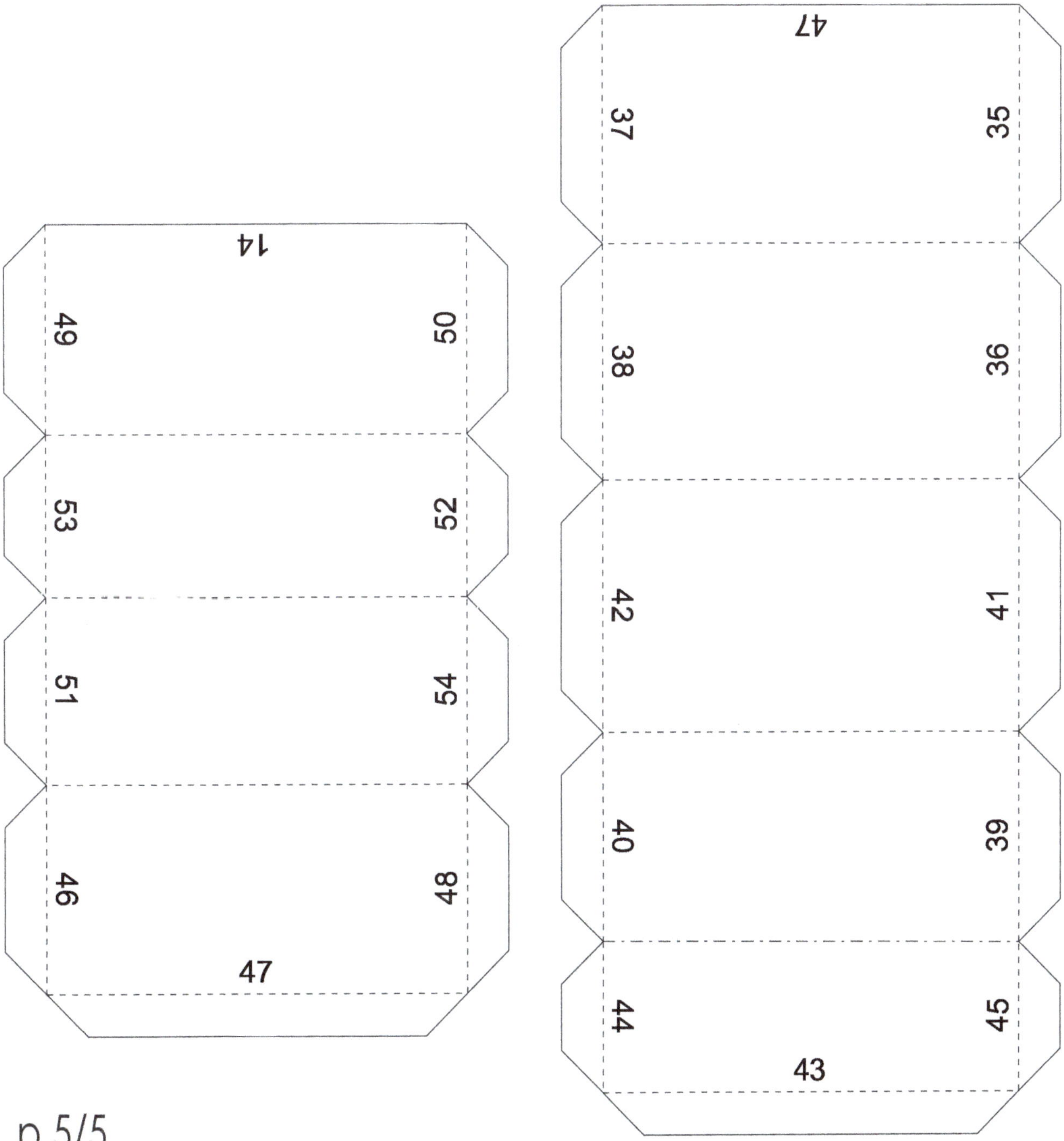

47

37

35

38

36

42

41

40

39

44

45

43

14

49

50

53

52

51

54

46

48

47

p.5/5

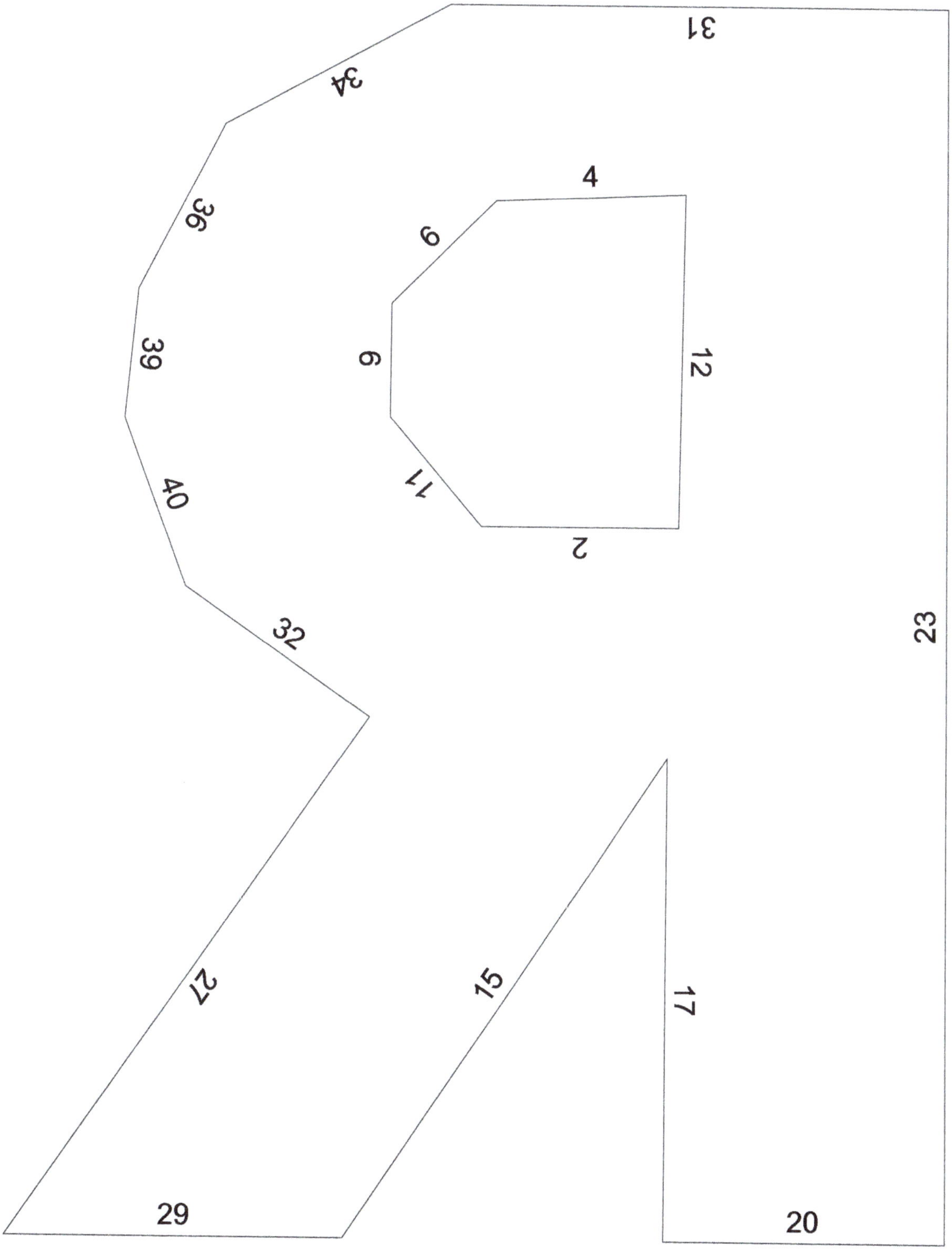

31

34

4

6

36

6

39

12

11

2

40

23

32

27

15

17

29

20

R by sofs

p.1/5

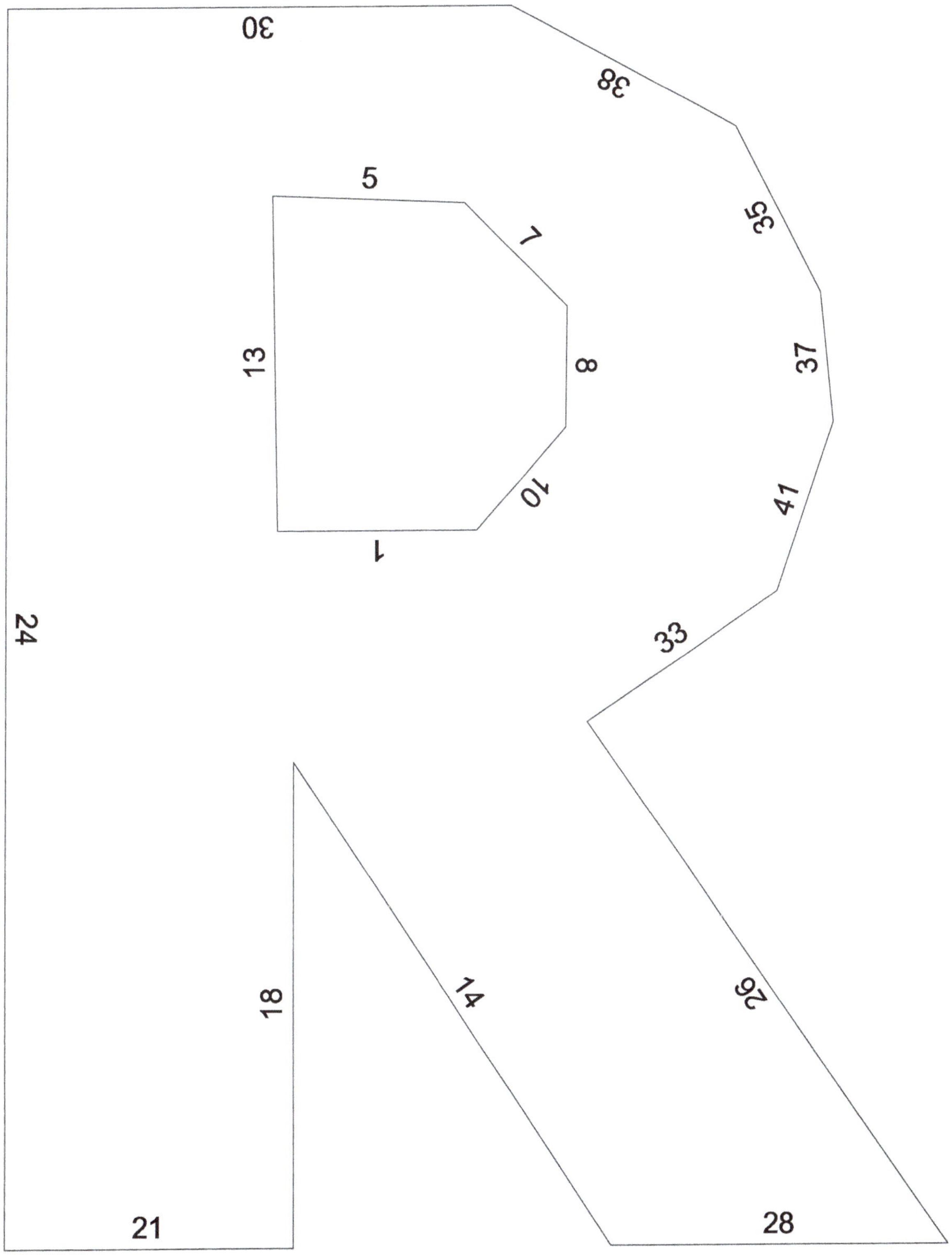

30

38

5

7

35

13

37

8

41

10

1

33

24

26

18

14

21

28

R by **Sofs**

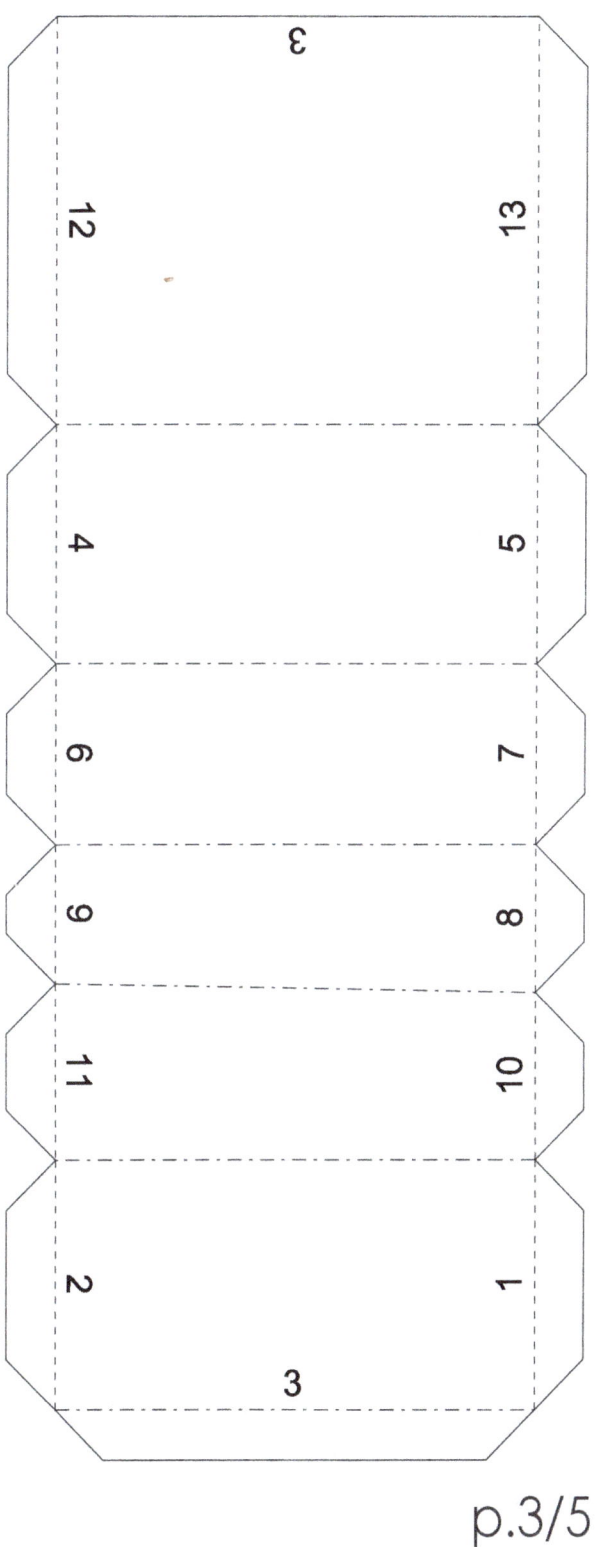

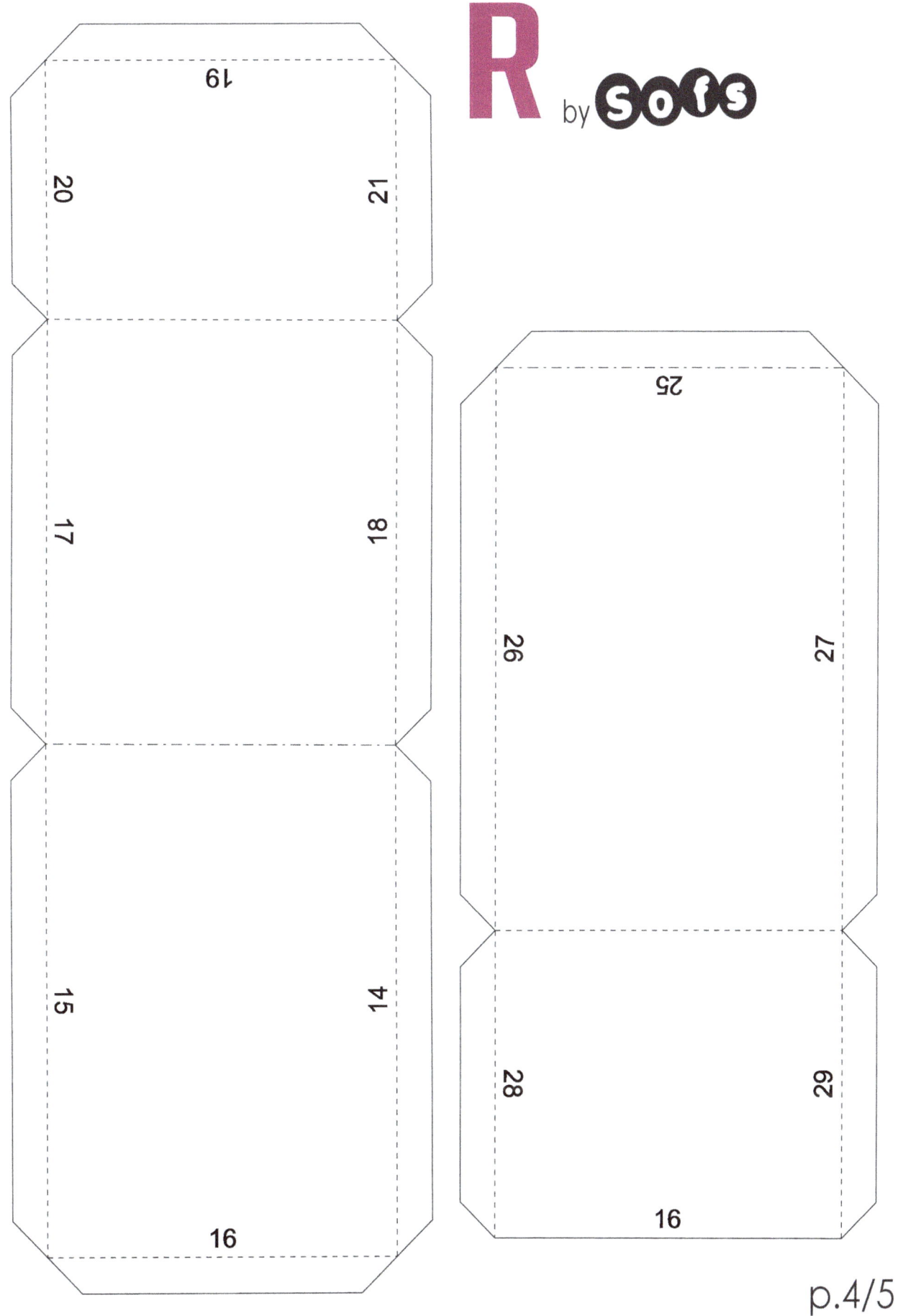

R by Sofs

p.4/5

R by sofs

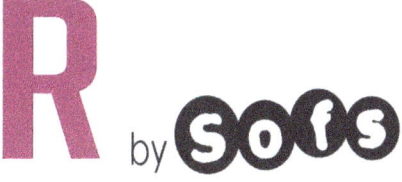

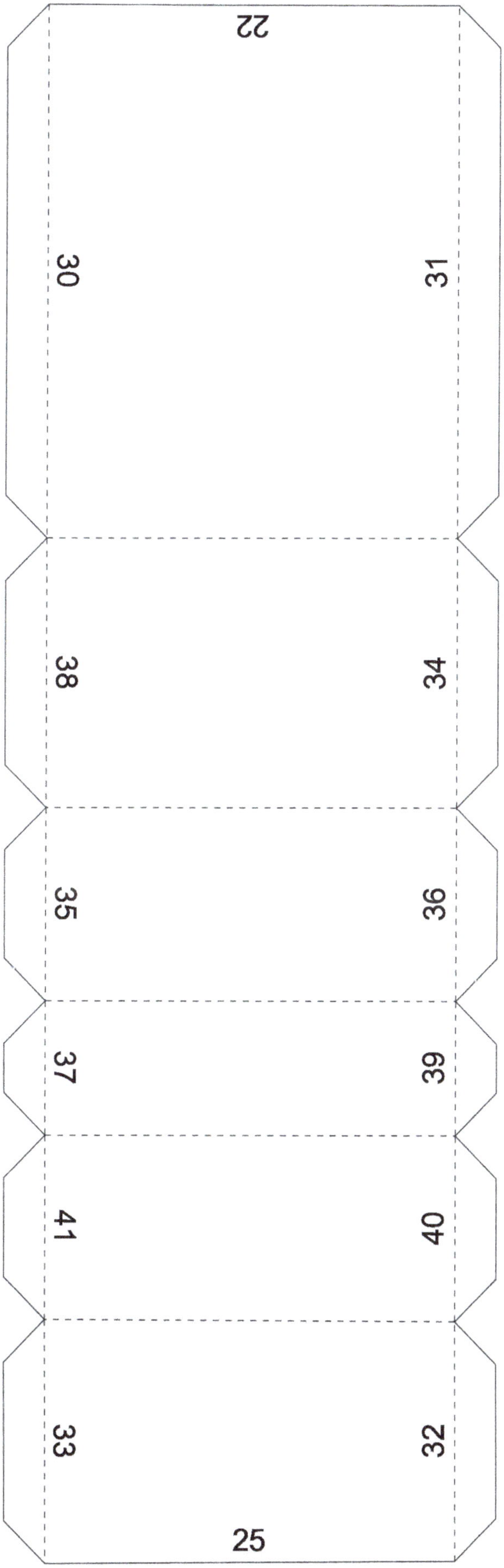

22
30
31
38
34
35
36
37
39
41
40
33
32
25

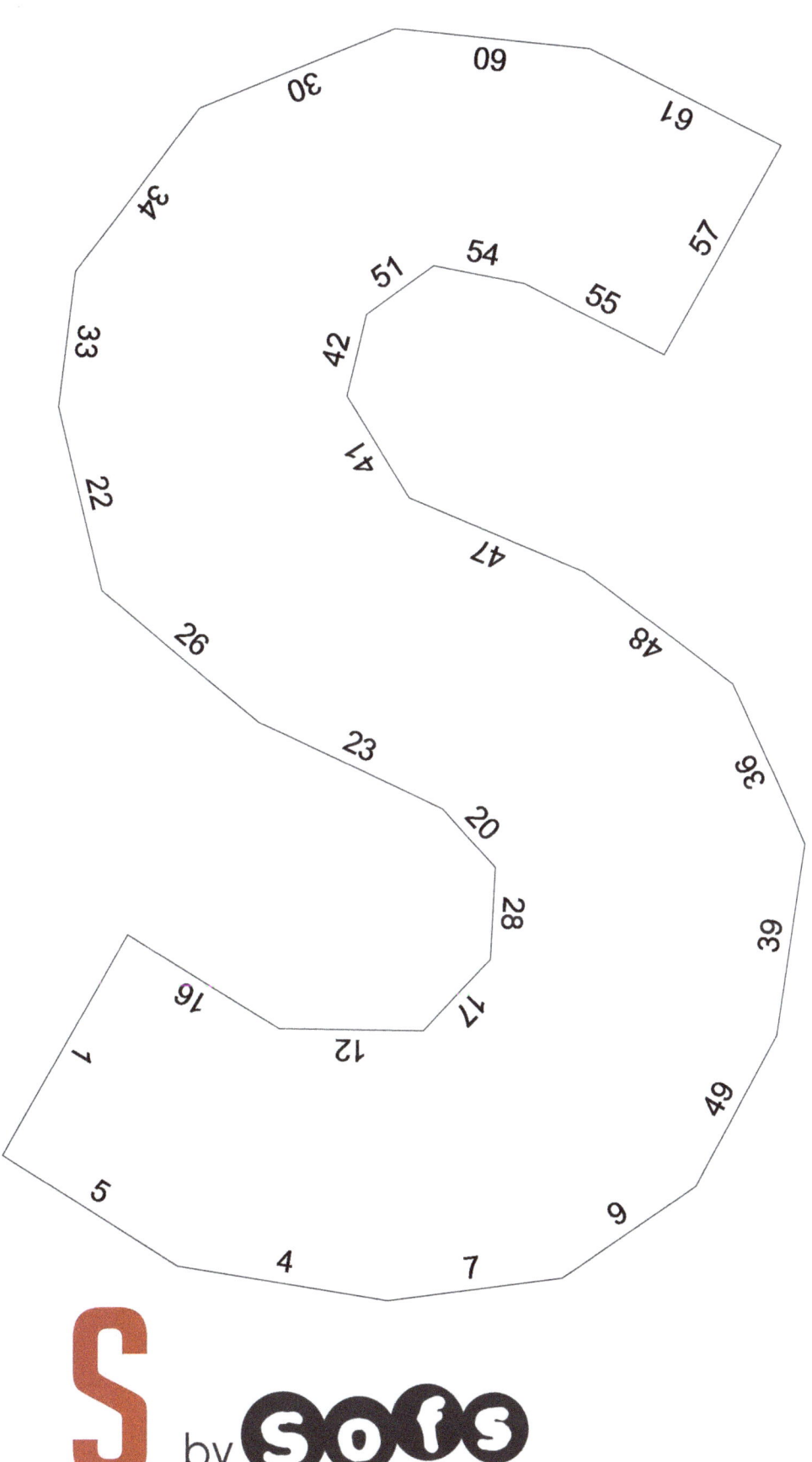

S by Sofs

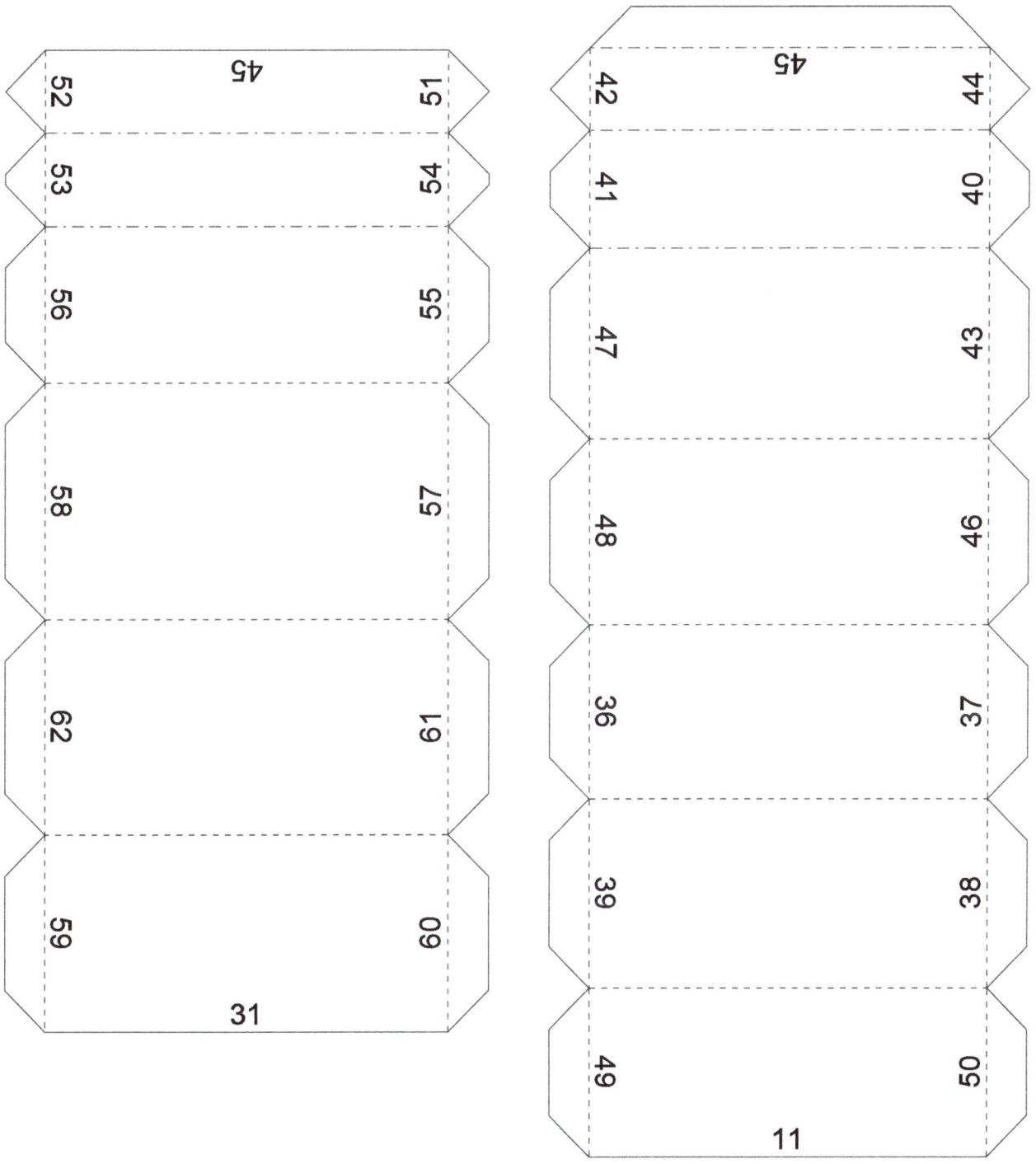

S by Sofs

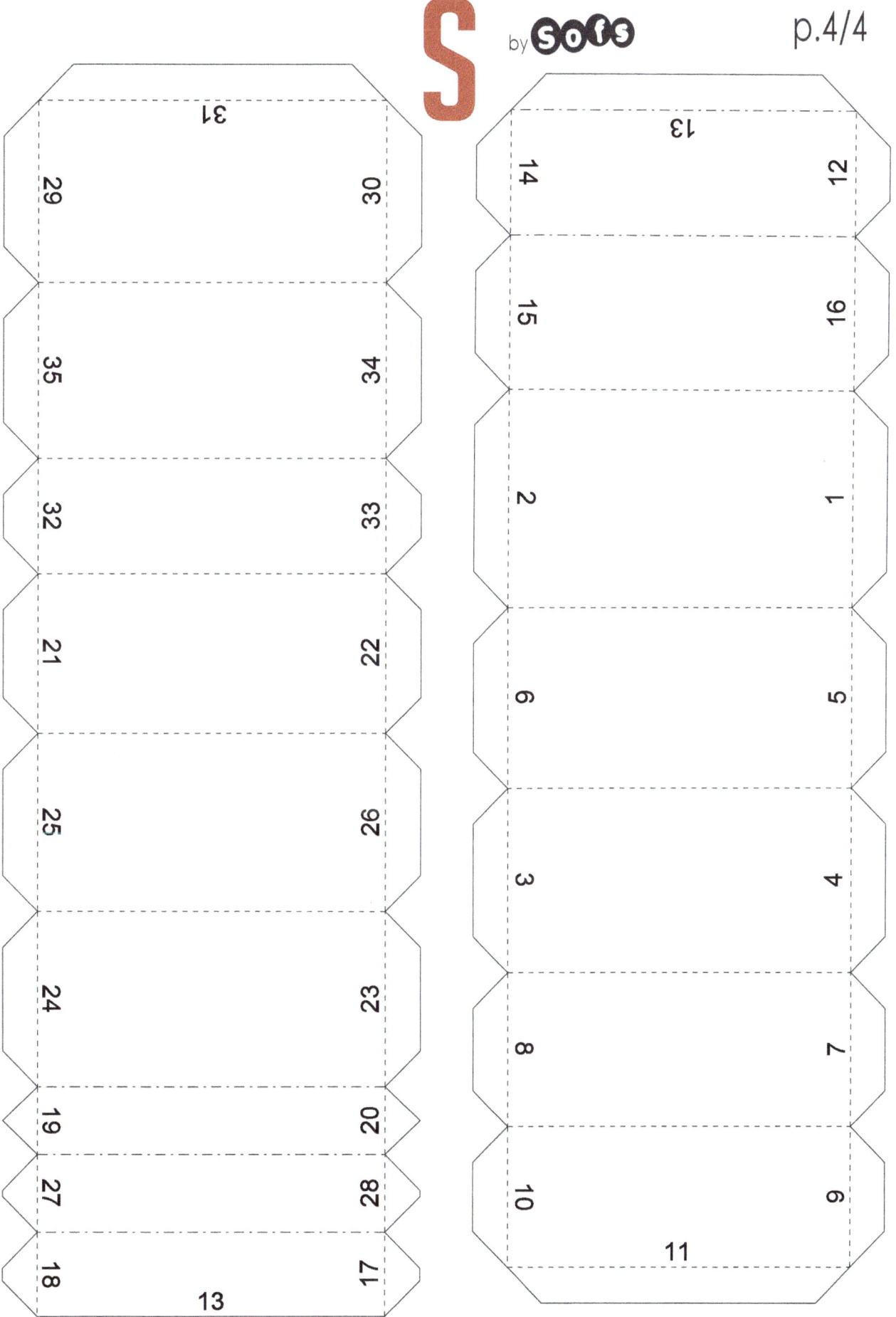

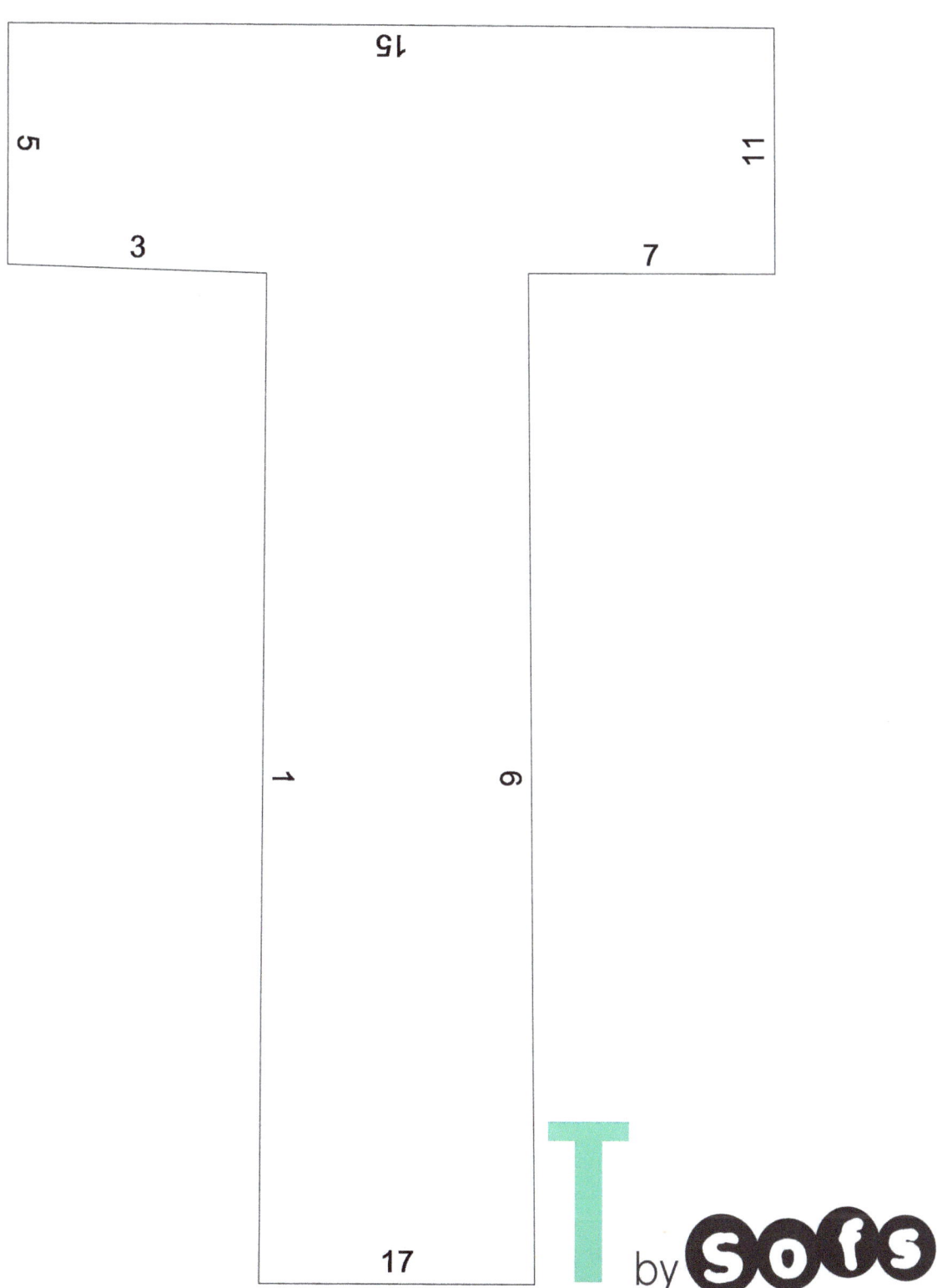

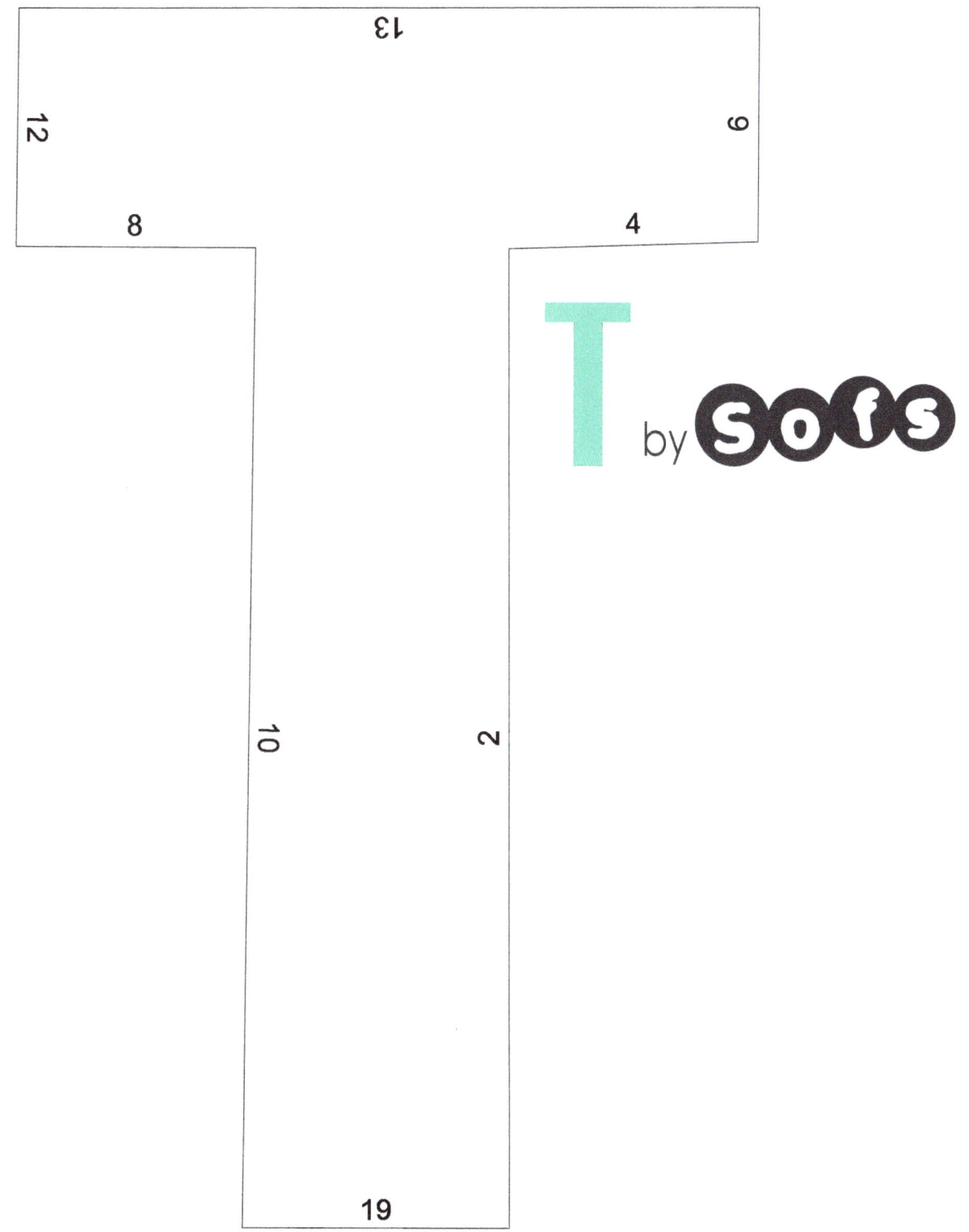

13

12

9

8

4

10

2

19

by Sofs

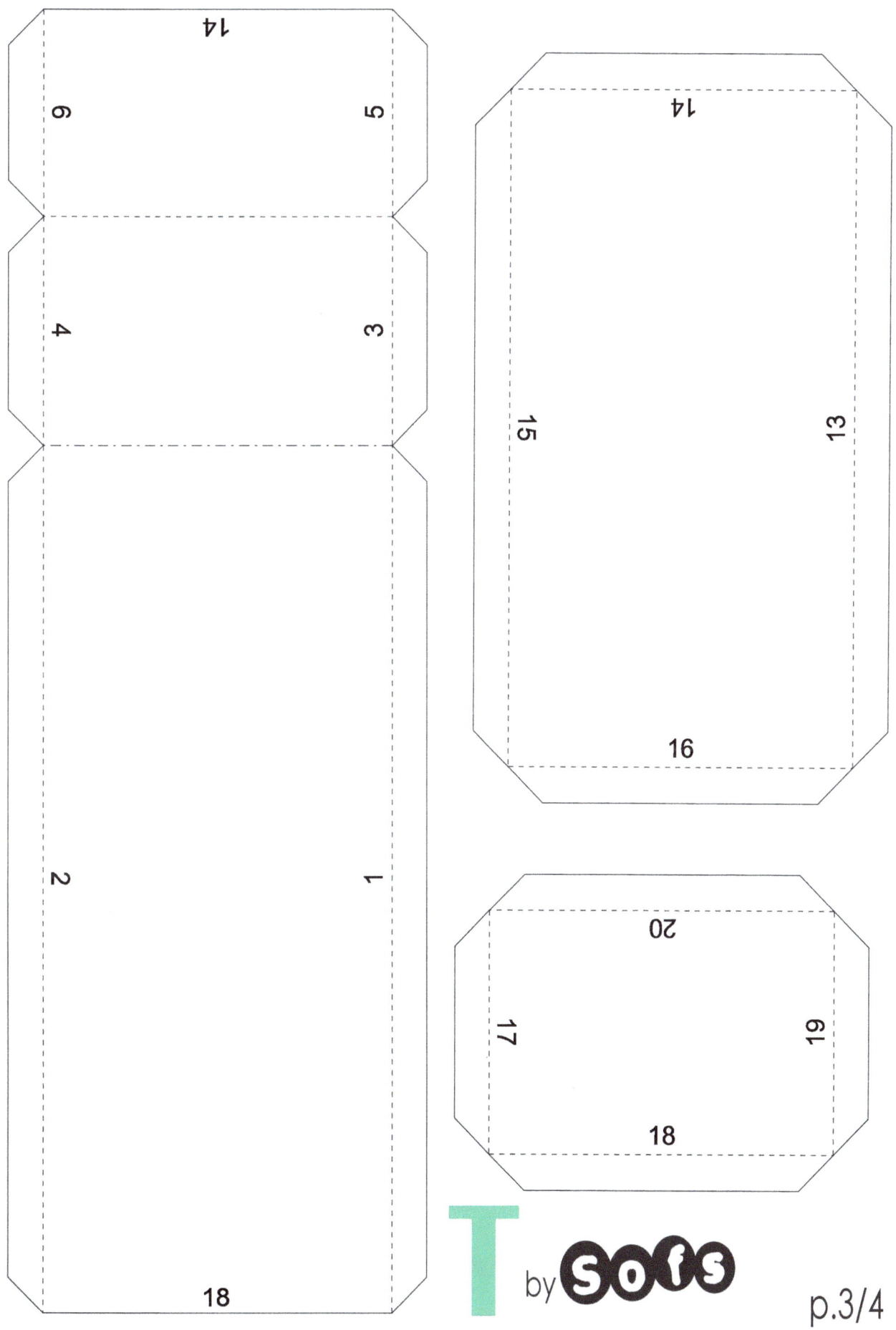

14

6　5

4　3

2　1

18

14

15　13

16

20

17　19

18

T by Sofs

p.3/4

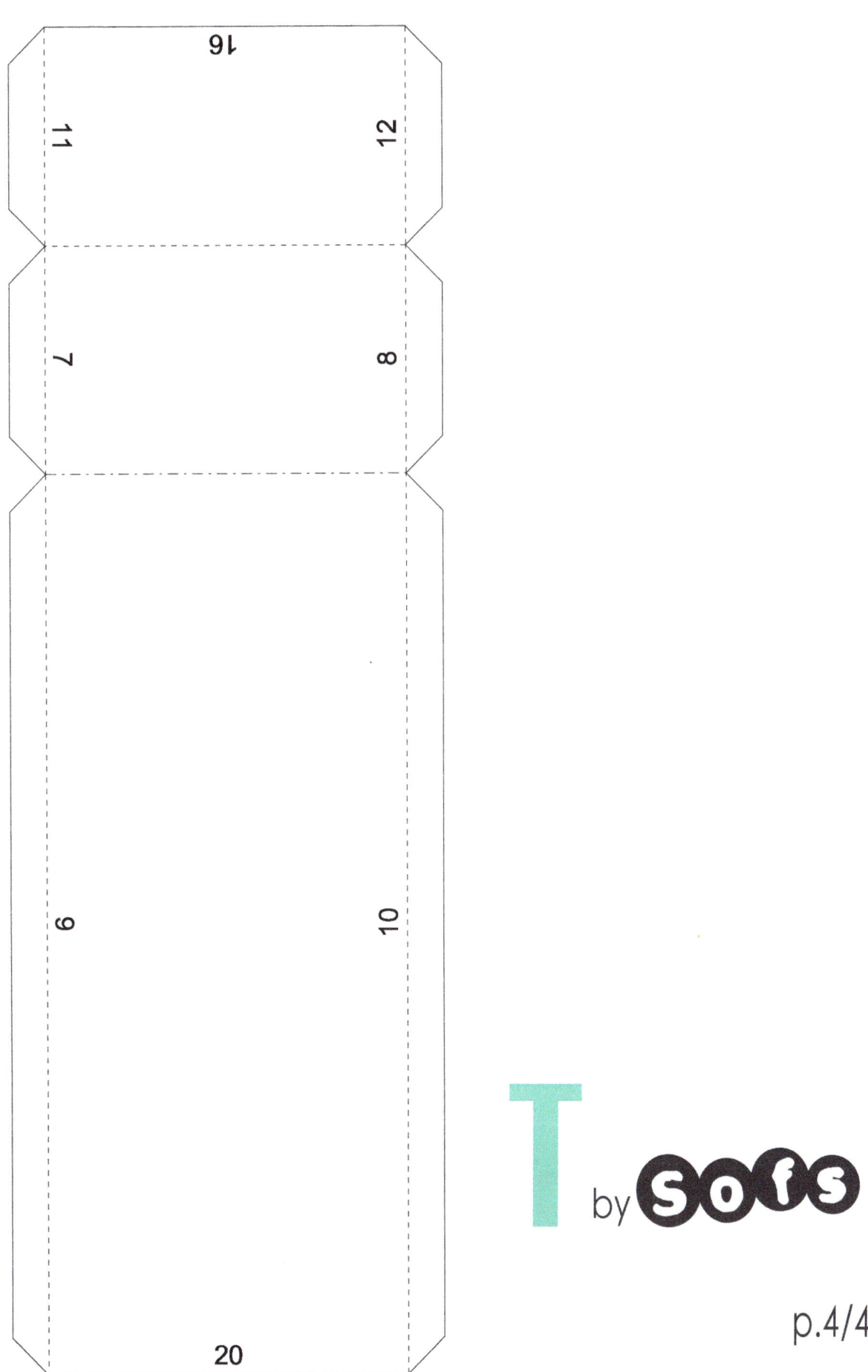

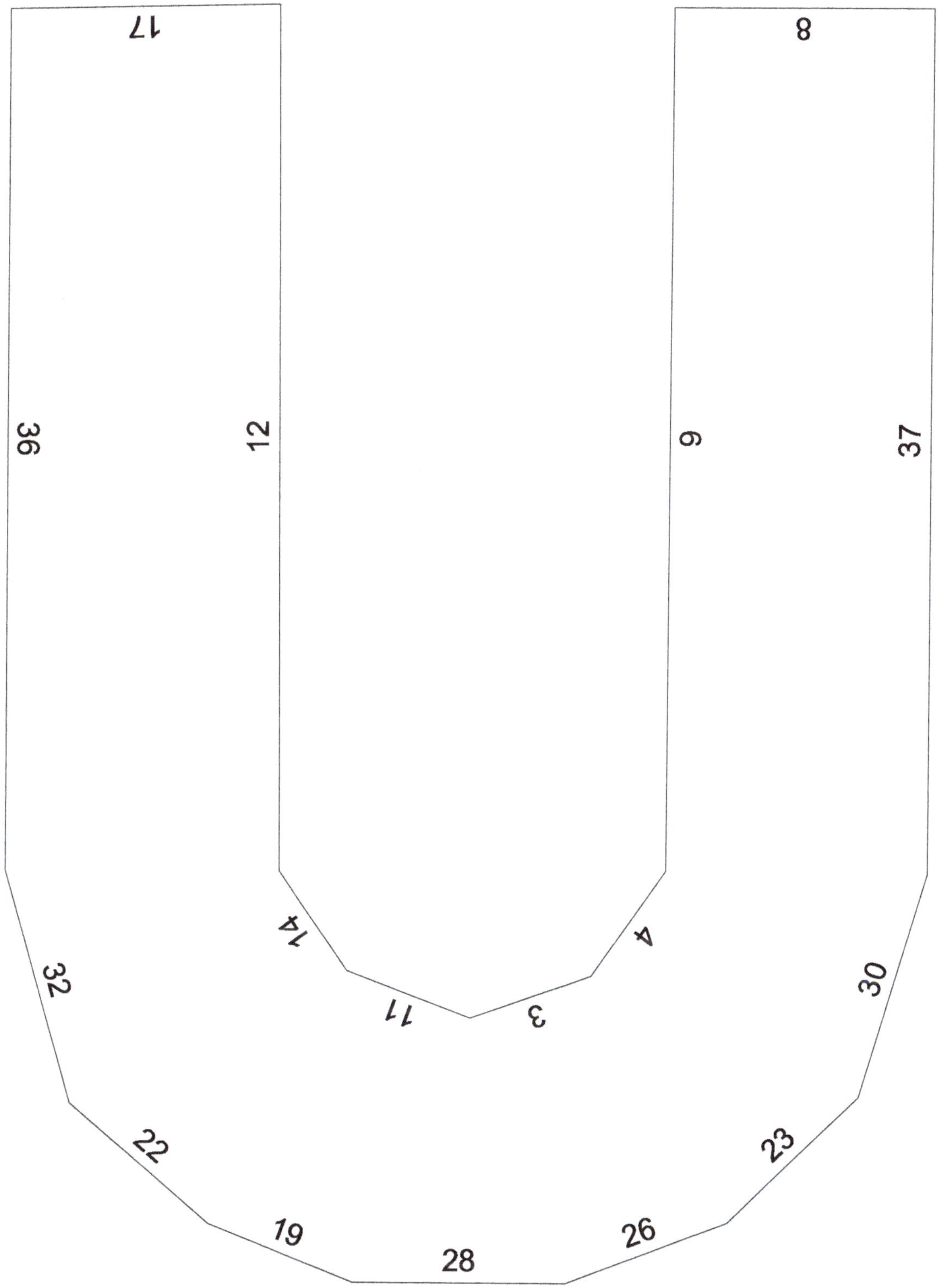

17

8

36

12

9

37

14

4

11

3

32

30

22

23

19

26

28

p.1`/5

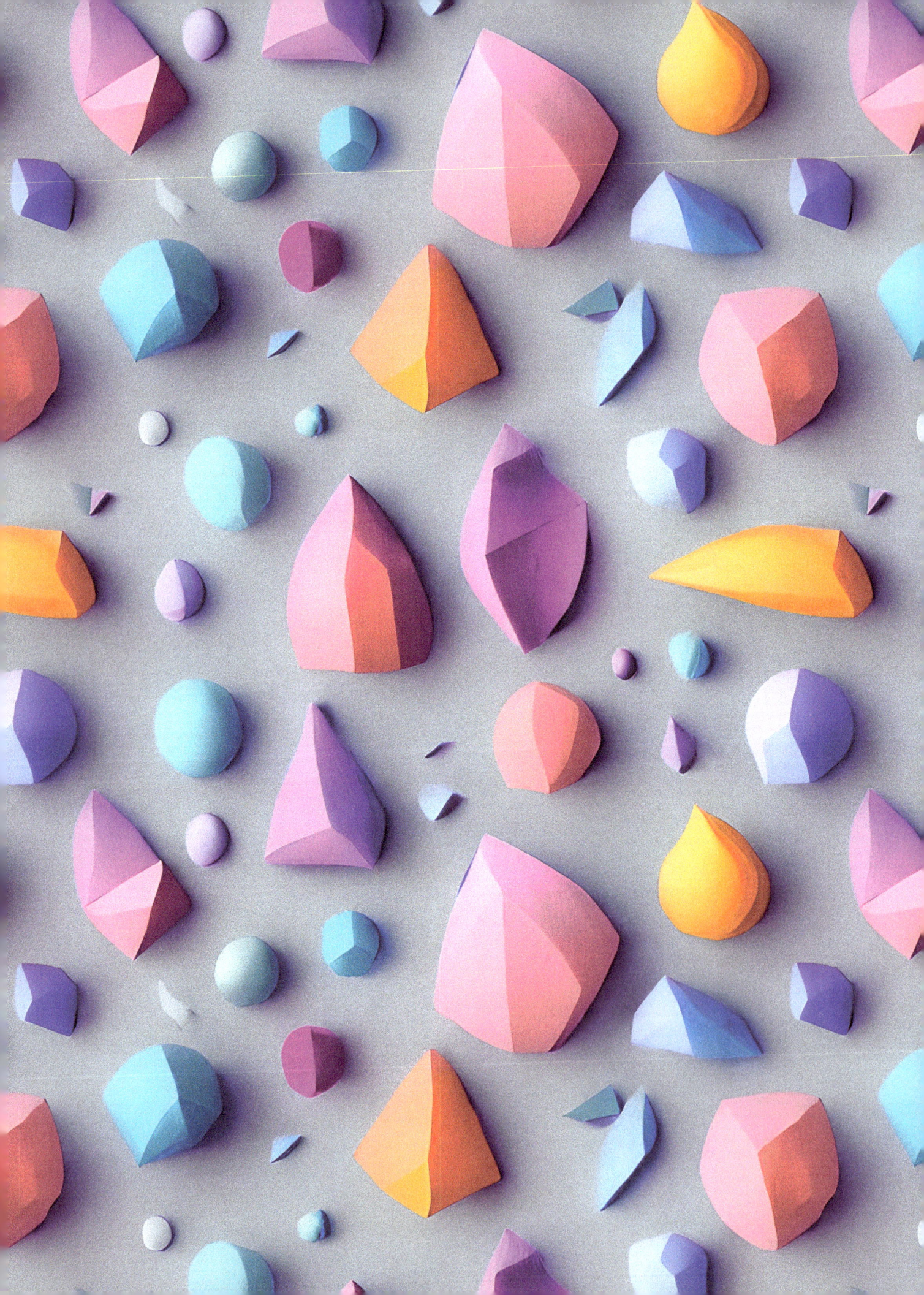

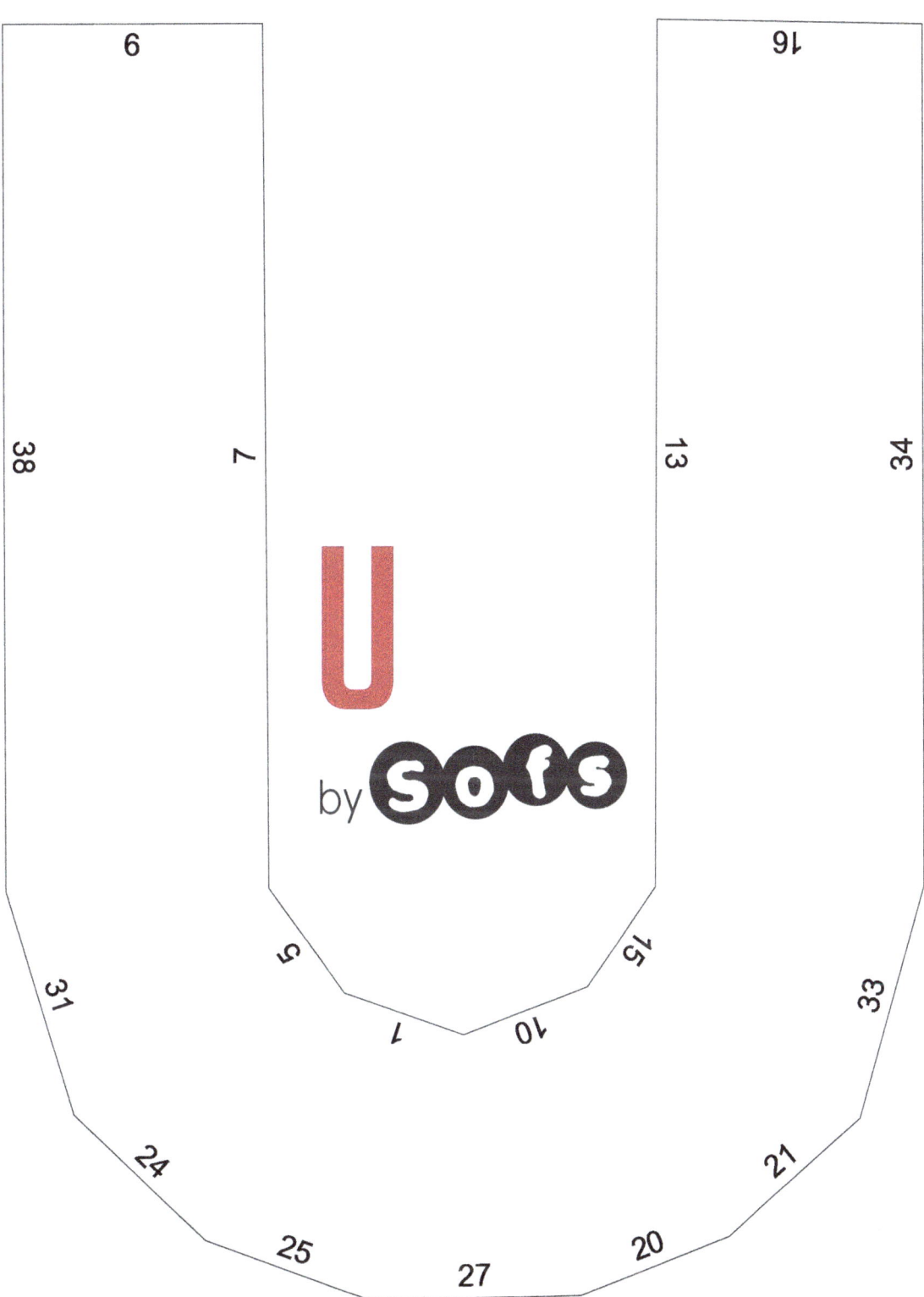

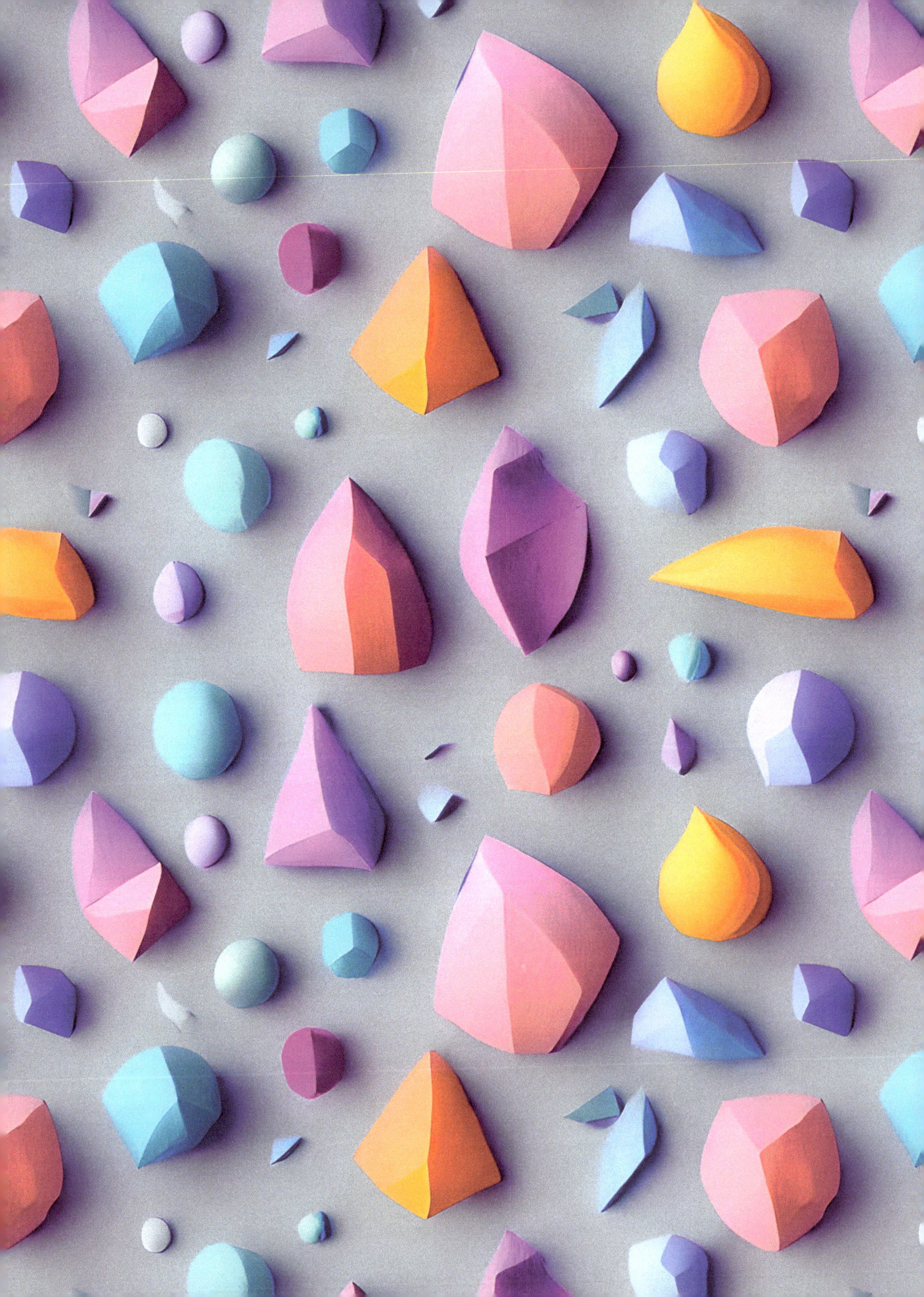

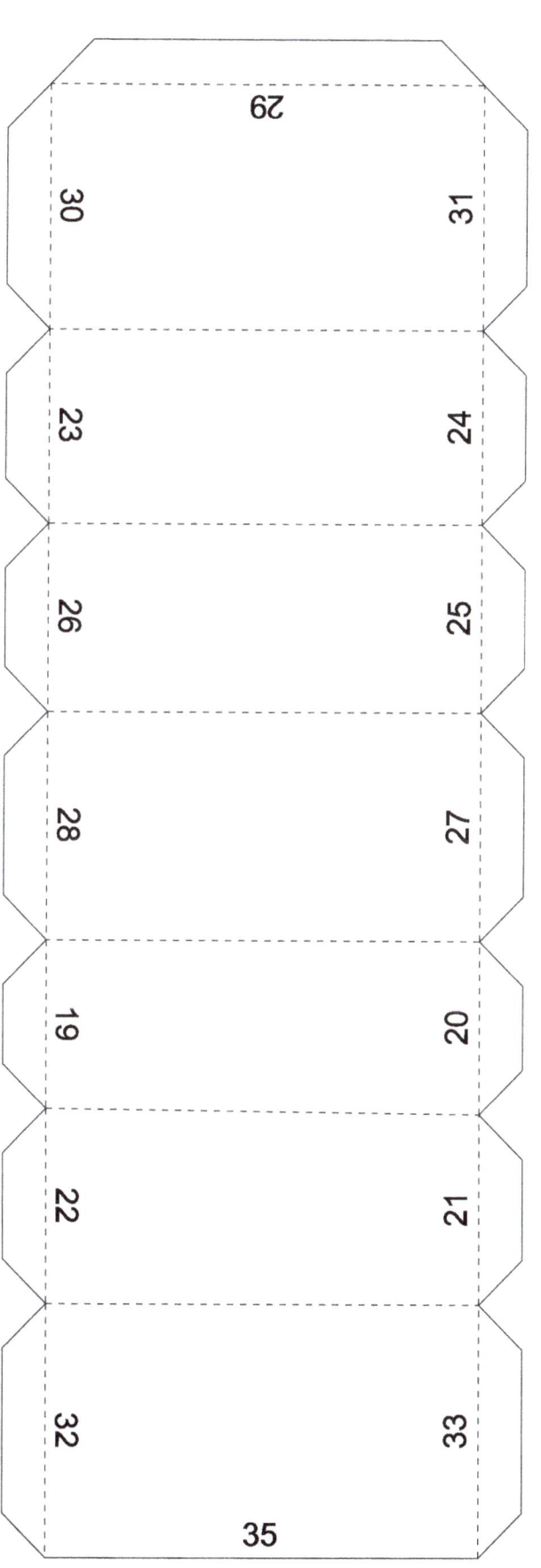

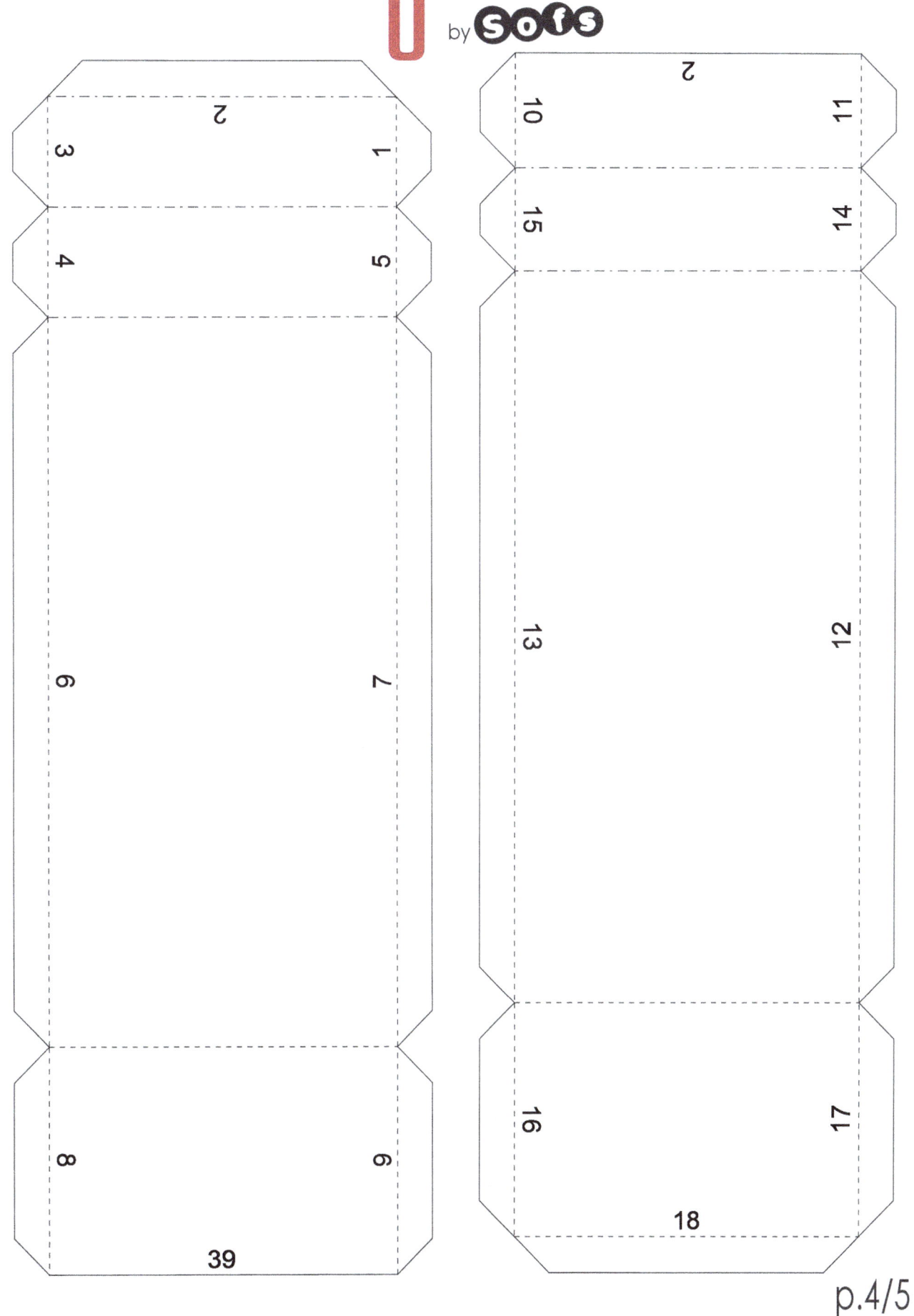

U by Sofs

p.4/5

29

38

37

39

35

36

34

18

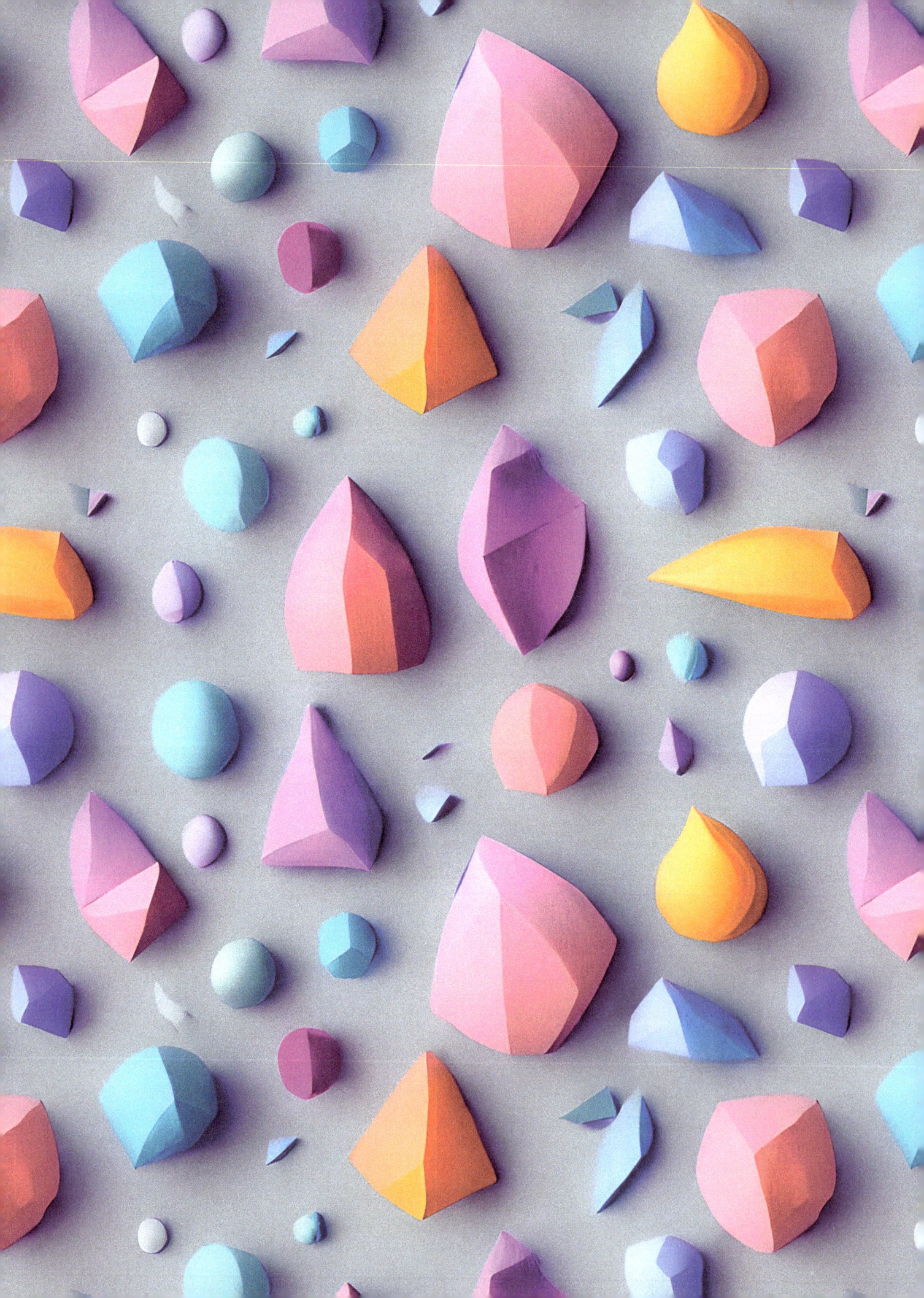

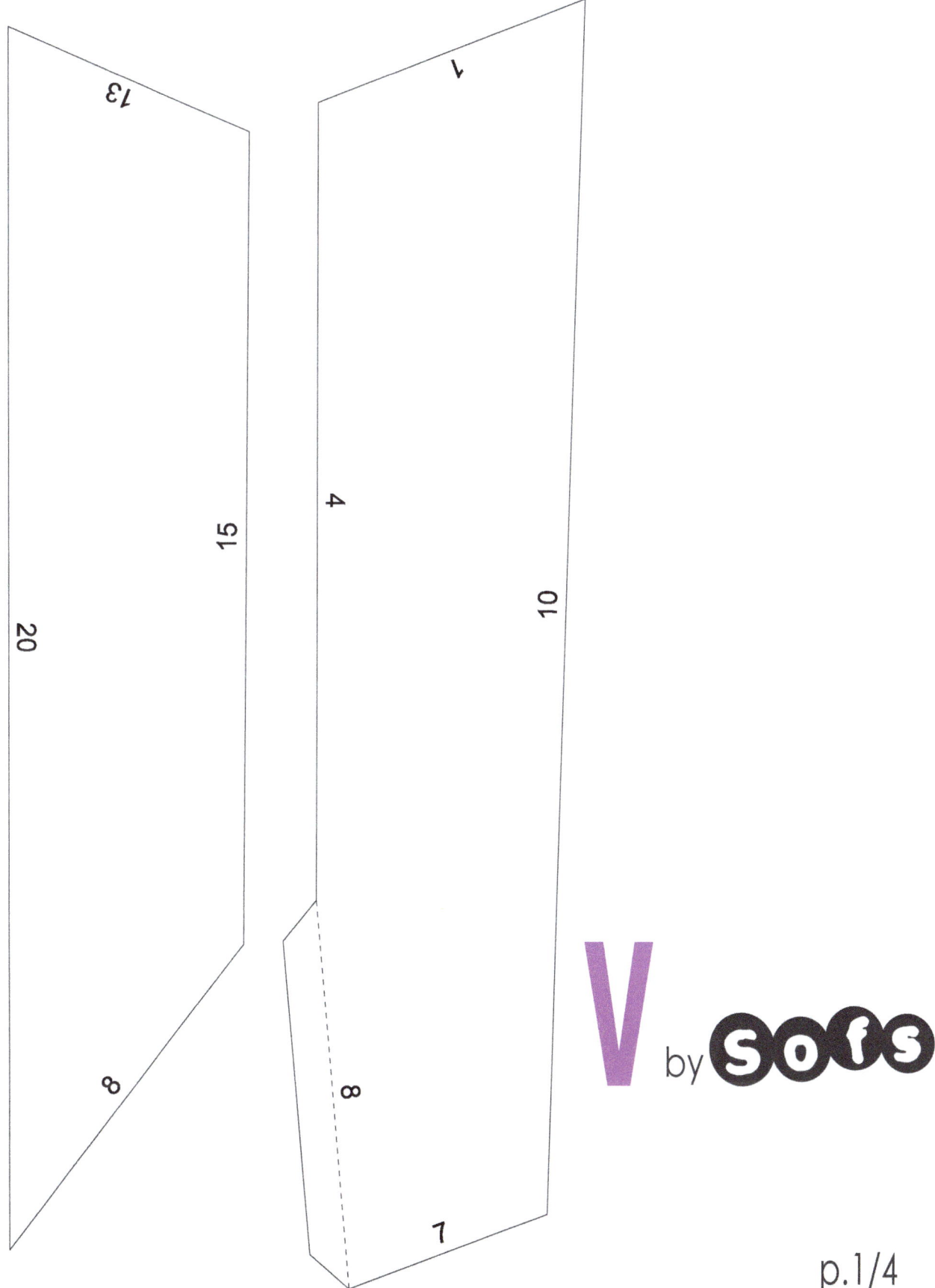

13

1

20

15

4

10

8

8

7

V by Sofs

p.1/4

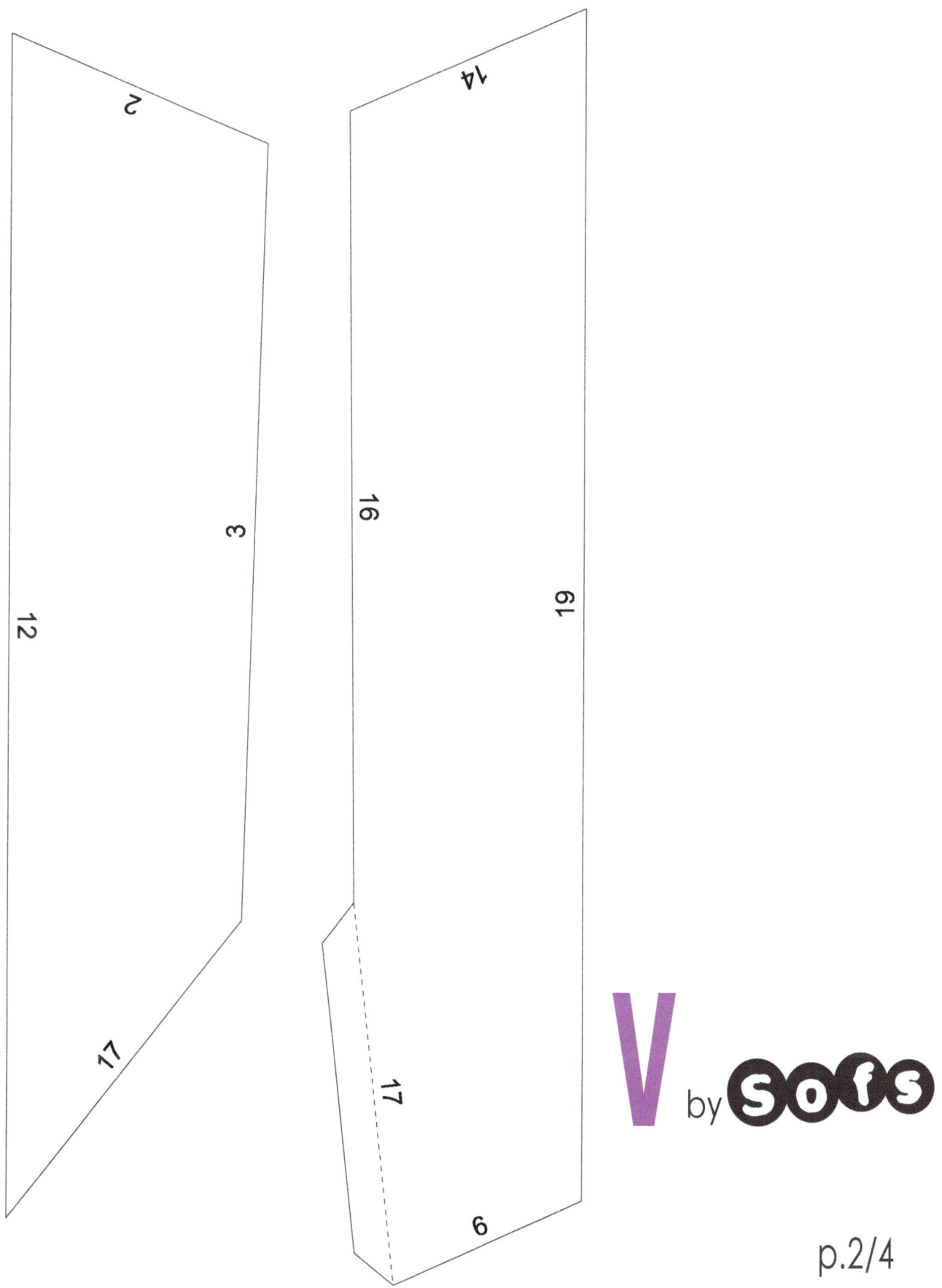

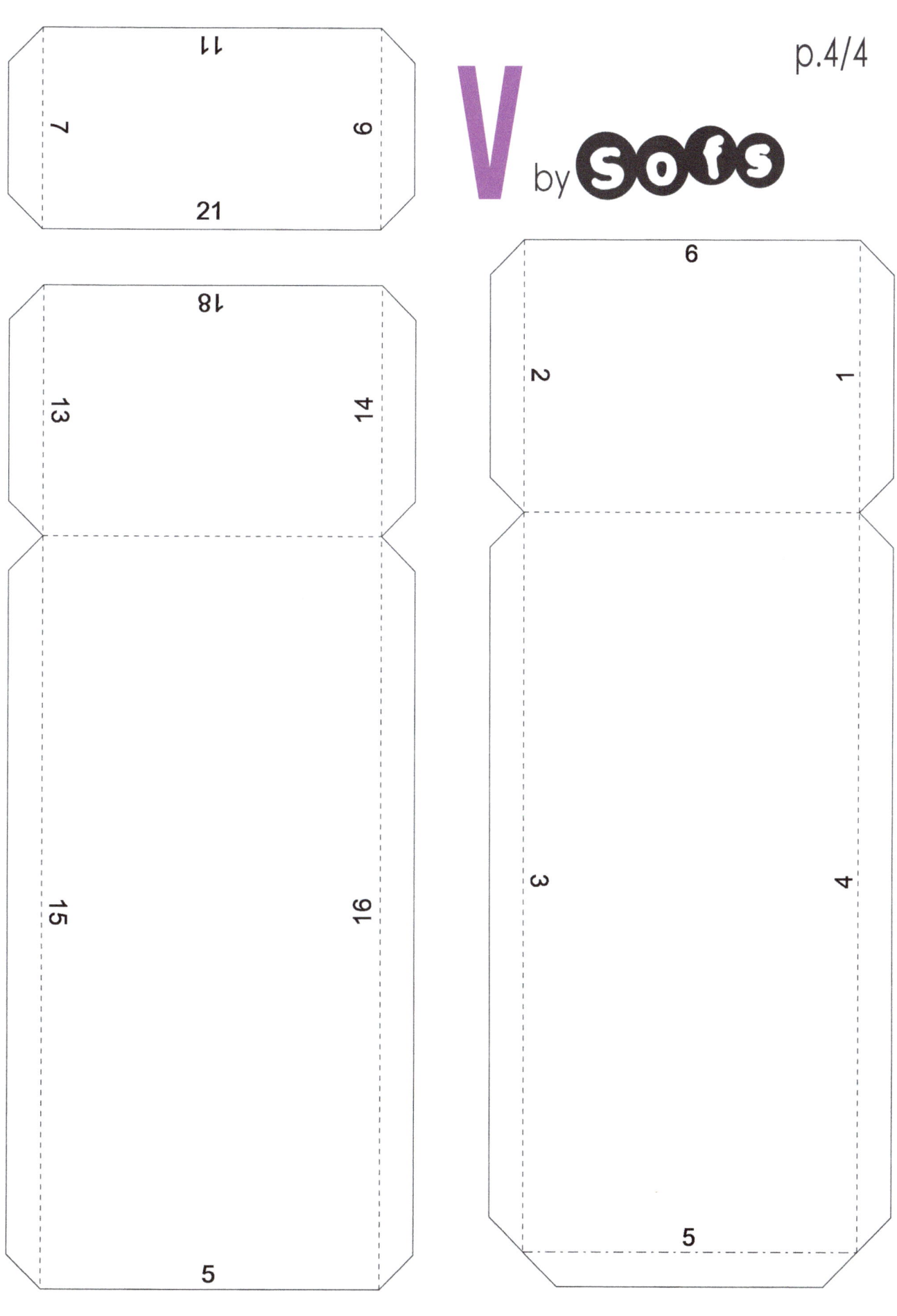

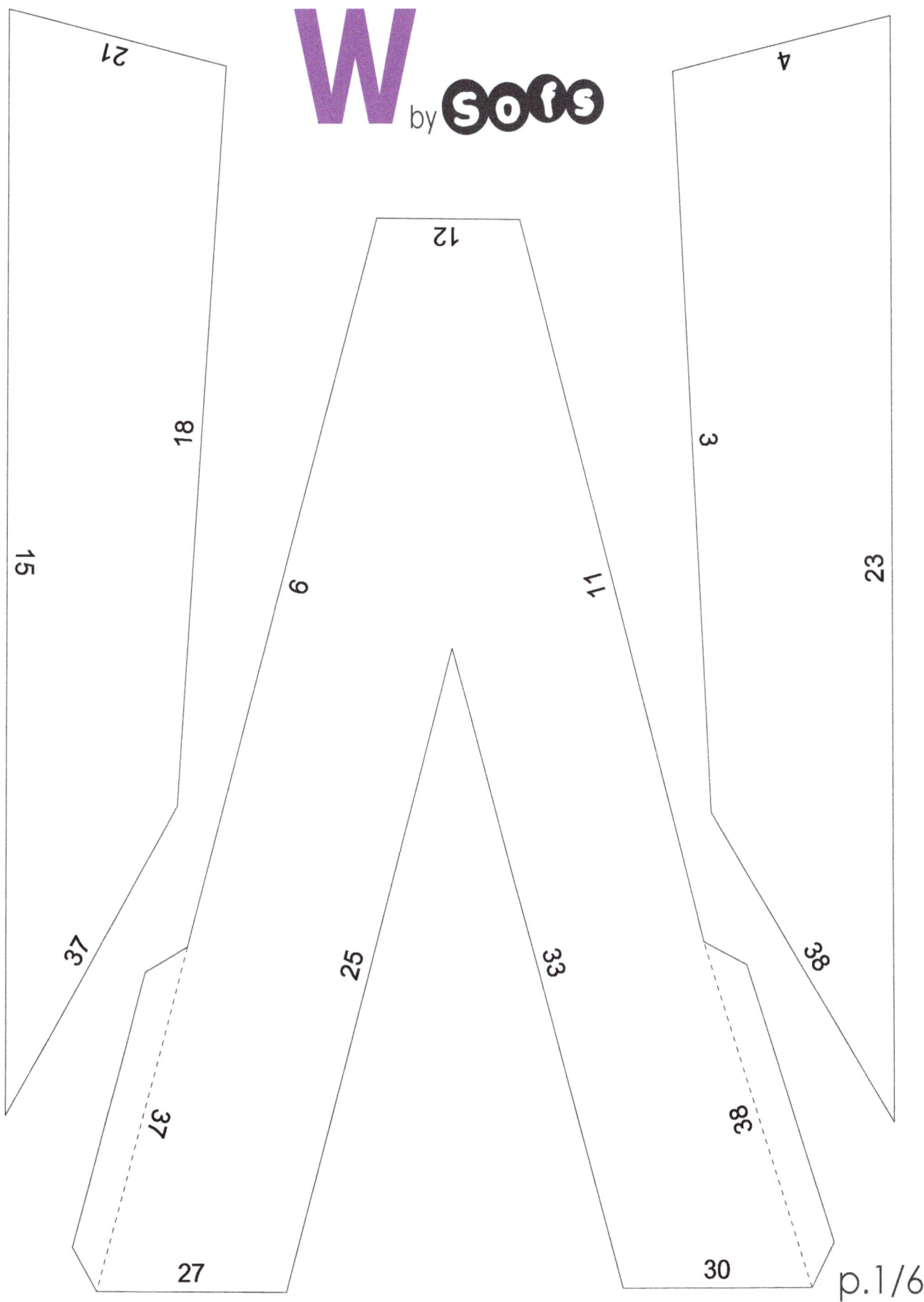

W by Sofs

p.1/6

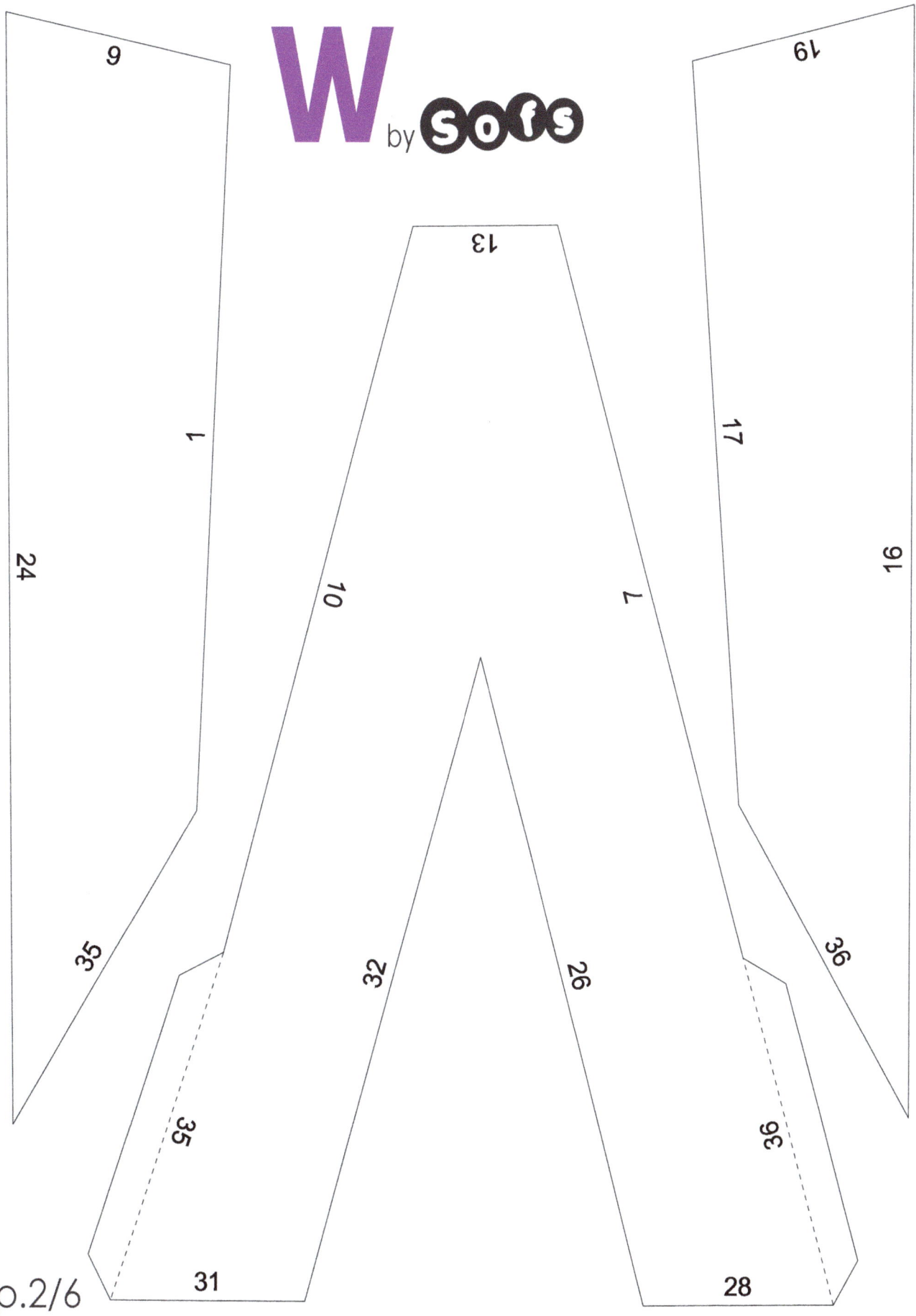

W by Sofs

9

19

13

1

17

16

24

10

7

35

36

32

26

35

36

31

28

p.2/6

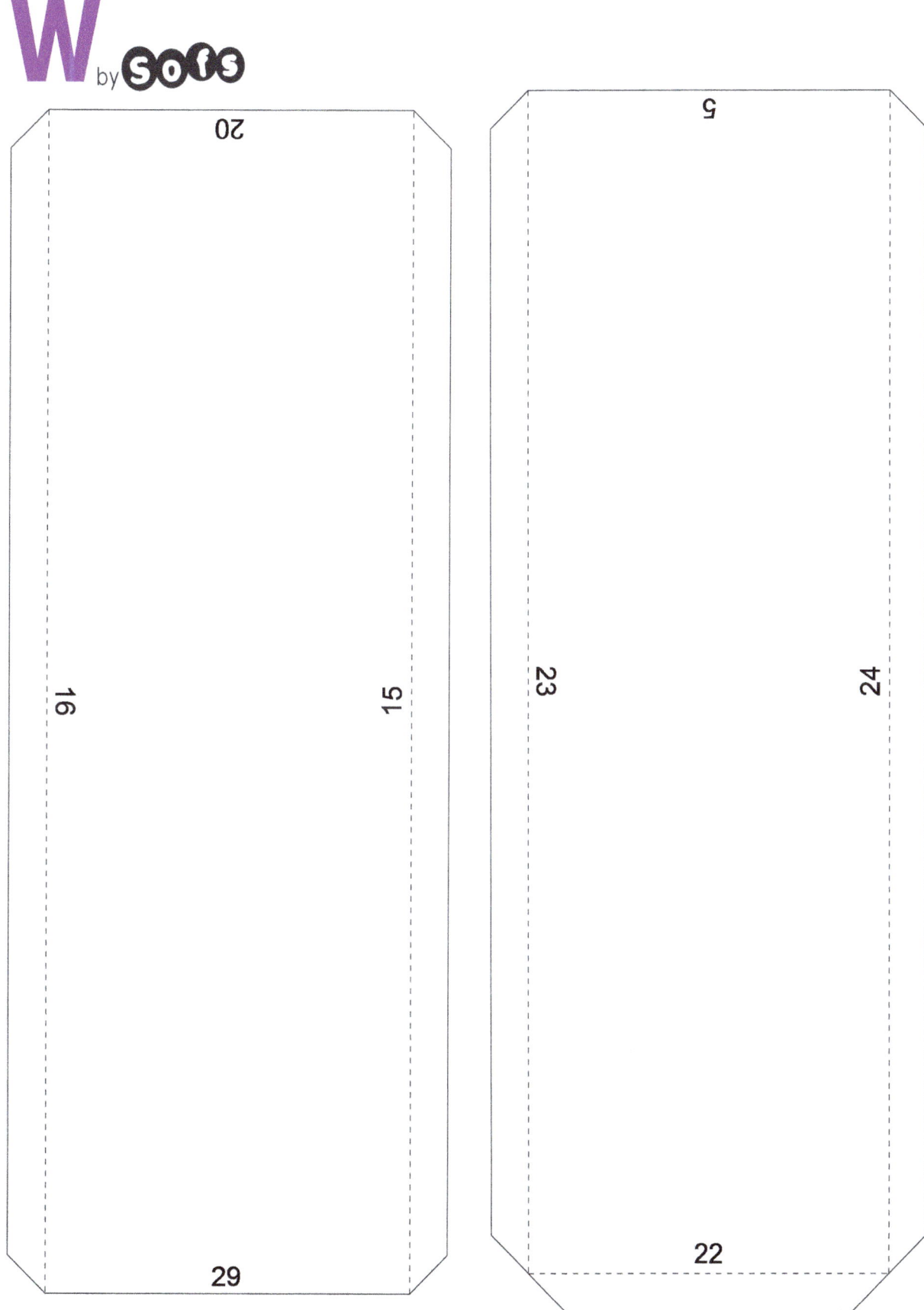

W by Sofs

p.3/6

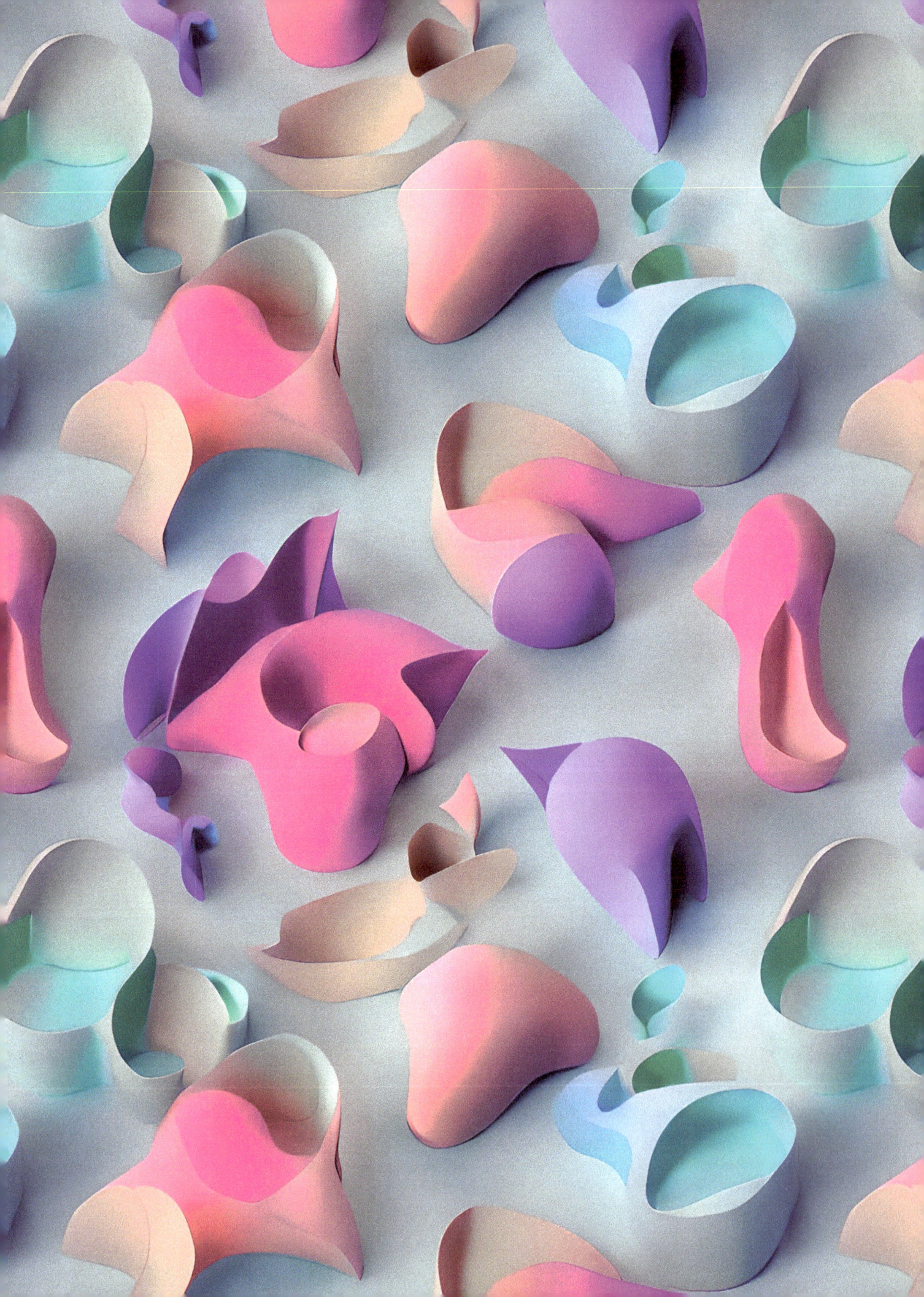

W by sofs

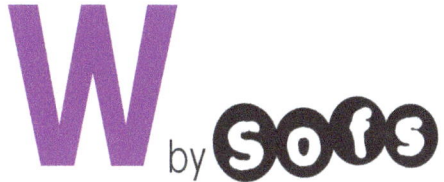

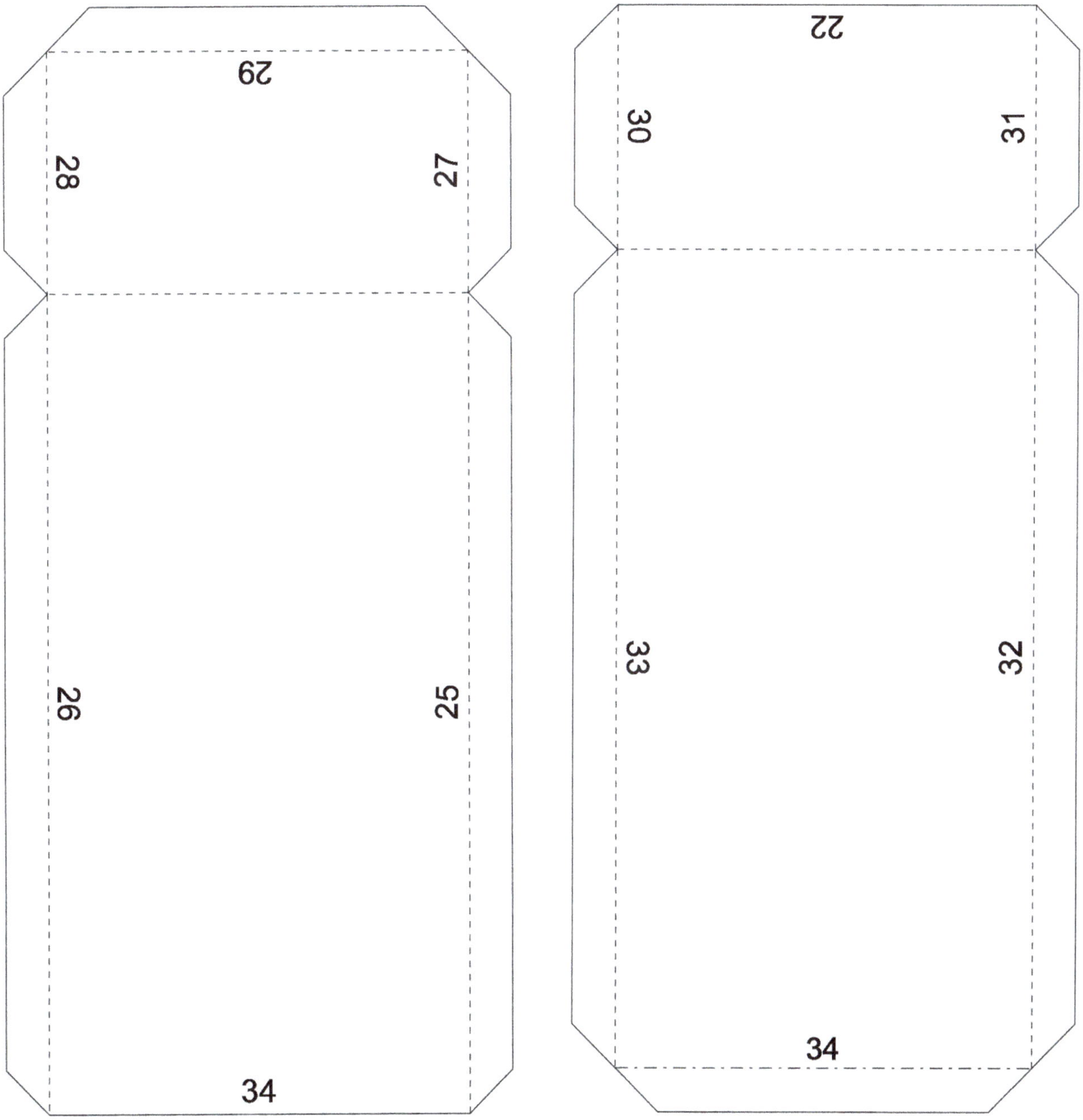
29
28
27
26
25
34
22
30
31
33
32
34

5

6

4

20

21

19

1

3

18

17

2

8

p.5/6

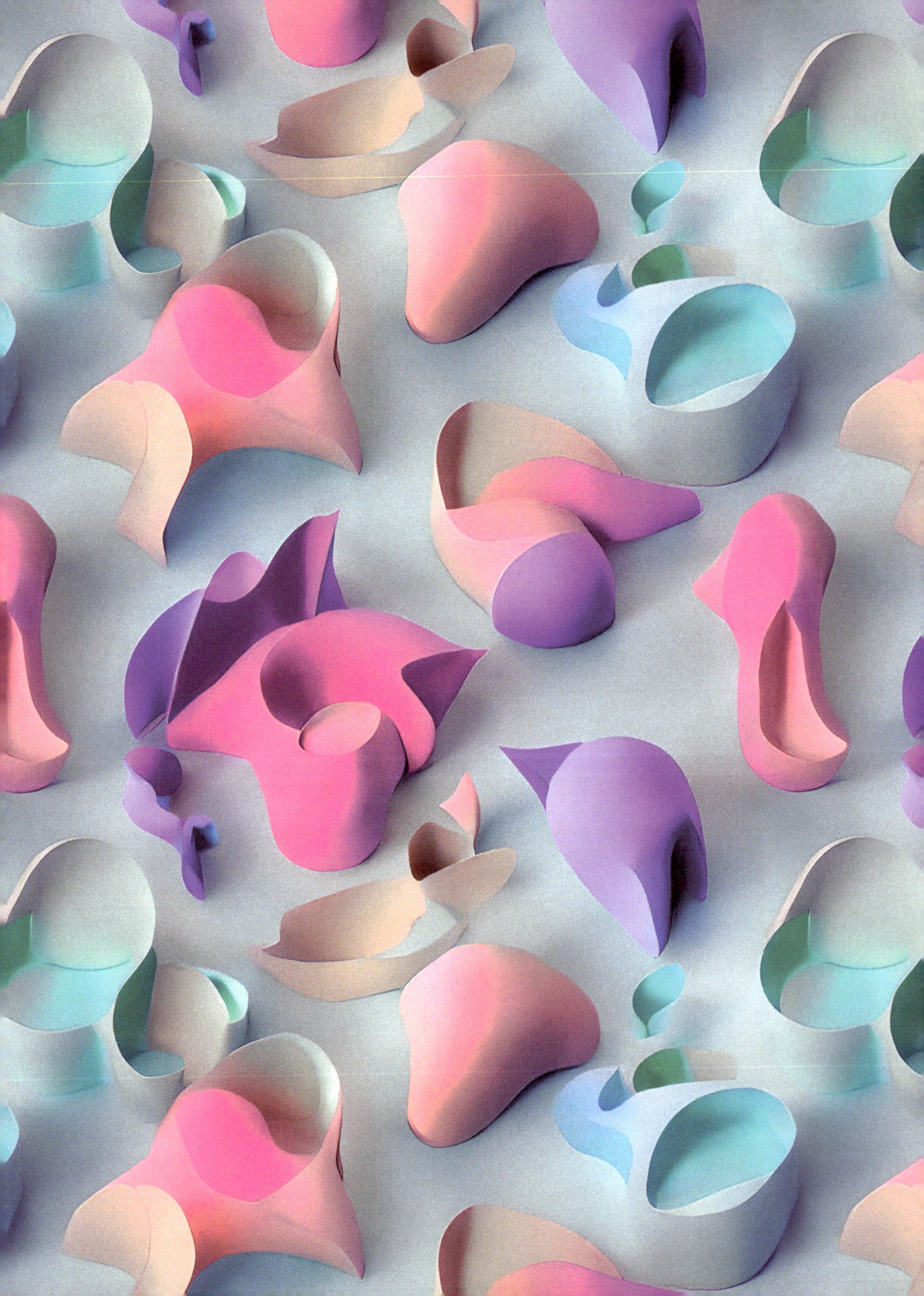

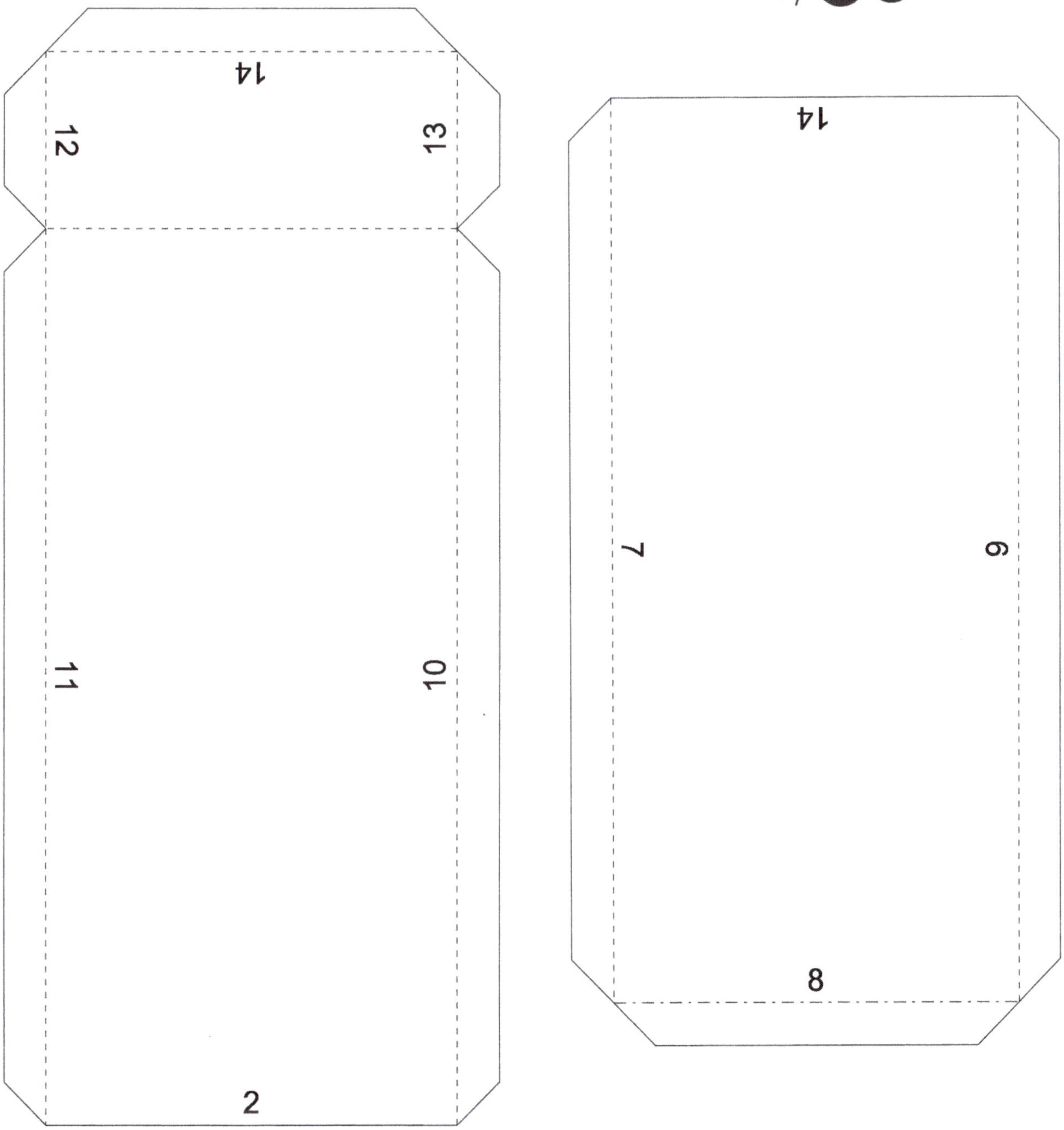

14

12

13

11

10

2

14

7

6

8

p.6/6

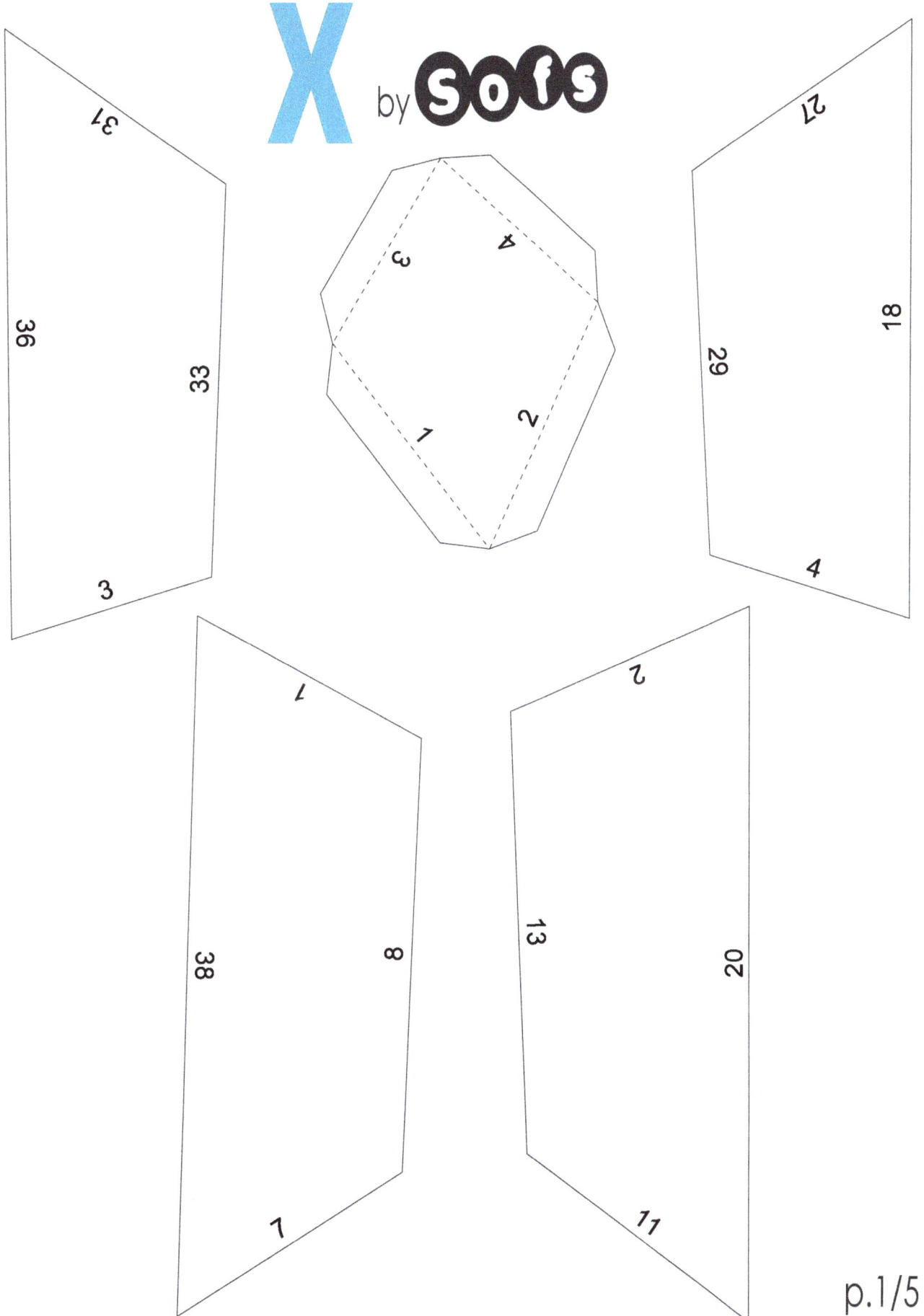

X by Sofs

p.1/5

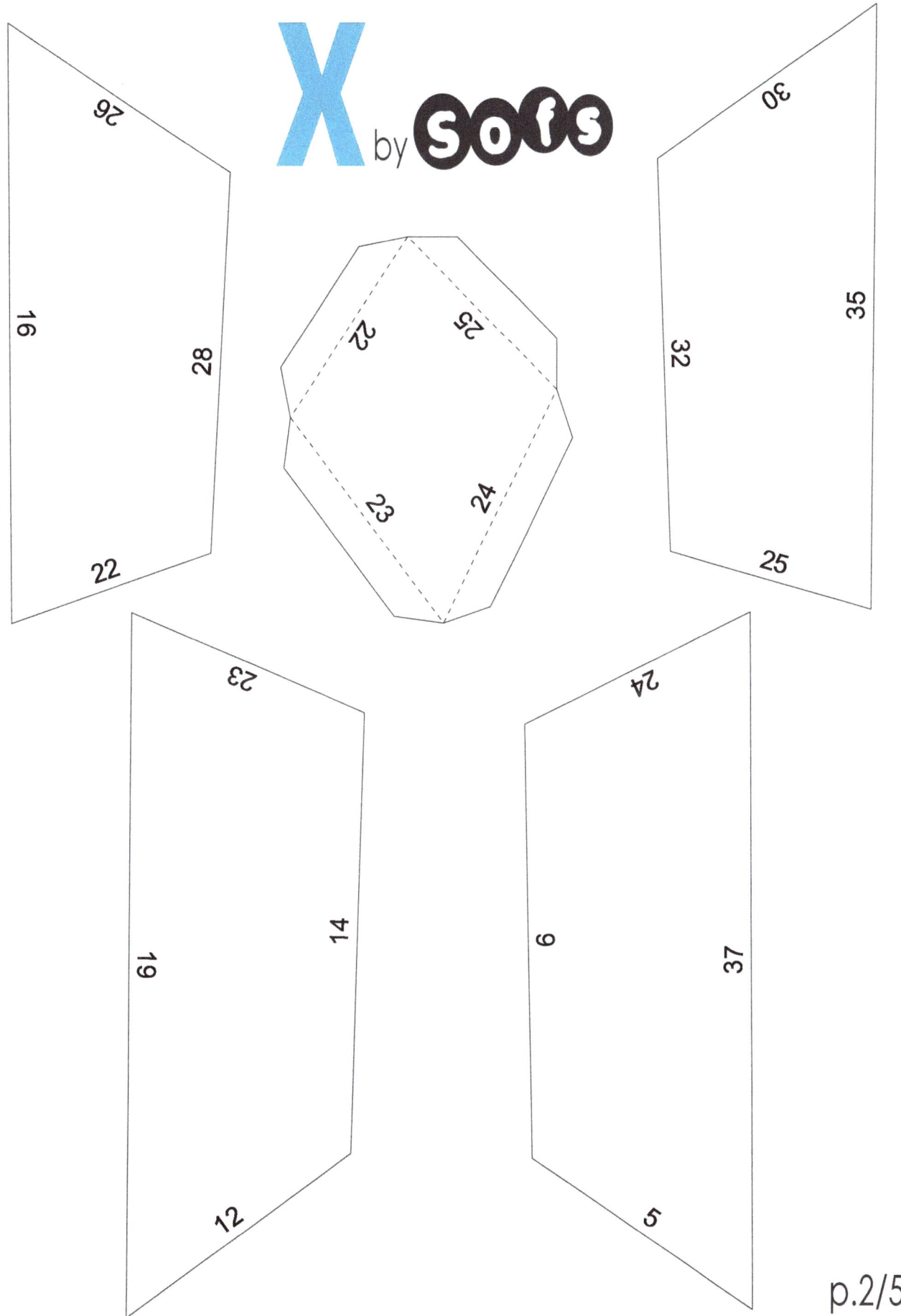

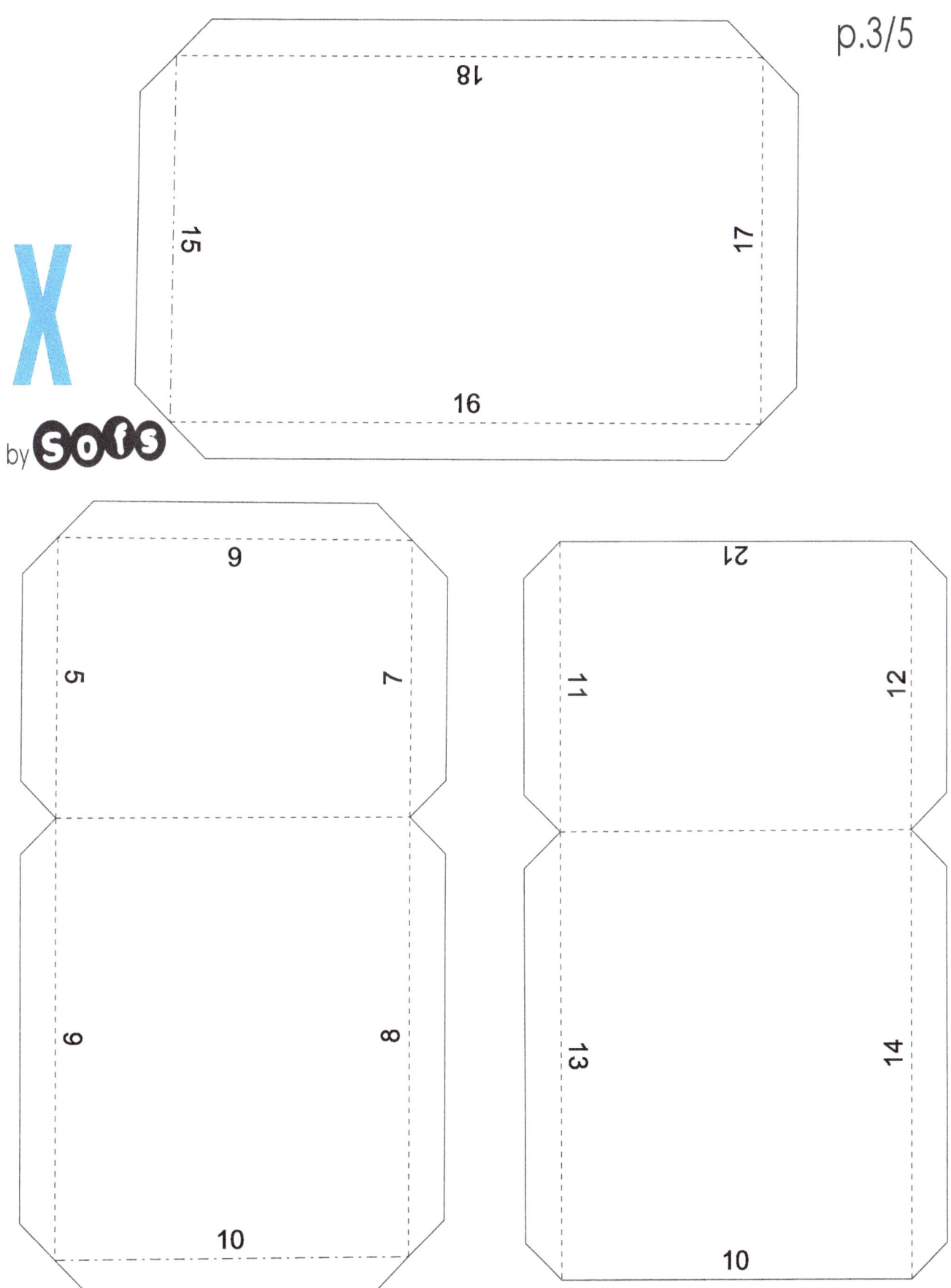

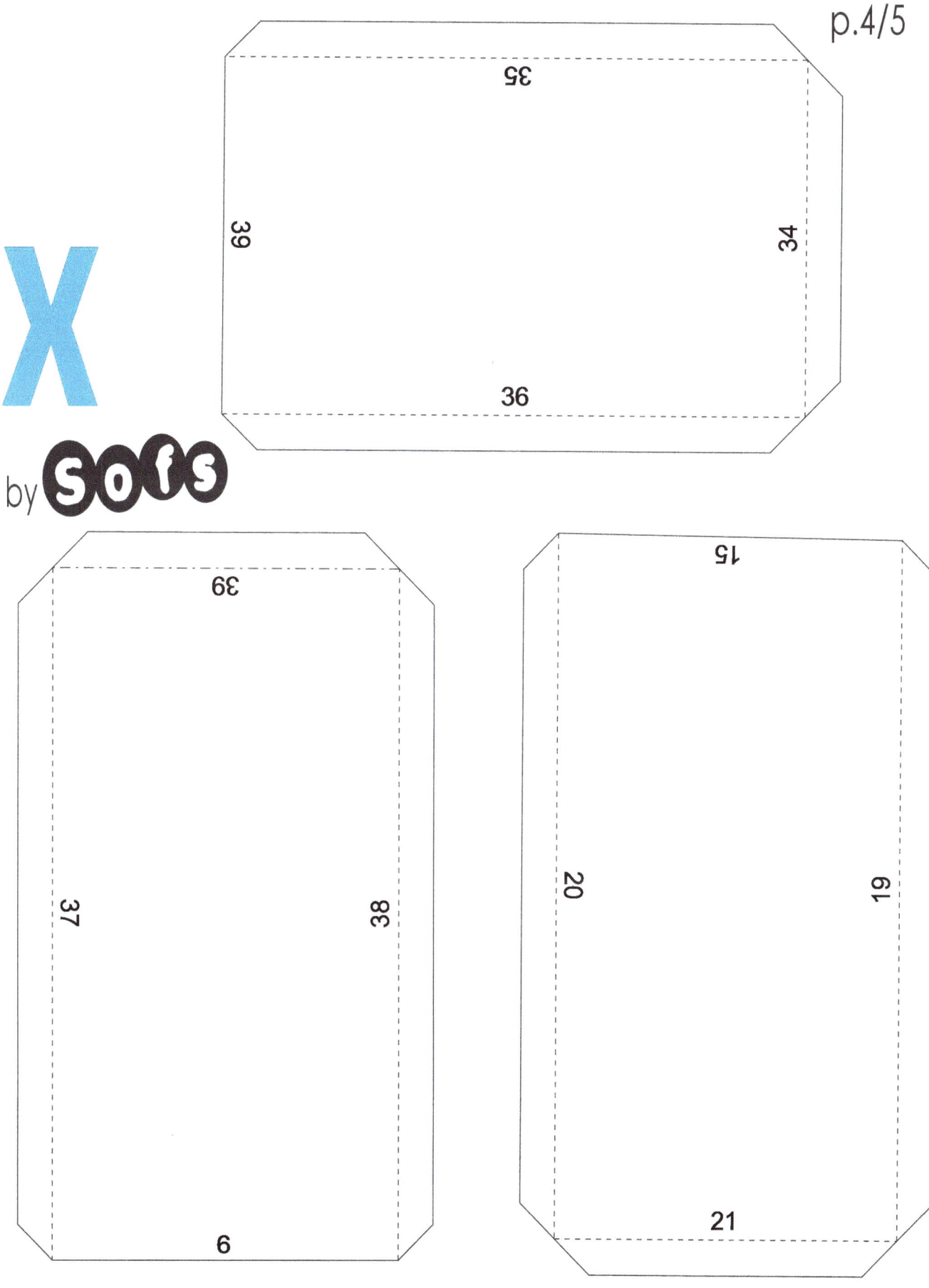

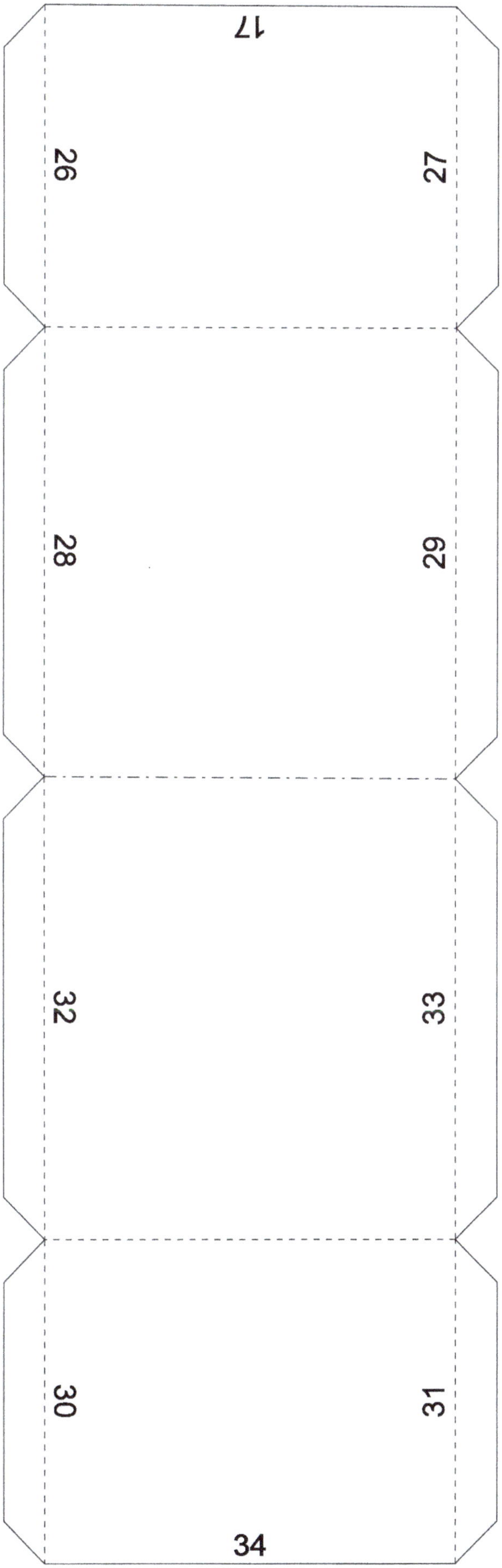

17

26

27

28

29

32

33

30

31

34

17

p.5/5

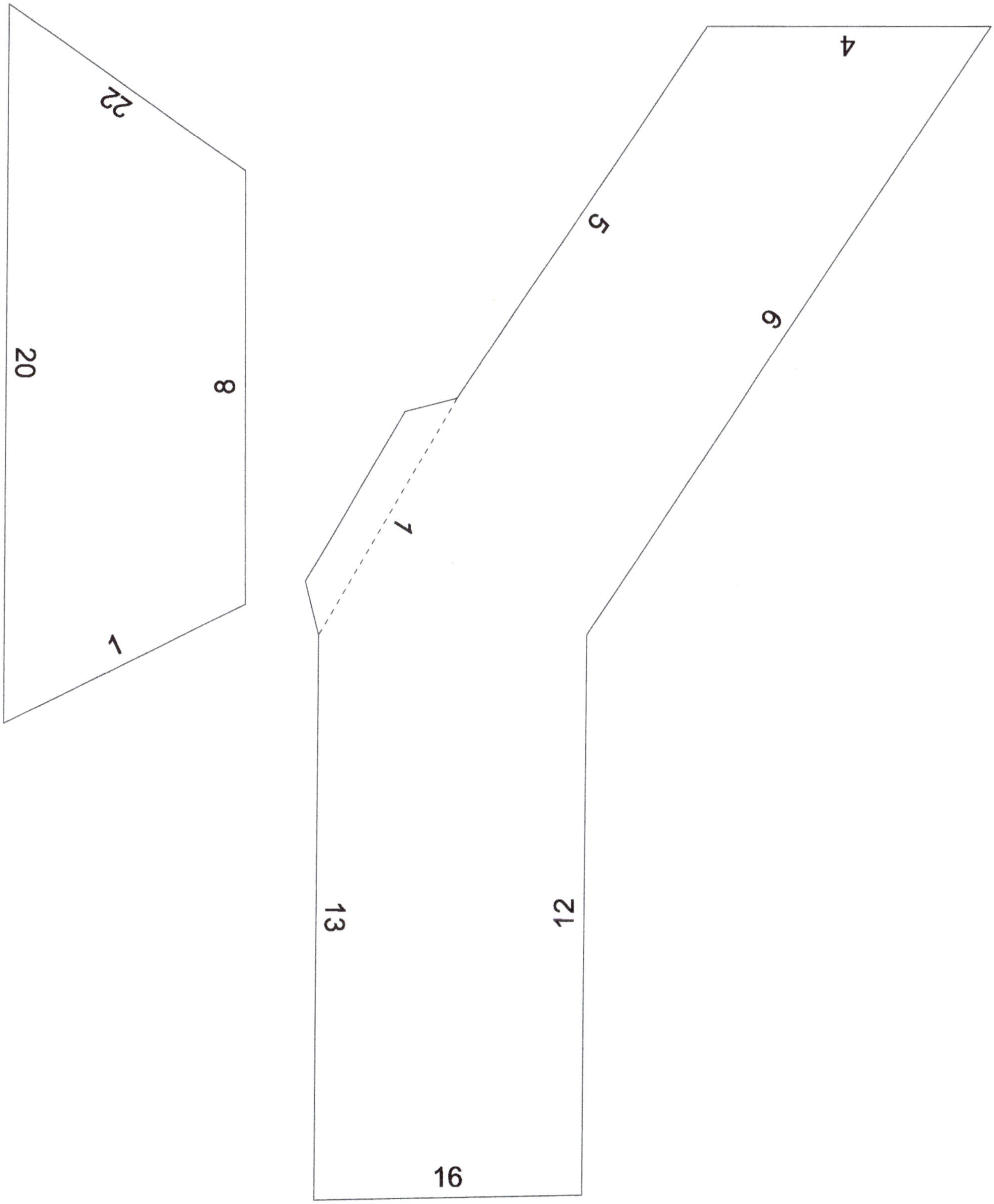

22

20

8

1

4

5

6

7

13

12

16

by Sofs

p.1/4

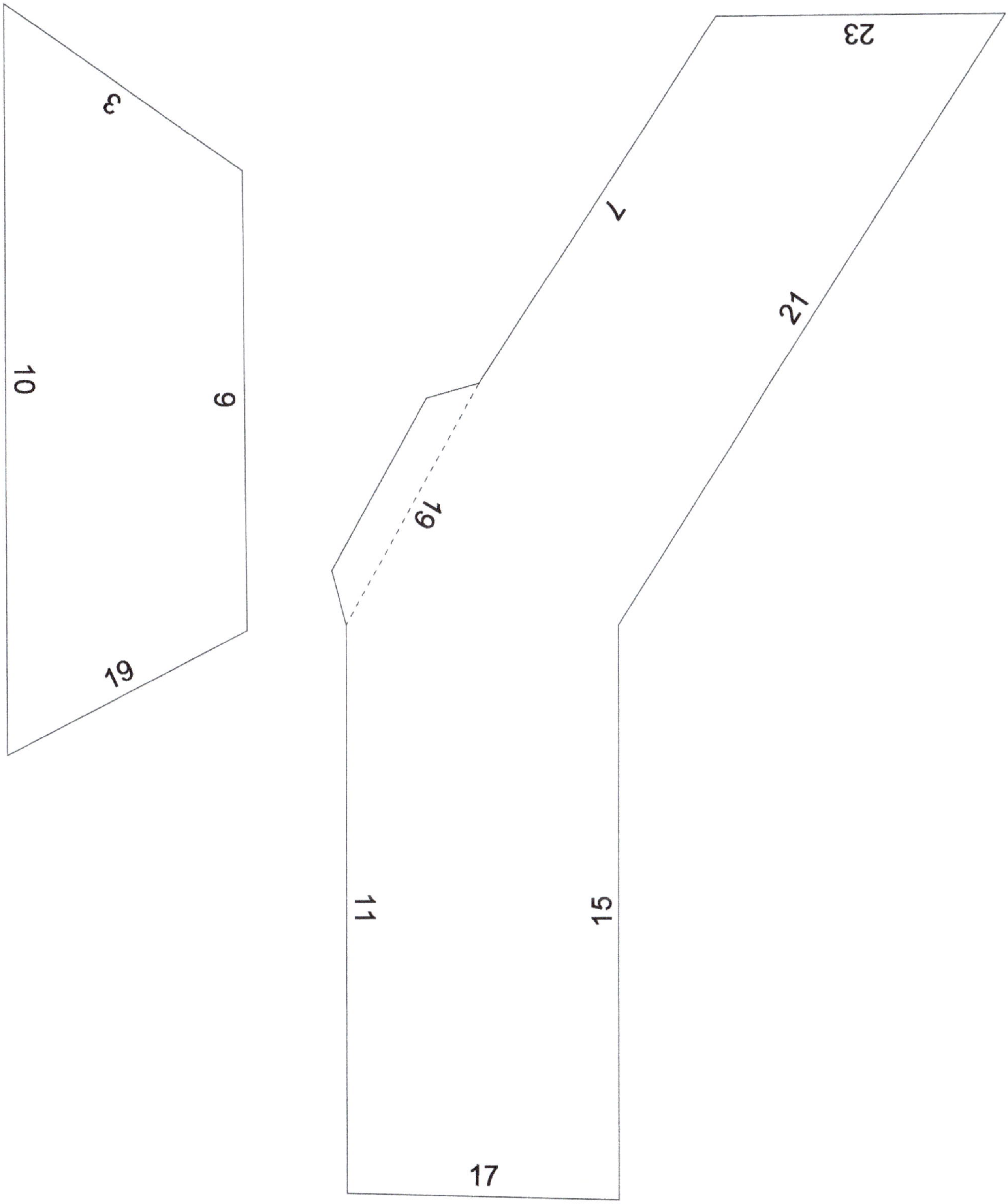

3

10

9

19

23

7

21

9

11

15

17

Y by Sofs

p.2/4

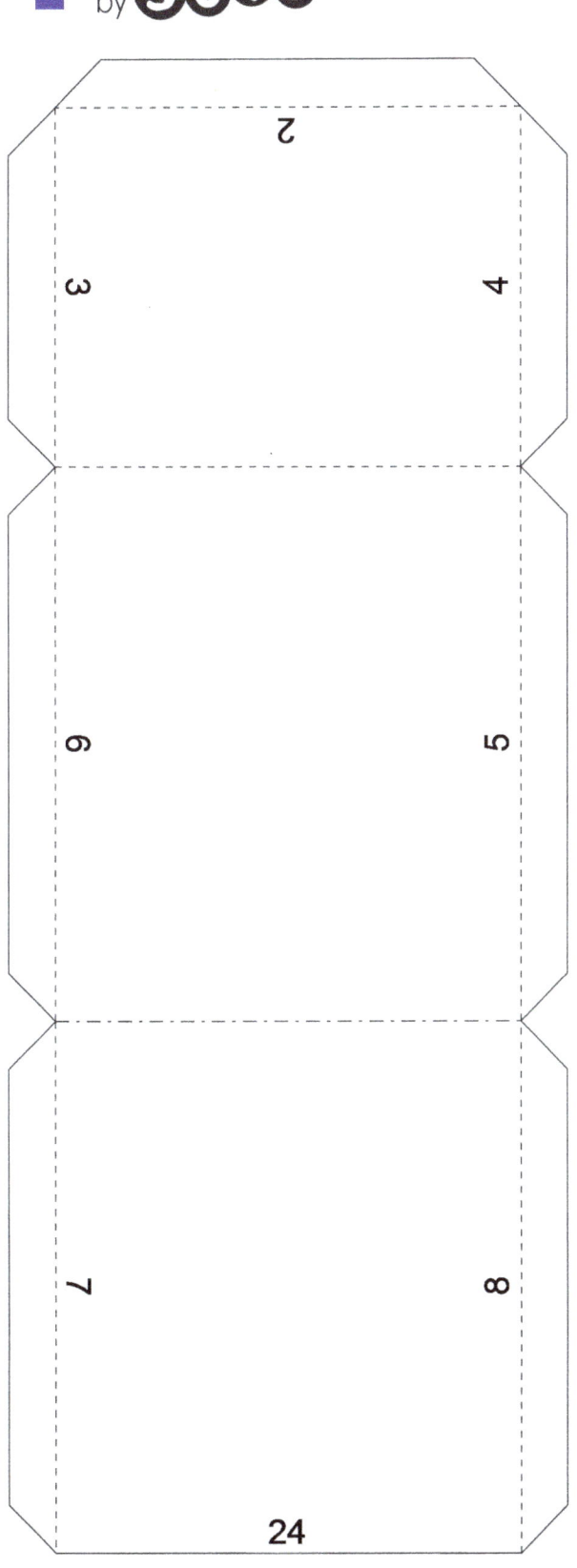

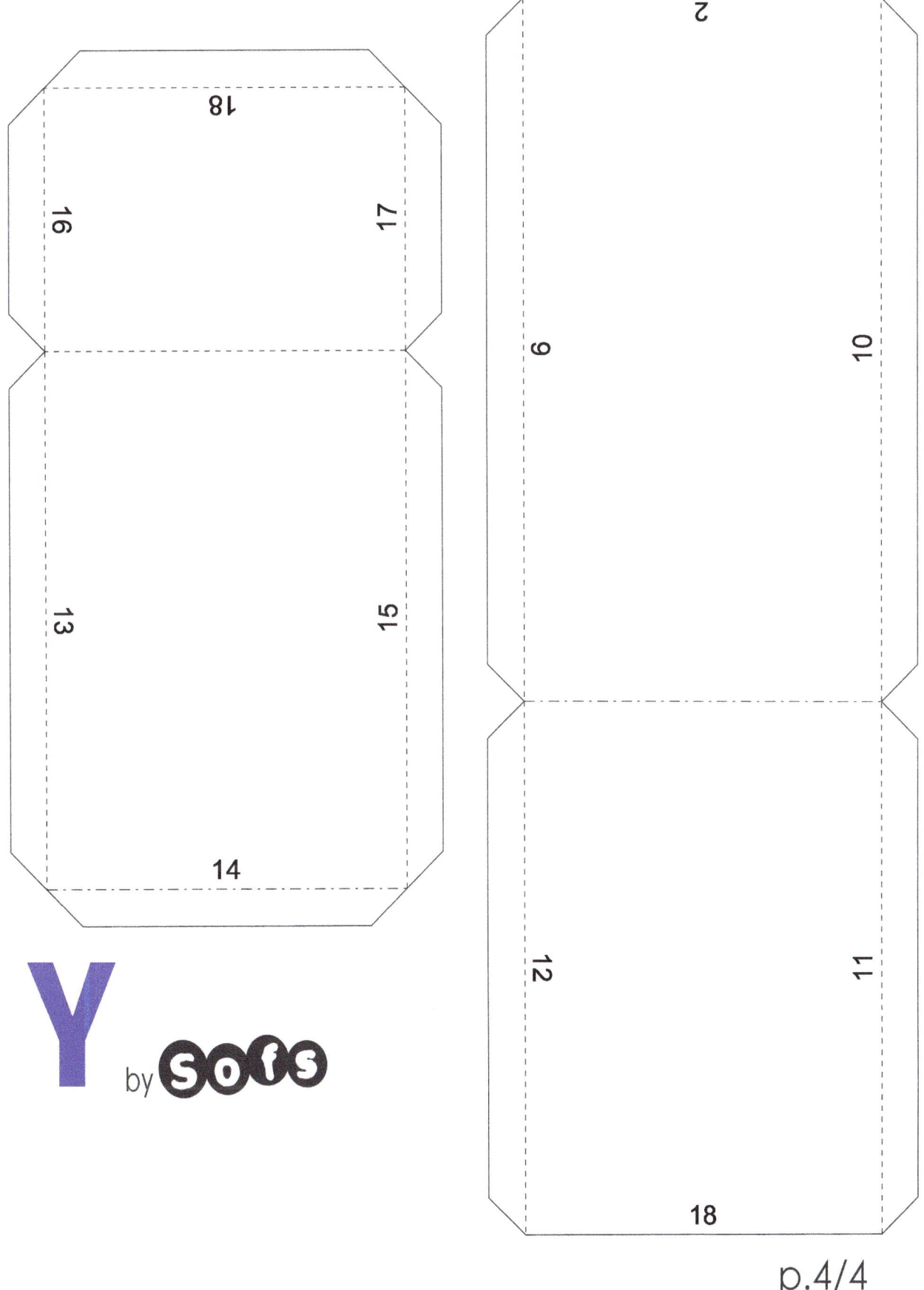

Y by Sofs

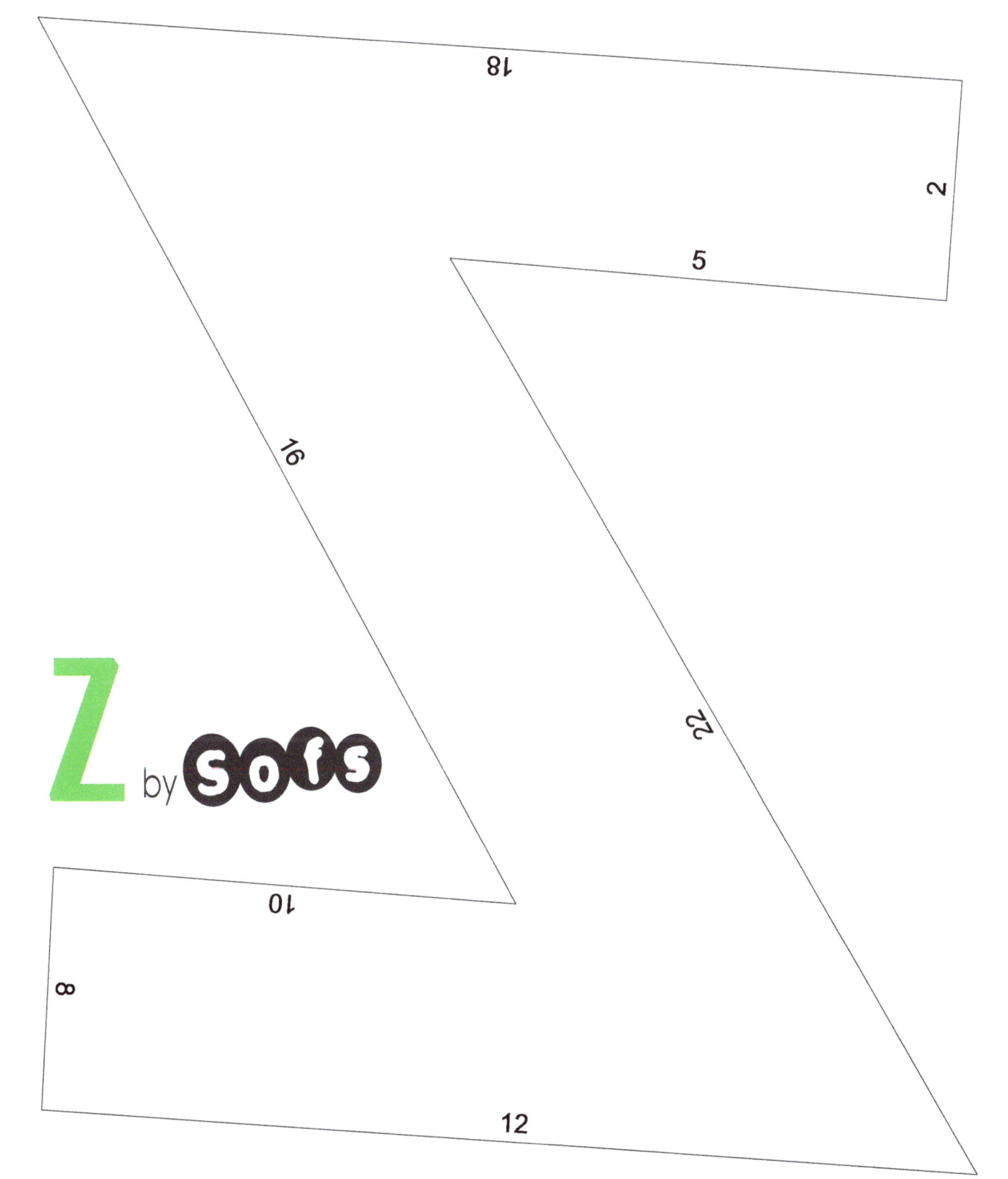

Z by sofs

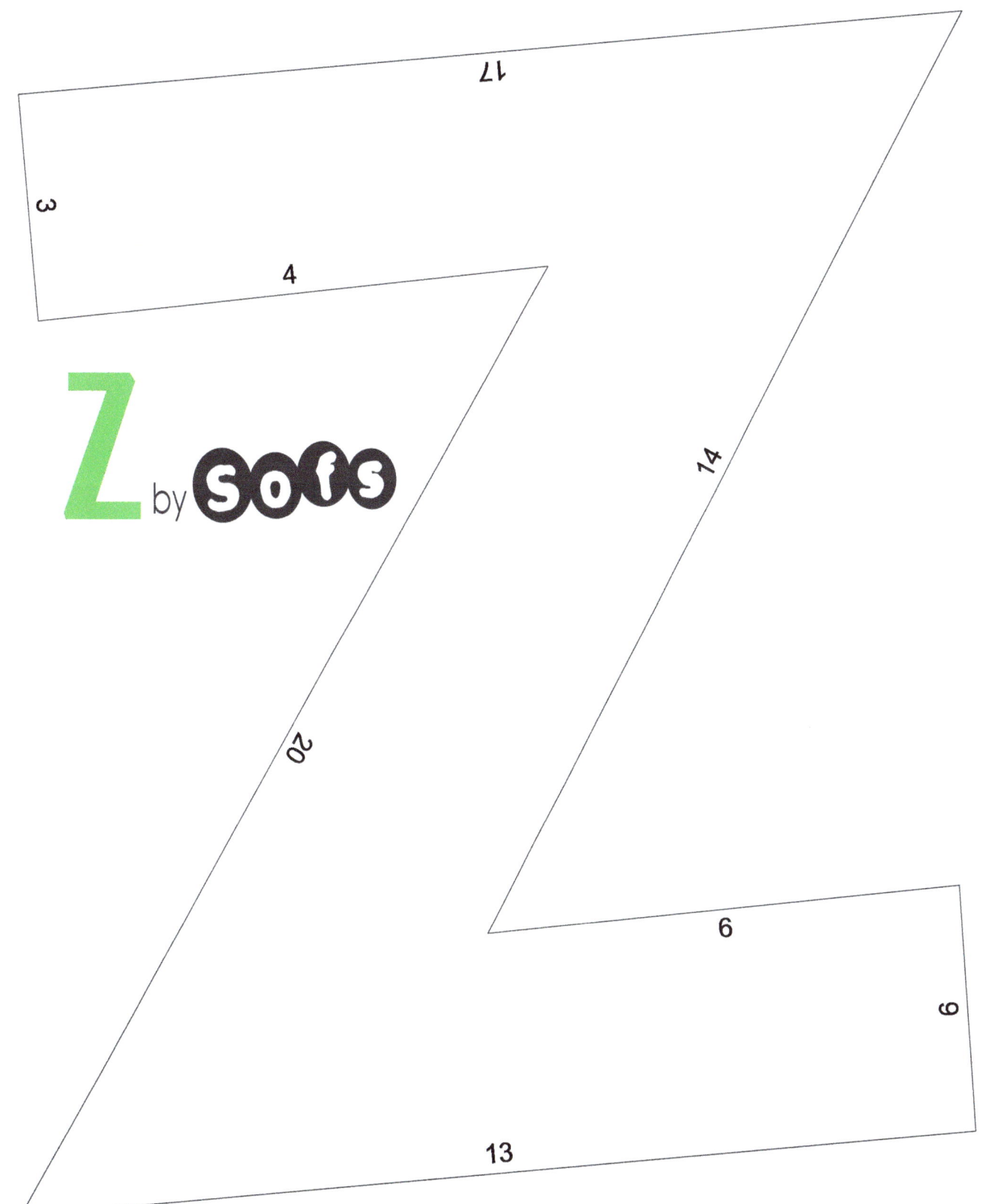

17

3

4

14

20

6

9

13

Z by sofs

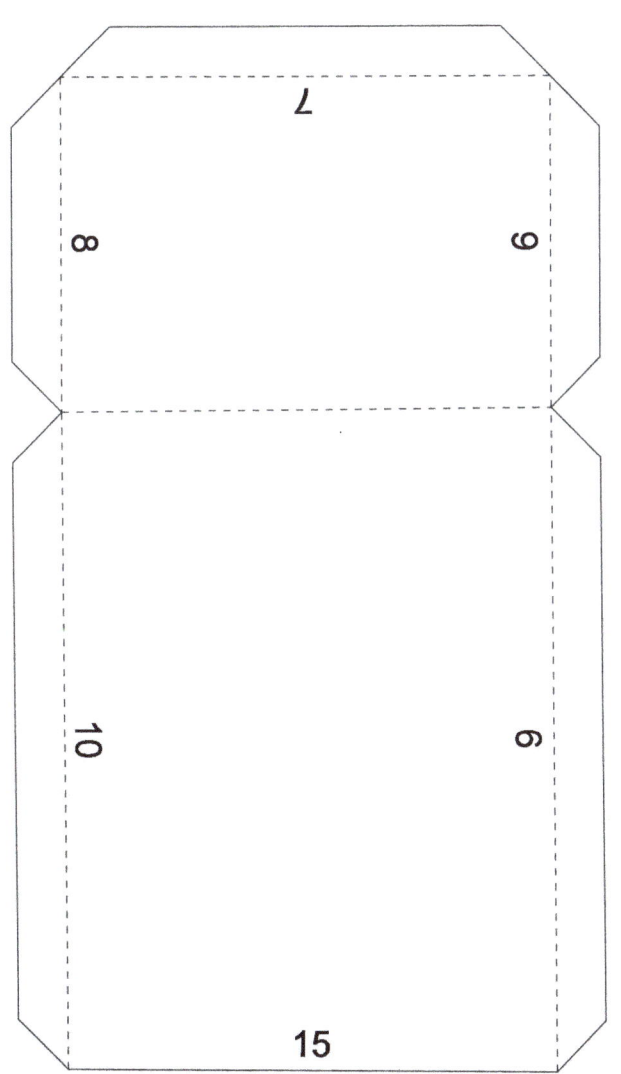

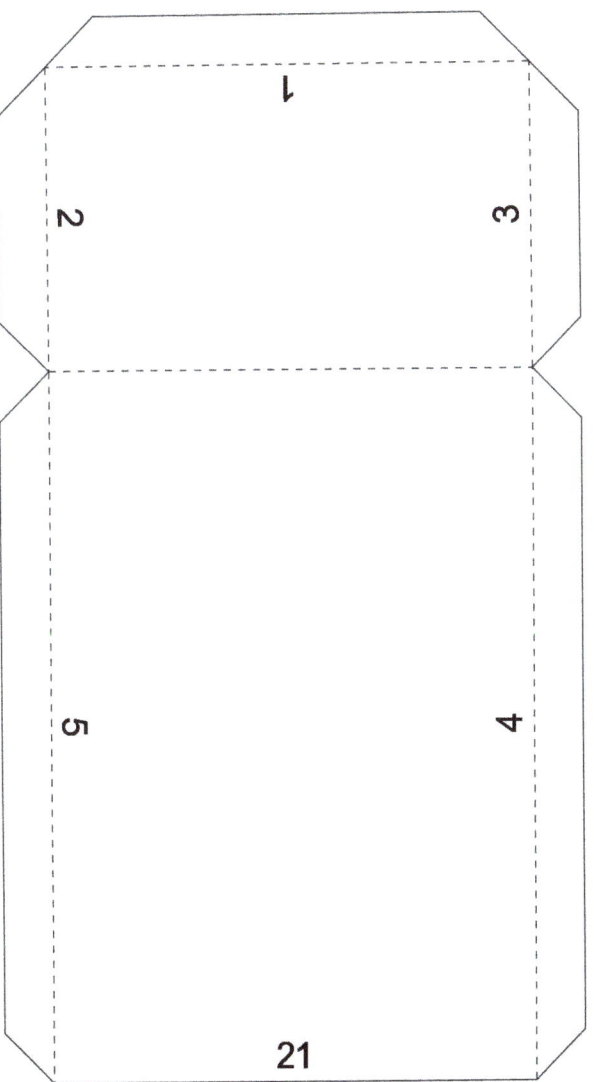

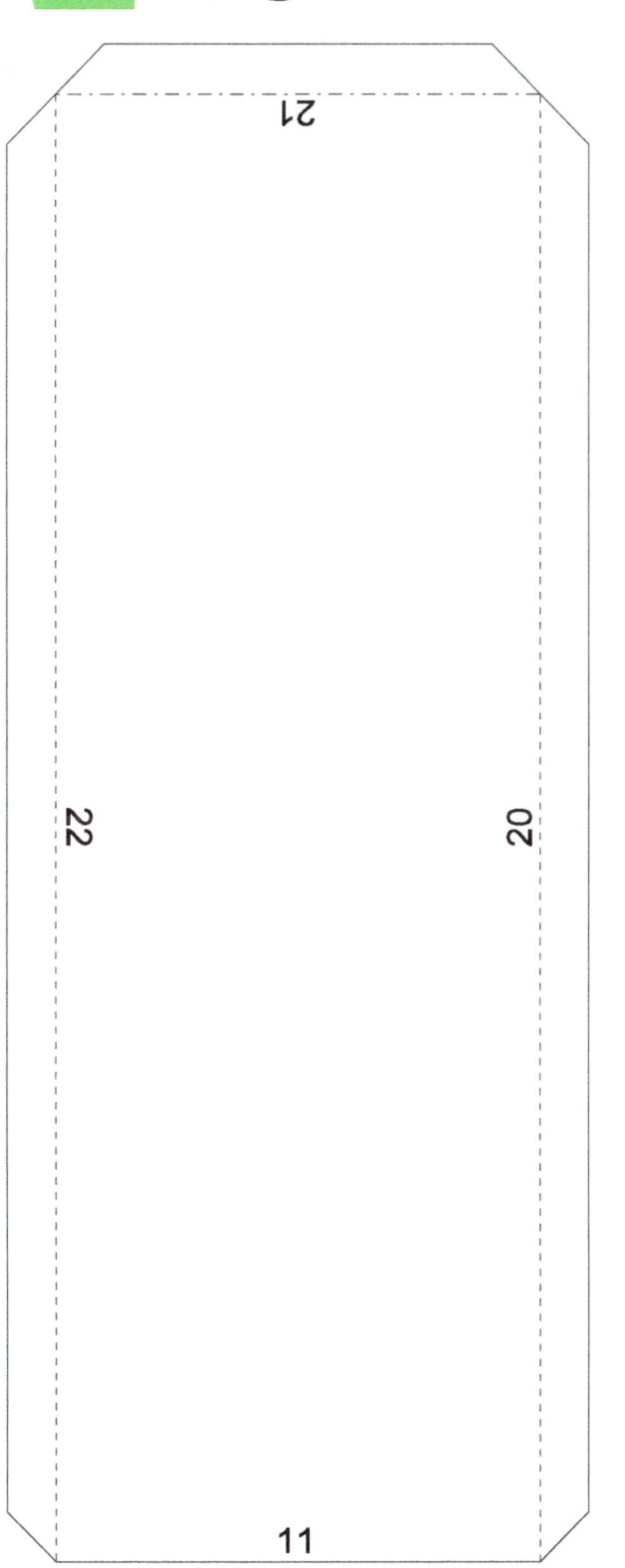

21

22

20

11

15

16

14

19

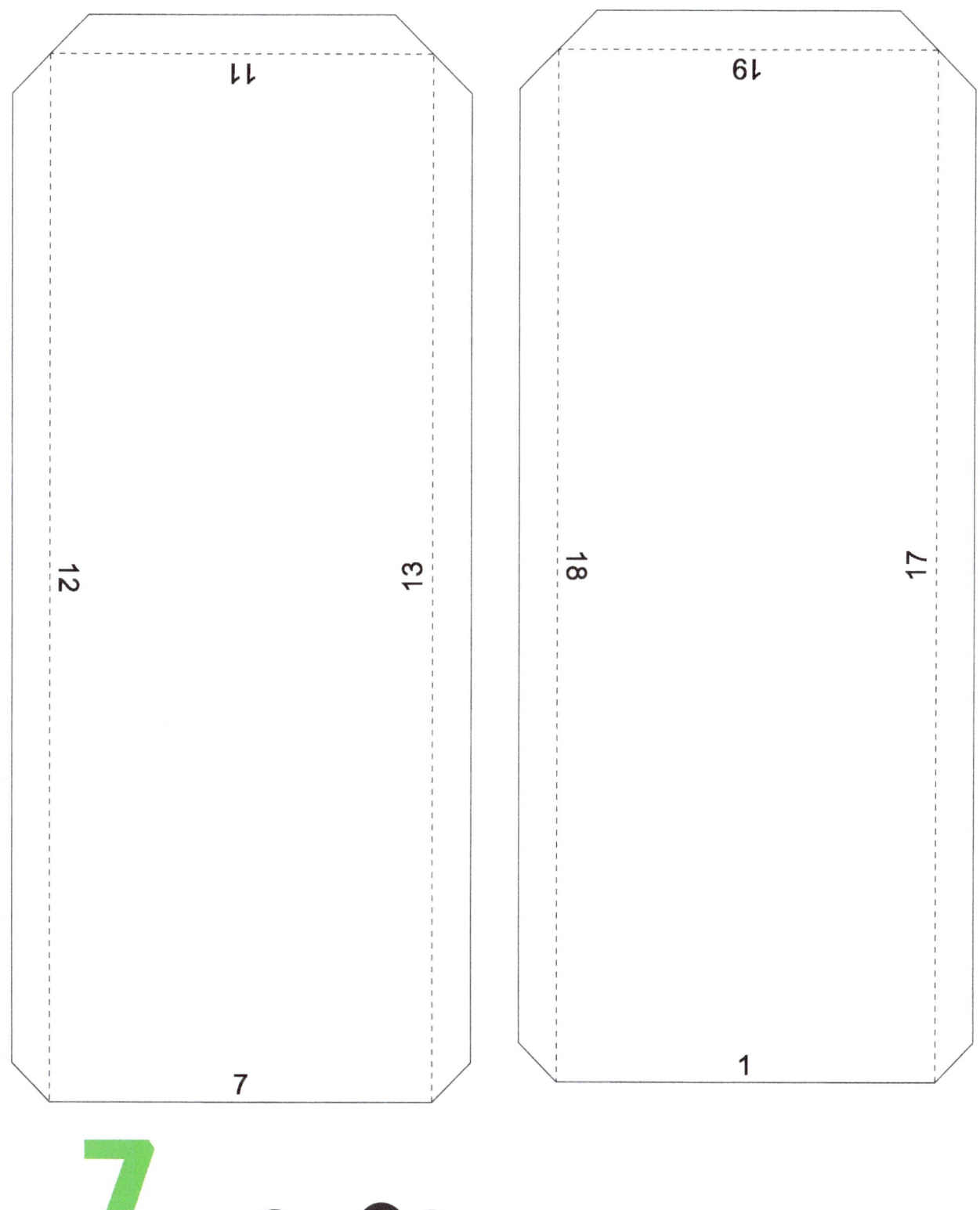

11

12

13

7

19

18

17

1

Z by Sofs

Sophie Marcoux is the creative designer
behind the 3D papercraft brand Sofs Designs.
Her work as amused and inspired people from
all over the world since 2012.
Based in Montreal Canada, Sophie feels
empowered when making stuff and in turn,
loves to empower herself and others while
on journey. Feel free to visit
www.sofsdesigns.com for more project ideas.

Sofs Designs 2023
First Edition FEb 2023
ISBN 978-1-998930-15-9
Cataloging data available from
Library and Archive Canada

www.ingramcontent.com/pod-product-compliance
Lightning Source LLC
Chambersburg PA
CBHW040513150626
46551CB00034B/2688